Reading the Everyday

Joe Moran

Routledge
Taylor & Francis Group

LONDON AND NEW YORK

A · H · R · B

arts and humanities research board

First published 2005 by Routledge
2 Park Square, Milton Park, Abingdon, Oxon OX14 4RN

Simultaneously published in the USA and Canada
by Routledge
270 Madison Ave, New York, NY 10016

Routledge is an imprint of the Taylor & Francis Group

© 2005 Joe Moran

Typeset in Perpetua and Bell Gothic by
Florence Production Ltd, Stoodleigh, Devon
Printed and bound in Great Britain by
MPG Books Ltd, Bodmin, Cornwall

British Library Cataloguing in Publication Data
A catalogue record for this book is available from the British Library

Library of Congress Cataloging in Publication Data
Moran, Joe, 1970–
    Reading the everyday/Joe Moran
        p. cm.
    Includes bibliographical references.
    1. Sociology, Urban.   2. Civilization, Modern.   3. Popular culture.
    I. Title.
    HT153.M668 2005
    307.76–dc22   2004029206

ISBN 0–415–31708–8 (hbk)
ISBN 0–415–31709–6 (pbk)

Contents

Illustrations

Preface and acknowledgements

This book is about everyday life in contemporary societies. It focuses on those mundane, 'boring' aspects of the daily (what the French call *le quotidien*, with more precision than the English 'everyday') that have been theorized by European critics such as Henri Lefebvre, Michel de Certeau, Siegfried Kracauer and Marc Augé, but have received relatively little attention within Anglophone cultural studies. As the book's title suggests, it aims to extend the primarily theoretical emphasis of recent, groundclearing works in everyday life studies[1] through detailed readings of the spaces, practices and mythologies of the quotidian. Indeed, one of the central arguments of *Reading the Everyday* is that the everyday is always already read: its lived culture cannot be easily separated from its representation in architecture, design, material culture, news media, political discourse, film, television, art and photography.

The book explores the ways in which important changes in Western societies over the last few decades – such as the privatization of public services, the deregulation of markets, the managerial revolution in the workplace and the promotion of homeownership – have been articulated through these practices and representations of daily life. I want to argue that everyday life has become a space for a new kind of 'post-political' politics, in which the quotidian coalesces with the political in unnoticed but pervasive ways. Many of the examples I discuss are British, although there is frequent cross-referencing to European and American culture. At a time when the subject matter of cultural studies is being increasingly internationalized, I want to argue that the study of mundane life demands a necessary concreteness and specificity alongside an awareness of the increasing globalization of everyday practices. Just as many of the pioneering theorists of daily life (Lefebvre, Certeau, the Situationists) used Paris as a *locus classicus* in their writings, several of my case studies are linked to London, an increasingly global city whose everyday life still has its own distinctive landscapes and mythologies. I aim to show that quotidian spaces – offices, call centres, subway systems, traffic jams, new towns, suburbs, motorways and housing estates – are caught up in global processes while remaining tied to resilient local conditions and histories.

The introduction, 'Waiting, cultural studies and the quotidian', begins with a common daily experience – waiting for a bus – and uses it to suggest that the concept of the everyday in academic, media and political discourse has often neglected or obscured the specifically quotidian. The book is then divided into four main sections, each dealing with particular types of actual and discursive everyday space. Chapter 1, 'Workspace: office life and commuting', examines the representation of work culture and commuting in the context of recent changes in neo-liberal, globalized economies. Chapter 3, 'Urban space: the myths and meanings of traffic', discusses pervasive mythologies about vehicles and pedestrians in relation to questions of politics and the public sphere in the modern city. Chapter 4, 'Non-places: supermodernity and the everyday', investigates the dispersal of quotidian activity into liminal or peripheral spaces such as motorways, service stations and new towns, and explores the historical contexts and cultural politics of these supposedly blank environments. Chapter 5, 'Living space: housing, the market and the everyday', analyses ideas and representations of housing in contemporary capitalist societies, arguing that they serve both to romanticize and to conceal the everyday reality of the house. My conclusion, 'The everyday and cultural change', discusses the uneven development of daily life in a global context, in relation to colonialism, terrorism and social capital.

I would like to thank the Arts and Humanities Research Board, which granted me a research leave award for a semester to allow me to complete this book. I am also grateful to my colleagues in the departments of American Studies and Literature and Cultural History at Liverpool John Moores University, who covered my duties during this semester and a matching period of departmental leave. Rebecca Barden, Ross Dawson, Elspeth Graham, Michael Moran, Jonathan Purkis, Gerry Smyth and several anonymous reviewers for Routledge kindly read and commented on draft chapters of my book. Other people offered advice, information and various forms of help: Timothy Ashplant, Jo Croft, Rick Fell, Colin Harrison, Ben Highmore, Bob Kettle, Annette Kuhn, Liam Moran, Glenda Norquay, Joanna Price, Hazel Rayner, Cathy Wainhouse, Kate Walchester and members of the e-mail list, TheBusStopsHere. I am very grateful to the artists, filmmakers and photographers (Patrick Keiller, Martin Parr, Tom Phillips, David Rayson and Tom Wood) who have given me permission to reproduce images, helped supply me with film transcripts and reproductions and took the time to answer my questions about their work. Some brief sections of Chapter 5 appeared in my article 'Housing, Memory and Everyday Life in Contemporary Britain' in *Cultural Studies* 18, 4 (July 2004) (http://www.tandf.co.uk/journals), and I thank the editors and publisher for permission to use this material again. Peter Wilby also allowed me to publish some of the research for this book in a very different form in the *New Statesman*.

This book is dedicated to my brother Liam, with love and respect; and my fellow passengers on the number 82 bus, with heartfelt sympathy.

Chapter 1

INTRODUCTION

Waiting, cultural studies and the quotidian

IN HIS *CRITIQUE OF DIALECTICAL REASON*, Jean-Paul Sartre describes a queue forming early one morning at a bus stop on the Place Saint-Germain in Paris. He argues that those lining up at the stop 'achieve practical and theoretical participation in common being' because they have a shared interest, as people who regularly use the bus service and who all have business that day on the Right Bank (Sartre 1976: 266). But compared to people gathered together for some collective purpose such as a street festival or popular uprising, these bus-stop queuers produce only a 'plurality of isolations' (1976: 256). The bus passenger does not know how many people are going to be at the stop when he (*sic*) arrives or how full the next bus will be, and so is encouraged to see his fellow queuers as competitors for a potentially scarce resource. He takes a ticket from a machine by the stop, which indicates the order of his arrival and assigns him an order of priority when the bus arrives. By accepting this system, he acknowledges that his identity is interchangeable with that of the other passengers, a 'being-outside-himself as a reality shared by several people', which assigns him a place in a 'prefabricated seriality' (1976: 265).

What seems clear from this passage is that Sartre is not very interested in the actual experience of waiting for a bus. Indeed, the passage is typical of the slightly begrudging, tangential way in which the quotidian has emerged as a subject of intellectual inquiry over the last century. Sartre uses the bus queue as an easily understood example, raw material for a thought experiment that allows him to move on to weightier matters of politics and philosophy. He sees it as an abstraction of the laws of political economy, based on the competitive quest for a limited resource – in this case, seats on the awaited bus. The actual queue itself is devoid of any wider meaning: 'This unity is *not* symbolic . . . it has nothing to symbolise; *it* is what unites

1

everything' (1976: 264). The example only works because of the nature of the queue that Sartre describes. This orderly cohort of people taking tickets from a machine would certainly seem very strange to a contemporary British bus queuer.

The ability to queue patiently is often seen as part of the British, or more especially English, national character. The Hungarian humorist George Mikes argued in *How to be an Alien* (1946) that 'an Englishman, even if he is alone, forms an orderly queue of one'. For Mikes, uncomplaining queuing was 'the national passion of an otherwise dispassionate race' (1958: 48) and was symptomatic of other characteristics of Englishness: politeness to strangers, respect for order and deferral to absent authority. Writing in the early 1990s, though, Patrick Wright noted the more elaborate protocol of the London bus queue. While conservative commentators were lamenting the decline of the well-ordered bus queue as symbolic of national decline and social anarchy, Wright suggested that the reality was more complex. The West End was indeed a 'sordid scrum', in which unprincipled natives pushed past tourists with impunity. But in quieter, residential areas, aggression and cheek did not always win out, as 'each time a bus pulls up the crowd negotiates a messy but still intricately structured settlement between the ideal of the orderly queue and the chaotic stampede' (Wright 1991: 125). Wright's argument about the disintegration of the queue into less obvious, fragmented forms of social behaviour proved to be prescient. In 1994, a London Passenger Transport bylaw introduced in 1938, which made it illegal to stand more than two abreast at a bus stop, was repealed because it was no longer seen as workable (Jones 1994).

In the centre of London, since 2003, passengers have had to pre-purchase their tickets from kerbside machines before boarding the bus, but this does not assign them any order of precedence in a queue. One problem with the modern bus queue is that it lacks what Barry Schwartz calls the 'ecological supports' of waiting, such as 'queue this side' signs or queuing channels created by cords and metal poles (1975: 99). These supports are increasingly common in commercial environments such as supermarkets, banks and cinemas, where they are often supplemented by buzzers, digital displays and recorded voices saying 'cashier number 5 please'. Bus queuers, though, are left to improvise their own waiting arrangements. On my own bus route, I have seen this lead to near-fistfights, as hordes of passengers clamber on to already packed buses in no particular order, and drivers with half-full buses speed past stops teeming with angry commuters, because they know they will have to let everyone board or no one at all. The bus queue is a reminder that even the most mundane routines incorporate complex spatial politics and cultural meanings.

This introduction has five main sections. First, it examines the bus stop as a way of considering the unspoken economic and political contexts of everyday life. Second, it argues that cultural studies has downplayed these aspects of the everyday through an emphasis on popular culture, consumption and lifestyle. Third, it explores the ways in which an understanding of the quotidian can help to make sense of contemporary political culture, with its particular notions of the relationship between the market, the public sphere and 'ordinary people'. Fourth, it looks at how ideas of everyday life developed by French theorists in the immediate postwar era can be adapted to make sense of this new political culture. Finally, it discusses questions of methodology, 'ways of reading' that might be particularly useful in addressing these questions.

Reading the bus stop

Waiting for the bus may be a well-known British tradition, but it is about as unglamorous an experience as you can get. It is not just that the unreliability and bunching up of buses makes passengers feel that they do not have ownership or control over their own lives (hence the familiar complaint: 'You wait for ages and then three come at once'). It is that the second-rate service confirms their status as second-rate citizens. Buses are the most widely used form of public transport in Britain, and account for more than twice the number of journeys taken by rail (*Social Trends* 2004: 188). But they have low cultural status, because they are disproportionately used by (and, just as importantly, are associated with) women, children, students, the elderly and the poor. Although 86 per cent of British households are within six minutes' walk of a bus stop, a recent social attitudes survey found that nearly two-thirds of people agreed with the statement: 'I would only travel somewhere by bus if I had no other way of getting there' (Department for Transport 2004: 42; *Social Trends* 2004: 189). It is hard to stand at a bus stop, as the single-occupant cars stream by, without feeling somehow denied full membership of society. Insofar as it forms part of cultural representation at all, the bus is the vehicle that cannot keep up with the pace of modernity, that 'splutters along behind, picking up all those people who will never quite make it into either "History" or "Tomorrow"' (Bonnett 2000: 27).[1]

Just before beginning this book, I read a newspaper report about Britain's first queuing agency, Q4U, which aims to relieve Londoners of the hassle of queuing. For £20 an hour, the report said, its employees would line up for anything from passports to theatre tickets. Q4U recruits its workers from the ranks of the long-term unemployed, who, according to a company spokesman, are used to queuing: 'It's a job that doesn't require a lot of skill or experience. All you need is plenty of patience' (Eden 2001). I have seen no evidence of Q4U since then; it may have overestimated the demand for queuing services. In fact, a queuing agency has a fairly obvious problem. The economics and practicalities of the more tiresome forms of waiting, such as standing at bus stops, do not support a market for surrogate waiters. In these contexts, it is difficult to separate the experience of waiting from its surrounding cultural practices and meanings.

In his classic study of queues, Schwartz argues that the experience of waiting and our attitudes towards it embody social differences (1975: 22). For the poorest members of society, waiting is simply a daily experience as they queue for public transport, state benefits and doctors' appointments. For the more affluent, waiting is less time-consuming and may be expected to come with compensatory props such as comfy chairs, bottomless coffee pots and reading matter. The changing fortunes of the British bus over the last two decades offer a case study in this differentiated experience of waiting. Under the 1985 Transport Act, the Thatcher government disbanded the National Bus Company and deregulated all local bus services outside London. To the act's supporters, it replaced inefficient local authority monopolies with healthy competition and consumer choice. To its detractors, it carved up the bus services into a morass of holding companies and private firms, with no integration of timetables or ticketing, less provision for unprofitable routes and nobody to blame when the bus did not show up. The view that deregulation confirmed the social marginalization of bus users was reinforced by a remark attributed, perhaps apocryphally, to Thatcher: 'If a man finds himself a passenger on a bus having attained the age of twenty-six, he can account himself a failure in life' (Grayling 1999).

When the Labour government came to power in 1997, it combined a new concern with the delivery of public services with an unwillingness to alter the economic and political landscape created by Thatcherism. As urban traffic congestion became a significant electoral issue, the Department for Transport published *From Workhorse to Thoroughbred: A Better Role for Bus Travel*, which set a target to increase bus use by 10 per cent by 2010. The government aimed to achieve this not through re-regulating the buses but through a 'Quality Partnership Approach' in which local authorities would work more closely with private companies to improve services (Department for Transport 1998: 2). It is a classic New Labour strategy: policy-making is not about weighing up competing priorities, but about public and private agencies working together to achieve pre-agreed ends, with 'everybody concentrating on what they do best' (1998: 2). While the local authorities could integrate and coordinate services, the private operators could show 'responsiveness to the customer', 'flexibility' and 'incentive to innovate' (1998: 22). The current status of bus travel suggests the limitations of such a policy. Labour is on course to achieve its target of increased bus use, but only because it has risen dramatically in London, which accounts for about a third of all bus journeys in Britain (*Social Trends* 2004: 188). The buses were never deregulated in the capital, and the Greater London Authority formed in 2000 has exercised considerable central control. Almost every-where else in the country, bus use is static or falling (Office for National Statistics 2003).

It would be difficult to find a piece of modern architecture that inspires less interest than the bus shelter. It is an omnipresent object of everyday life that, when it registers in the public consciousness, is usually only associated with graffiti and vandalism. But there has been an unnoticed bus-shelter revo-lution in recent years. Many of the world's shelters are now supplied by just two companies, both of which deal with outdoor advertising: Clear Channel Adshel and JCDecaux. These firms have built themselves into global brands since the 1990s, winning thousands of street furniture contracts throughout the world. As more and more local authorities contract out their public services to private companies, bus-shelter design has become an adjunct of the advertising industry.

In Britain, Adshel is the market leader with an 80 per cent market share. It supplies and maintains its shelters free of charge, in return for the right to display advertising on some of them in backlit '6-sheet' panels. Bus shelters will normally have just one advertising panel, but on prime sites in city centres they can have two or more, with rotating displays to maximize income. Adshel bus shelters are architect-designed, with trendy names for particular ranges: Metro, Classic, Skylight, Avenue. The company takes pride in the high quality of its shelters, which use graffiti- and etch-resistant materials, reinforced glass, bright colours and courtesy lights. A 2003 government White Paper on combating anti-social behaviour commended Adshel for its success in cleaning bus shelters and removing graffiti, and working with the police to reduce vandalism (Home Office 2003: 70). It is a public–private partnership that seems to benefit all parties: Adshel gets free advertising, while the local authority gets free shelters, and does not have to spend thousands of pounds cleaning them, removing graffiti and sweeping up broken glass. It is, according to Adshel's managing director, 'a win-win business model for all concerned' (France 2002).

But the sponsored bus shelter is also a case study in the colonization of urban landscapes by the market. Adshel has been supplying advertising in bus shelters since the 1970s, but it really began to boom because of two key devel-opments in the late 1980s. The first was the installation of illuminated posters called 'Adshel Superlites'. The second was the advent of a data system called OSCAR (Outdoor Site Classification and Audience Research), providing infor-mation on vehicle and pedestrian traffic near poster sites (Sutherland 1989). These innovations allowed advertisers to direct their campaigns beyond the unglamorous target market of the habitual bus user. The ads are now also aimed at passing pedestrians and motorists, which is why they are big on visual impact and short on copy.

The economies of scale created by multinational advertising companies, combined with the need for these companies to sell attractive packages to city councils, have produced an interesting tension between global standardization and local difference. In Liverpool, the city where I work, there is a surprising variety of bus shelters built around the standard steel frame (see Figure 1.1). The contracts between the advertising companies and local authorities stipulate that the former will provide a certain number of shelters if they can advertise in an agreed proportion of them. The 'de luxe' shelters, with barrelled glass roofs, glass walls on all sides and dot-matrix displays with real-time passenger information technology letting passengers know when the next bus is due, do not have advertising. The shelters with adverts, which tend to be in the prime city-centre sites or the main routes into town, are much more rudimentary. They have a cantilevered roof or windbreak ends extending only part of their width, so that the ads can be seen by everyone. The outdoor advertising companies have understandably expended their energies not on prioritizing warmth and comfort for bus-stop waiters, but on developing new forms of advertising, such as talking adverts, triggered by motion sensors, and 'dynamic image' posters in which, for example, steam appears to rise from cups of Heinz soup (Clear Channel Adshel 2004).

Figure 1.1   Adshel bus shelters, Liverpool.
Photographs by the author.

In several British cities, we can see the logical culmination of this commodi-fication of public space: redundant bus shelters built solely for advertising, where no buses stop and no bus users wait – unless, of course, they have been cruelly misinformed (Mintowt-Czyz 2000: 22).

Several recent news stories have suggested that innovative technologies will improve the experience of waiting for a bus. Twelve-foot poles with pro-pellers on top will use wind power to generate electricity to heat the seats in bus shelters (BBC News, 16 January 2002). Buses4U, a pilot scheme funded by the Department for Transport, will allow passengers to book a bus by text message up to 30 minutes in advance, allowing them to wait in a nearby pub rather than the shelter (Monro 2004). Touch-screen bus shelters using plasma technology will be able to show timetables, maps and weather forecasts (Pearson 2002). Networked computers placed in shelters will allow bus passengers to access local news, council websites and e-mail accounts (*Daily Mirror* 1999).

The important point about these stories is not that they are untrue – in two cases they refer to schemes already in operation – but that such innova-tions are applied unevenly. For most people waiting in bus shelters, they remain in the realm of science fiction. The bus shelter is a kind of prism through which we can read the uneven modernization of everyday life and the changing priorities of society. It is no longer primarily a functional piece of architecture, still less a civic space; it is a marketing opportunity. Bus shel-ters may be more interesting to look at than they used to be, but waiting for a bus remains an unpredictable, low-status activity. Doreen Massey suggests that the practice of standing at a bus stop counters the more excitable visions of contemporaneity in cultural theory, which emphasize its restless mobility and pervasive mediatization. 'Much of life for many people, even in the heart of the first world', she argues, 'still consists of waiting in a bus-shelter with your shopping for a bus that never comes' (Massey 1992: 8).

Cultural studies and everyday life

I have begun this book with the experience of waiting for a bus because it encapsulates some of the theoretical and methodological problems of 'reading the everyday'. Waiting is frustrating because it is both an unavoidable and marginalized experience: an absolutely essential feature of daily life that is nevertheless associated with wasted time and even shameful indolence. In a society in which market imperatives increasingly invade the most routine oper-ations, waiting makes economic sense. If servers are only occupied for half the time, if railway platforms are half-empty and buses half-full, then those who provide the service are losing money somewhere. Henri Lefebvre suggests that everyday life is increasingly made up of this 'compulsive time', a kind of limbo between work and leisure in which no explicit demands are made on us but we are still trapped by the necessity of waiting (1971: 53). The very conditions that make waiting inevitable, though, give it low economic and cultural value. Wealth and status in advanced capitalist societies rest on the capacity to accumulate resources such as money, skills, knowledge and information. Waiting is the opposite of this kind of accumulated resource: it is simply the passing of time, time that could be spent doing something more useful.

For Lefebvre, waiting is a seminal experience because it encapsulates this essential tension in everyday life, between its inescapability and its dismissal as boring and marginal. His work sees a closely linked relationship between the lived experience of daily life and the meanings, ideas and mythologies that circulate around it. In both its practice and representation, he argues, the everyday exists as a kind of 'residual deposit' that lags behind the more glamorous, accelerated experiences of contemporary society, a 'great, disparate patchwork' that modernity 'drags in its wake' (Lefebvre 2002: 57; Lefebvre 1991a: 192). He suggests that the relative neglect of everyday life within the traditional academic disciplines is part of this same process of residualization. The everyday is a kind of remainder which evades conventional divisions of knowledge: it is 'defined by "what is left over" after all distinct, superior, specialized, structured activities have been singled out by analysis' (Lefebvre 1991a: 97).

This value system is reinforced by people outside academia who expect scholars to engage in research projects of established significance. While they are happy to recycle statistics and surveys from obscure journals for light-hearted news stories, journalists often combine this with a dig at the 'boffins' who have little better to do with their time than focus on the trivia of everyday life. This dismissal takes on a ritualistic quality in the media coverage of the Ig Nobel Prizes, an annual event at Harvard sponsored by the Annals of Improbable Research, for academic projects that 'first make people laugh and then make them think'. The winner of the 2003 Literature Prize was John W. Trinkaus, an American social psychologist who specializes in brief papers on topics such as shoppers who exceed the number of items permitted in the express checkout lane, conversations between strangers in elevators and motorists who cut through store parking areas to avoid red traffic lights. One commentator summed up the general mood by describing this work as 'daft science cashing in on the bleeding obvious' (Henderson 2003). For some deadline-driven journalists, this pained attentiveness to unpromising material is nothing more than a form of tenured trainspotting. The problem with such research, though, is not that it is undertaken, but that it tends to work within the constraints of disciplinary science, reducing the quotidian to controlled experiments and statistical configurations without looking at broader social questions. Waiting for a bus is precisely the kind of commonplace activity unclaimed by the established disciplines, which might reveal unnoticed connections between everyday experience, cultural representation and issues of power, resources and public policy.

One of the key aims of cultural studies has been to develop an inter-disciplinary project that will address these practices of everyday life. The evolution of cultural studies as an academic subject, though, has tended to militate against a concern with boring, routine activities – such as waiting at bus stops. In both its general and academic usage, the word 'everyday' refers to a wide range of practices undertaken by ordinary people, and specific subject areas have tended to define it differently according to their own concerns. As John Hartley argues, cultural studies has understood the every-day in relation to its own interest in the political-cultural construction of identity and meaning, and has therefore seen it 'as a symptom for something else – struggles, ideologies, oppressions, power structures' (2003: 121). At the risk of oversimplifying a diverse field, I would suggest that there have been two main ways in which the emerging discipline of cultural studies has thought about everyday life over the last few decades: as ritual and as popular consumption.

The first of these approaches was strongly influenced by an ethnographic notion of ritual as semi-formalized, symbolic action. Traditional ethnography sought to capture the minute detail of ordinary life through extensive field-work involving participant observation and in-depth interviews. It focused on specific activities that, if they could not be formally articulated, could at least be symbolically expressed. As Nancy Ries argues, the convention within ethnographic studies of 'primitive' societies was to begin with the mundane details of demography, work and daily life and move 'up' to 'the seemingly more esoteric realms of kinship patterns, exchange, religious belief, and ritual' (2002: 728). The ethnographer's main interest was in 'the symbolically charged practices which bridge the ordinary and the extraordinary': initiation rites, marriages, burials, communal feasts and other ceremonies. By exam-ining the role of these rituals in establishing systems of social stratification, kinship relations and cultural identities, the ethnographer saw the everyday as '*the* preeminent temporal/spatial domain where nonalienated, culturally and existentially meaningful productivity occurs' (2002: 732).

The research conducted in the Centre for Contemporary Cultural Studies (CCCS) at Birmingham from the late 1960s onwards shows the influence of this ethnographic understanding of the everyday. In Paul Willis's words, the CCCS's work on subcultural groups such as skinheads, bikers and punks iden-tified forms of 'symbolic creativity' that were both embedded in daily routines and separate from them (1990: 1). This partly explains the CCCS's particular interest in youth cultures. Willis's *Learning to Labour* (1977) focuses on the socializing forces of education and school-leavers' jobs in all their oppressive mundanity, but in his later work he also suggests that young people are adept practitioners of the 'dramaturgy and poetics of everyday life' because they are not yet locked into the 'routinized roles of adult life' (1990: 22). This ethnographic notion of ritual sees it as difficult to communicate verbally but nevertheless symbolically charged, a 'grounded aesthetics' (1990: 21) that responds to the dullness and insecurity of dead-end work with the meaning-making of leisure time.

The second of these approaches to the everyday within cultural studies was influenced by *Arts de Faire*, the first volume of Michel de Certeau's *L'Invention du Quotidien*, translated as *The Practice of Everyday Life*. In this book, Certeau argues that ordinary people can undermine centralized power systems with a form of consumption characterized by 'its poaching, its clandestine nature, its tireless but quiet activity, in short by its quasi-invisibility' (1984: 31). He means consumption in its broadest sense rather than simply the buying and using of consumer products. Certeau examines cultural practices located quite specifically in the quotidian, the repetitive tasks that people do every day, such as walking, cooking, commuting and working in an office. For example, he argues that train journeys are a peculiar mix of freedom and imprisonment, a kind of 'incarceration-vacation' (1984: 114) in which people can improvise creatively by daydreaming and gazing out of the window. He is interested in forms of *savoir-faire*, a term that in English is associated with the possession of sophisticated social skills, but in French simply means the know-how involved in the habitual performance of everyday tasks. In English, the word 'everyday' does not capture the specificity of this French *quotidien*, with its particular emphasis on daily routine.

Anglophone cultural studies, while making use of Certeau's work, has tended to shift its focus on to actively resistant readings of popular culture by individual consumers.[2] One of the most influential readings of Certeau's work in this vein is John Fiske's notion of everyday life as a form of 'micro-politics' that resists the 'macropolitics' of political and cultural institutions. Fiske argues that leisure and consumption offer the best opportunities for resistance in everyday life, because they are less heavily controlled than the classroom or office, where those in power have more to lose (1989a: 213). Once the cultural commodity has been sold, he suggests, it becomes detached from its more controlled meanings and becomes 'a resource for the culture of everyday life' (Fiske 1989b: 35).

When Fiske discusses the habitual acts of daily life, it is by way of celebrating the individuals who subvert these routines: pedestrians who take shortcuts across the grass instead of keeping to the path, office workers who steal company stationery for their children, window shoppers who enjoy the visual stimulation of malls without buying anything. When Fiske deals with domestic activities such as housework and cooking, he argues that they are disempowering to the extent that they are compulsory. Cooking *can* be pleasurable but 'the pleasure lies in its creativity, not in its necessity'. The voluntary

like Augé
with elegant
commuter.

routines of popular culture, such as watching the daily news or a soap opera on television, reproduce the repetitions of cooking and cleaning in more inventive form: 'Routine lives require routine pleasures' (Fiske 1989b: 65). Fiske's work contrasts the creative practices of everyday life with the dull monotony of quotidian routine.

Susan Willis's *A Primer for Daily Life* is in part a critical response to Fiske and others who see the everyday primarily as a space for individual creativity and subcultural resistance (Willis 1991: 13). Like Fiske, though, she equates daily life with the individual consumption of commodities, in the form of women's workout videos, children's toys, supermarket brands and theme parks. Willis makes a brief reference to Lefebvre's and Certeau's writings on '*la vie quotidienne*' at the beginning of her book, but argues that, while their work is a response to European urban experience, her own is written in an American and suburban context (1991: vi). This means that she focuses on the atomized consumer lifestyles made possible by the shopping mall, the car and the high-tech home. 'The bottom line in daily life', she argues, 'is the commodity form. Herein are subsumed all the contradictions of commodity capitalism and our aspirations for their utopian transformation' (1991: vi). Willis aims to show how commodity fetishism conceals or reinvents the use value of products, transforming the mundane into the desirable. It turns work into play in the form of children's toy cookers and shopping baskets, or historical theme parks promoting the authenticity of traditional crafts; or it taps into the needs and desires – for energy, abundance, democracy and community – that daily life does not usually provide. Willis argues that this commodified everyday always precludes the possibility of socialized consumption: 'Almost everything we do in daily life, we do as individuals' (1991: 175).

I want to argue that this emphasis on ritual or consumption in cultural studies has produced a limiting notion of the everyday that values the creative and recreational over the banal and boring. This has no doubt helped in the development of a relatively young discipline: the forms of symbolic creativity involved in our interaction with new forms of media, technology and consumption are rather more enticing topics for prospective students than quotidian routines. But it has tended to overlook a vast area of social life whose very 'boringness' makes it a significant arena for an unacknowledged cultural politics. It is significant that some of the most interesting reflections on everyday life in recent cultural studies have been on the uses of television, in which consumption has become relatively routine and domesticated, melded with daily patterns and behaviours (see Silverstone 1994; Gauntlett and Hill 1999; Moores 2000: 57–104); and on suburbia, where the separation of public from private space is often similarly linked to mundane practices and mythologies (see Silverstone 1996; Spigel 2001). My own book seeks to explore this routinization not so much in the sphere of domesticity and leisure time as in the banal, communal sites of everyday life such as the office, commuter train, traffic jam and housing estate. If it is mainly concerned with exterior spaces, this is partly because I feel that the domestic and related realms of the everyday (cooking, housework, shopping) have already been well explored elsewhere, and partly because I want to focus on collective routines where the possibilities for consumerist reinvention are most limited.

As Meaghan Morris argues, the history of the word 'banality' partly 'inscribes the disintegration of old ideals about the common people, the common place, the common culture'. It was not until the late eighteenth century that 'banal', a word that had previously referred to compulsory feudal service, came to be associated with the workaday and routine (Morris 1990: 40). When banality is evoked in cultural studies, Morris argues, it is often a way of resisting these historically contingent, hierarchical value judgements. Employing a primarily ethnographic frame, with 'the people' as informants and critics as their translators, cultural studies has promoted a 'myth of trans-formation' of the banal as a way of challenging elitist distinctions between official and vernacular culture (Morris 1990: 35). In cultural studies, the banal is usually turned into something else, made interesting and significant by acts of subaltern resistance or semiotic reinvention. Morris's own work on motels and shopping malls, by contrast, has shown that these environments are not simply 'privileged sites of a road-runner *Angst*' (1988a: 2) or playgrounds for the 'cruising grammarian' (1988b: 195), but can also be non-recreational, semi-domestic and routine.

This approach is reminiscent of the work of some of the founding figures of cultural studies. Raymond Williams's essay, 'Culture is Ordinary' (1958), for example, begins with an account of a bus journey taken from Hereford into the Black Mountains, and goes on to criticize those who dismiss the ordinary comforts of modern working-class daily life such as 'plumbing, baby Austins, aspirin, contraceptives, canned food' (Williams 1989: 10). Richard Hoggart's *The Uses of Literacy* (1958) deals with run-of-the-mill aspects of working-class culture, such as allotment-keeping, pigeon-fancying and pub-singing. Although the early work of these critics has its own implied distinctions between valued ritual and humdrum routine, and between 'good' and 'bad' popular culture, it is still informed by a notion of the banal as shared and communal.[3] As Ben Highmore points out, this is a difficult notion for contemporary cultural studies, with its crucial investment in the politics of identity, difference and otherness (2002b: 2–3). My book is an attempt to move beyond this difficulty without simply dismissing it, by focusing on widely practised, increasingly globalized routines that nonetheless produce difference and inequality in the way they are lived and represented. The apparently universal, taken-for-granted nature of quotidian culture makes it a powerful grounding for what Antonio Gramsci calls 'spontaneous philosophy' (1971: 323) – those forms of lay knowledge that, by virtue of being so firmly embedded in specific social contexts, conceal resilient power relationships.

In this context, 'the everyday' is a space where practice and representation are complexly interrelated, where the lived reality of the quotidian co-exists with clichés, mythologies, stereotypes and unsourced quotations.[4]

In *Fast Cars, Clean Bodies*, her study of French daily life between the mid-1950s and mid-1960s, Kristin Ross offers a model for this study of the dialectical relationship between practices and representations of the everyday. Ross uses a wide range of cultural texts – advertisements, novels, films, mass-market magazines, material culture – to suggest that the category of 'the everyday' in this period was a way of both imagining social change and defusing its politics. This new understanding of the everyday rested on a separation of public from private life, typified by the work and commuting routines of a new, status-conscious class of *jeunes cadres* (young executives), and the 'democracy of consumption' of the Ideal Home. These new life patterns became a way of celebrating but also 're-enfolding' modernization, naturalizing it and making it unthreatening to the middle classes, allowing it to function as 'the alibi of a class society' (Ross 1995: 89, 13). Ross argues that this version of everyday life served as both a distraction from the traumas of decolonization and a reproduction of colonial logic in its dispersal of the working classes to the suburbs and its policing of domestic space in the form of new concerns about household management. Like Ross, I am less concerned in this book with the ethnographic investigation of daily life per se than with 'the everyday' as a category that brings together lived culture and representation in a way that makes sense of, but also obscures, the reality of cultural change and social difference.

The everyday and the public sphere

I want to examine, in particular, the extent to which representations of the everyday have helped to transform notions of the public sphere in Euro-American societies in recent years. From the late 1970s onwards, Britain and other Western countries experienced a decisive shift to the political right, the implications of which are still being felt, even in those countries that now have nominally centre-left governments. There has been a series of social and political changes, such as the expansion of homeownership, the deregulation of markets and the managerialist transformation of the workplace, that have had an untold impact on everyday spaces and routines. But these changes have rarely been acknowledged as the product of political processes. Indeed, they seem to have coincided with increasing popular disengagement from mainstream politics. The turnout at the British general election in 2001 was 59 per cent, the lowest since the wartime election of 1918. In such a context, as Nick Couldry argues, the representational boundaries that separate 'the political' from 'the non-political' are crucially significant (2001: 131–2).

These boundaries are consolidated in the increasingly significant intersection between media representation and political discourse, where the policy decisions that affect people's everyday lives are represented, caricatured or evaded.

One of the ways in which these boundaries can be understood is in the context of what Andrew Milner calls 'the strange death of class' in media and political representation (1999: 1). Thatcherism's supporters saw it as removing the spectre of class conflict from British society, shifting power away from organized labour and an old-school Establishment and towards an ever-expanding middle class of individual consumers and shareholders. More accurately, we could say that Thatcherism's class politics were redirected into a fundamental rethinking of the relationship between public and private space. In Britain and many other countries, the experience of national planning during and after the Second World War led to a broad acceptance of the state's role in the management of forms of collective consumption such as transport, public utilities and social housing. In the era of Conservative government between 1979 and 1997, though, this consensus disappeared as every major nationalized industry was privatized, and the revenue-raising and planning powers of local authorities were drastically reduced. The new consensus increasingly saw the public sector as 'the twilight zone of the second best' (Hutton 1996: 9), and a new politics of scarcity developed, which tended to blame public bodies for wasting taxpayers' money. Thatcherism's 'classlessness' was underpinned by the ideological construction of a normative everyday life separated from this residualized public sphere. Its iconic figures were homeowning, car-owning neo-suburbanites in the south-east of England, particularly the white-collar and skilled manual workers who were now seen as the key swing voters in elections.

Thatcher's successor, John Major, was often mocked for his faux-populist identification with ordinary people, most famously with his introduction of a Cones Hotline in 1993, which allowed drivers to ring up and complain about the rows of fluorescent plastic bollards that divert traffic on major roads. But in his championing of the individual motorist or consumer against bureaucratic controls, Major's political imagery owed much to Thatcherism's identification with 'Middle England', a term that gained wide media currency during his premiership. This term may be partly derived from 'Middle America', a similarly geographically indeterminate region populated by the silent majority of Americans whose 'moderate' opinions are supposedly unrepresented in mainstream media. 'Middle England' similarly suggests a vague geographical area in the south and Midlands and outside the major cities, but it refers less to a region than a particular group of people who have joined the expanding middle classes since the Thatcher years. The concept of 'Middle England' points to the complex relationship between organized politics and a carefully monitored but vaguely defined 'public opinion' in post-Thatcherite Britain. Significantly, its emergence coincided with that of another term, 'the chattering classes'. Coined in the early years of the Thatcher era, this phrase is usually taken to mean a cadre of metropolitan, left-liberal intellectuals, spouting off about the country's problems at dinner parties. It suggests people who are detached from both the centre of political power and the straightforward, sensible aspirations of Middle England.

New Labour updated the imagery but essentially consolidated this construction of everyday life. Tony Blair's Third Way politics attempted to identify the instincts and interests of Middle England with apolitical common sense and a supposedly inexorable process of 'modernization'. The number of nicknames coined for the inhabitants of Middle England in recent years – 'Basildon Man', 'Mondeo Man', 'Sierra Man', 'Galaxy Man', 'Granada Woman', 'Worcester Woman', 'Pebbledash People' – is a testament to their perceived electoral importance. These terms identify people according to their mid-range cars, semi-detached houses or towns in the south-east or the West Midlands. They have supplanted the 'man on the Clapham omnibus', a once ubiquitous but now seldom-used phrase, coined by a High Court judge in 1903 to describe the average citizen. (The gentrified area of Clapham in south-west London is no longer the embodiment of ordinariness, and the bus passenger is not the sort of average citizen with whom politicians are keen to identify.) Increasingly testing and defining its policies through market research among focus groups of key voters, New Labour has aimed to short-circuit political processes and speak directly to a nominally homogeneous, but actually carefully targeted, 'people'. The courting of 'Soccer Moms' and 'Nascar Dads' (after the National Association for Stock Car Auto Racing) in recent American presidential elections is part of a similarly circular process involving media caricature, popular psephology and policy-making.

This political reconstruction of everyday life in recent years has been crucially connected with its media representation. The predominantly right-wing British tabloids, particularly the two bestselling newspapers, the *Sun* and the *Daily Mail*, have been extremely effective in setting the agenda for the rest of the media in a country where newspaper reading is still widespread and television news is relatively non-partisan. In the 1980s and early 1990s, the *Sun* perfectly caught the mood of the aspirational working classes who supported Thatcher by speaking up for 'ordinary people' against the meddlesomeness of politicians and bureaucrats. In its famous 1992 election cover story, which it later claimed had swung the election for the Tories, the *Sun*'s banner headline pithily summarized the plight of mortgage-holders under an economically incompetent Labour government: 'Nightmare on Kinnock Street – He'll Have a New Home, You Won't' (*Sun* 1992).

The *Daily Mail*, the only tabloid newspaper whose circulation has risen in recent years, sees itself as the voice of 'Middle England'. Its perennial topic is the victimization of the middle classes, who it celebrates as the country's most economically dynamic, revenue-generating, law-abiding citizens. According to the *Mail*, 'Middle England' is always being 'ripped off', 'mocked', 'ignored', 'oppressed', 'ground into the dust', threatened by 'tax bombshells', 'creeping burdens' and 'tinpot Trotskyists'. In its identification with the middle classes, the *Mail* hypes up 'good' news about house price rises, opposes high income-tax burdens on 'ordinary' families, supports motorists' protests against petrol taxes and criticizes many forms of traffic management such as speed cameras, road tolls and congestion pricing. The *Mail*'s editor, Paul Dacre, has said:

> I think some newspapers and a lot of the radio and television media are now run by liberal, politically correct consensors [*sic*] who just talk to each other and forget that in the real world there are people who feel differently.
>
> (Hagerty 2002)

Dacre's comment is typical of the ways in which competing media elites wage battle over the ideological terrain of everyday life. These elites often identify with 'ordinary' people by dismissing their opponents as out-of-touch metropolitans. It is interesting, though, that the most discussed, mythically tedious spaces of British daily life – such as the M25 London Orbital motorway, the London Underground, south-east commuter trains and gridlocked London traffic – are in the capital city and its environs. Of course, the south-east has particular transport problems because of its status as the country's economic powerhouse, but centralized media elites also help to define the typicality of particular everyday experiences. It is not just that commuter travel is a special concern in Greater London, a region that relies greatly on trains to transport its workers, but also that commuting is a disproportionately middle-class concern. Those in managerial and professional occupations are most likely to drive themselves to work and to travel by mainline or underground trains, and they travel furthest and most often on commuting or business trips (*Social Trends* 2004: 186; Department for Transport 2004: 36).

The difficulty with interpreting these media stories is that they deal with something more opaque than the sorts of 'folk devils and moral panics' (to borrow Stanley Cohen's phrase) that are more usually the subject of critical analyses of the news media. The media and political discourses that demonize youth gangs, welfare cheats, single mothers and asylum seekers tend to focus on specific social problems and clearly defined enemies. By contrast, these media stories about everyday life involve the construction of normalcy without *obvious* signifiers of otherness, although as I will argue later on, they can produce low-level folk devils – transit van drivers, traffic wardens, school-run mums, estate agents. In his preface to the third edition of his book, Cohen suggests that in recent years 'some of the social space once occupied by moral panics has been filled by more inchoate social anxieties, insecurities and fears'.

In part he attributes this to the development of a 'risk society', the new forms of technology, mobility and interdependence that create anxieties about food safety, health, transport and terrorism (Cohen 2002: xxv).

These anxieties are more likely to be exploited in the competitive and crowded environment of 24-hour news production, which produces what one commentator has called 'avalanche journalism'. The media focus all their energies on the issue or controversy of the moment, which is quickly forgotten when the next story comes along (Rawnsley 2001: xvii). In a British context, recent examples of these issues include housing (rising or falling property prices, new building on greenfield sites), food (genetically modified (GM) crops, 'mad cow' disease), commuter travel (motorway jams, fuel prices, the dilapidated rail network) and work ('fat cat' executive salaries, shortfalls in pension funds, the 'work–life balance'). Unlike social problems such as crime, drug addiction, poverty and homelessness, these issues directly affect the daily lives of the majority of the population. The appeal of such media stories lies in their ability to connect with these issues but also to address them in a way that defuses their more problematic aspects, closing off important questions about politics, class and social difference.

What is often at stake here, in fact, is the definition of 'ordinary'. In his etymology of this word, Raymond Williams identifies a slippage beginning in the seventeenth century when the original sense of 'ordinary' (that which is correct or standard, shared by everyone) was joined by a more unfavourable sense (that which is ranked lower in a hierarchy). Unlike the words 'banal' and 'mundane', though, the new sense of the word did not overtake the old one. 'Ordinary people', a phrase that only became common in the mid-nineteenth century, can mean the vulgar and uneducated masses or the decent and sensible majority. Williams notes that, whether it is used positively or pejoratively, the phrase 'ordinary people' is often 'an indication of a generalized body of Others . . . from the point of view of a conscious governing or administrative minority' (1988: 226).

In newspaper stories, the phrase 'ordinary people' and variations on it often denotes this form of sublimated politics, a way of silently evoking class without having to elaborate on it. Invocations of the 'ordinary' motorist, taxpayer or homeowner, often preceded by qualifiers such as 'beleaguered' and 'long-suffering', implicitly exclude certain sections of society, as well as signifying a more general hostility to forms of collective consumption and the public sphere. These invocations are implicitly concerned with negative liberty and are underpinned by an inferred opposition between political meddlers and the average citizens who should be left alone to enjoy their decent job, nice car and mortgaged home. This championing of 'ordinary people' in media and political discourse has served as ideological reinforcement for what Cornelius Castoriadis calls the privatization of social life in modern society, in which public matters – or more exactly, social matters – are seen not only as foreign and hostile but also as beyond people's grasp and not liable to be affected by their actions. It therefore sends people back into 'private life', or into a 'social life' in which society itself is never explicitly put into question.

(Castoriadis 1988: 238)

This retreat from politics is, of course, based on highly politicized assumptions about 'private life' and 'ordinary people'. The 'ordinary man' to whom Certeau dedicates *Arts de Faire* is also a mythic figure referred to by politicians and journalists *ad infinitum* (see Ahearne 1995: 187).

Rethinking everyday life

This shift in political and cultural life over the last few decades suggests that we need to find new ways of theorizing the everyday. The thoroughgoing analysis of quotidian life developed in France in the decades after the Second World War.[5] The work of theorists such as Lefebvre, Castoriadis and the Situationists centred on what they called 'bureaucratic capitalism', a new kind of intervention by public and private managers into everyday routines. It is worth noting that these French theorists were writing within a national tradition of *dirigisme* that is still quite strong compared to other Western countries, even after a wave of privatization reform in France from the late 1990s onwards. But they were also reflecting a more general shift in western Europe in the early cold war period, as the state became increasingly involved in housing, transport and urban reconstruction, producing what Lefebvre called 'a parody of socialism, a communitarian fiction with a capitalist content' (1969: 40).

After his expulsion from the French Communist Party in 1958, Lefebvre made these links between 'state socialism' and 'state capitalism' more explicitly. In both the planned economies of the eastern bloc and the welfare states of western Europe, he argued, technocratic planning had created blandly functional environments that allowed hierarchical societies to run smoothly and reproduce themselves. Lefebvre and other French theorists were also influenced by decolonization, a process that took place in several European countries at this time but was particularly traumatic and protracted for the French. For Lefebvre, the transformation of everyday life in France in the postwar era mirrored the spatial relationships of colonialism in its pull between homogeneity and hierarchy, between a controlling centre and a periphery to which otherness and marginality were expelled. The most intelligent leaders in capitalist societies, he writes, have 'succeeded in getting out of the dead-end of colonialism' (Lefebvre 1969: 40) by investing their surplus capital at home, in the rebuilding of cities, the development of suburban areas, and new consumer markets.

This French critique of everyday life was formulated during the massive rebuilding of Paris in the so-called *trente glorieuses*, the thirty years of social and economic reconstruction in France between 1945 and 1975. During this period, the city forced out its working-class and immigrant populations through compulsory purchase and rent increases, and built elaborate transport networks to allow them to commute to work from suburbs and new towns. A key symbolic element in this restructuring was the demolition in the early 1970s of Victor Baltard's beautiful nineteenth-century pavilions, which housed the old food market at Les Halles. This market, which was clogging up traffic by handling one-fifth of the country's meat and greengrocery (Ardagh 1988: 263), was eventually replaced in 1979 by a shopping centre-cum-interchange for the RER (the suburban express railway) and the Métro. Someone, perhaps a disgruntled *banlieusard*, wrote on a sign erected at Les Halles in the early 1970s: 'The centre of Paris will be beautiful. Luxury will be king. But we will not be here' (Baillie and Salmon 2001: 452). As city centres were increasingly given over to business, tourism and government, Lefebvre argued, the poorer members of society lived out an impoverished everyday life in peripheral areas. With their carefully zoned housing estates, and long, straight streets that could be easily surveyed and patrolled by police, these new suburbs even replicated the layout of colonial towns in an effort to control their populations (Lefebvre 1971: 59). The Situationists put it in typically emphatic fashion: 'Everyday life, policed and mystified by every means, is a sort of reservation for good natives who keep modern society running without understanding it' (Debord 1981: 70).

This body of work still offers significant insights that I have drawn on in this book, most importantly the notion that lived, social space is inextricably linked to represented, imagined space, and that both are central to an understanding of everyday life. But these theorists always imagined the everyday as a dynamic and historically evolving concept, and so they would not be surprised that more recent transformations in daily life have been bound up with different social and political problems. First, the uneven effects of globalization on the everyday lives of people throughout the world question the continued usefulness of Lefebvre's analogy of displaced colonialism – and, in any case, the primarily middle-class movement to the suburbs in Britain and America complicates his understanding of the shifting relationships between centre and periphery in urbanized society. Second, the resurgence of neo-liberalism in the last few decades brings a new perspective to the Lefebvrian critique of large-scale planning and technocratic expertise. This neo-liberal orthodoxy has evoked the history of state planning in the form of high-rise flats, new towns and transport monopolies as a caution against all sorts of big government, often supplementing this with crude comparisons with the former communist states. The New Right's ideological outmanoeuvring of the Left over the last few decades, in which it has appropriated an anti-statist rhetoric associated initially with progressive protest in the 1960s, has largely been fought on the terrain of 'everyday life'.

This political shift has been framed as an escape from the over-regulated public sphere into a private space in which we can all get on with our own lives, free from interference. The reality is that old-fashioned state regulation has been replaced by new forms of interventionism, usually termed 'the new public management', in which market imperatives increasingly colonize daily life. In Britain, this new public management has included the contracting out of public services to private firms under competitive tender; the establishment of internal markets in large public services such as the National Health Service; the regulation of these markets through the 'naming and shaming' of operators, quality incentive contracts, league tables and mission statements; the favouring of indirect taxes and private finance initiatives over direct taxation, which might be unpopular with key voters; and the valuing of the advice of managers and consultants over that of public-service professionals, now viewed as a self-interested elite protecting their own jobs and privileges.

The classic model for understanding the ideological landscape produced by Thatcherism is Stuart Hall's concept of 'authoritarian populism', first formulated in the late 1970s even before Thatcher came to power. Hall argued that Thatcherism owed its broad electoral appeal to its combination of traditionally conservative discourses of the nation, the family, the law and the 'enemy within' (trade unions, racial others) with populist notions of the free market, which appealed to the aspirational consumer and homeowner. Hall's work showed how Thatcherism grounded neo-liberal policies in an appeal to 'the little people' against 'the big battalions' (1983: 6). It seamlessly melded politics and everyday life, discovering 'a powerful means of translating economic doctrine into the language of experience, moral imperative and common sense' (1983: 28).

Bob Jessop and his colleagues criticized Hall's model of authoritarian populism, arguing that he overestimated Thatcherism's hegemonic hold over public opinion. For them, Thatcherism did not represent a new ideological paradigm but a much more pragmatic alliance between established power blocs and sections of the population benefiting quite specifically from low taxation and inflation, council house sales and rising consumer standards (Jessop et al. 1988: 68–98, 109–24). Their argument is partly confirmed by more recent studies of voter attitudes, which show that key Thatcherite policies, such as introducing market incentives into public services and accepting higher unemployment in return for lower inflation, never had majority electoral support (Heath et al. 2001: 31–57). Despite the moralistic rhetoric of many members of the Thatcher government, the economic liberalism of these years was also accompanied by increasingly liberal social attitudes. With the benefit of hindsight, it can be seen that the most important cultural shift produced by Thatcherism was not an intensification of greed, intolerance or racism, but a much more nebulous sense of disconnection from social life.

In the 1980s and 1990s, the archetype of the upwardly mobile worker who had been won over to Thatcherism was 'Basildon Man'.[6] In search of the real Basildon Man (and Woman), Dennis Hayes and Alan Hudson carried out two surveys of 500 skilled workers in this Essex new town during the election years of 1992 and 1997. They found that Basildonians felt little connection with political parties or institutions outside their immediate family, such as the Church, trade unions or workplaces. They also noted a stark contrast between personal optimism and collective pessimism in their informants. While most Basildonians saw themselves as reasonably happy and successful, they tended to view this success as a result of their own hard work, and thought that society as a whole was deteriorating.

Hayes and Hudson's most surprising conclusion was that, in this supposed hotbed of working-class conservatism, Thatcherism was 'skin-deep' (2001: 38). There was no major ideological shift among Basildonians in these years, and they gave only lukewarm endorsement to policies such as privatization, share ownership and income tax cuts. But while they broadly supported a non-Thatcherite agenda of improving public services through taxation, they tended to be sceptical of the ability of politicians and bureaucrats to bring about these improvements without interfering unnecessarily in people's everyday lives. Hayes and Hudson conclude that the real impact of Thatcherism was felt in its role as 'the corrosive agent which broke down the vestigial certainties of old forms of social life' and 'dealt a death-blow to important forms of collectivism in society' (2001: 42).

In the light of Hayes and Hudson's work, it could be argued that Hall's model of authoritarian populism is too concerned with partisan constructions of the 'nation' and 'people'. Few people identify themselves as residents of 'Middle England', a term endlessly reiterated but rarely defined in the media. The persuasiveness of this term relies not on a specific political agenda or even the sense of an imagined community but on the tacit acceptance of a certain notion of ordinary life. In a more important sense, though, this suggests that Hall's thesis turned out to be deadly accurate. Thatcherism achieved its aim of becoming 'the common sense of the age', according to the Gramscian notion of a deeply embedded mindset that 'shapes out ordinary, practical, everyday calculation and appears as natural as the air we breathe' (Hall 1988: 8). This 'common sense' has worked not by persuading everyone that it is desirable or right but that, in the often-repeated slogan, 'there is no alternative' to neo-liberal capitalism. Jessop et al.'s argument that Hall is too interested in the ideological productions of the media at the expense of the concrete workings of power blocs and the vested interests of the electorate thus seems anachronistic (Jessop et al. 1988: 73). In the intervening years, as the relationship between politics and the media has become ever closer and more complex, the New Right's success has largely been founded on these public discourses of an apolitical 'ordinary life'. A key issue for democracy, particularly in a majoritarian electoral system in which many politicians believe that a few thousand votes in a small number of marginal constituencies can determine their futures, is how we define and think about this 'ordinariness'.

Ways of reading

In *Mythologies*, one of the founding texts in the study of everyday life in cultural studies, Roland Barthes offers a series of readings of margarine advertisements, soap powders, cookery columns, cars and other ordinary phenomena in 1950s France. Barthes shows how these everyday things generate 'meta-languages', secondary connotations alongside their more obvious meanings, which support the dominant values of petit-bourgeois society. Arguing that myth is 'a type of speech', Barthes writes that 'the universe is infinitely fertile in suggestions. Every object in the world can pass from a closed, silent existence to an oral state, open to appropriation by society' (1993: 109). He is interested in the semiotically rich resources of an emerging consumer society, a world in which commodities are newly charged with value and significance. In his virtuoso readings, these phenomena are always brimming over with meanings, a potent vehicle for hidden messages and half-formulated desires.

The mundane everyday life with which my own book is concerned may not be so hermeneutically suggestive. As I have already argued, quotidian culture *has* inspired its own 'mythologies' – on the one hand, the myth of the false normativity of ordinary life, which serves to demarcate the boundaries between the political and the non-political; on the other hand, the anti-mythology of the everyday as marginal and unworthy of attention. But these mythologies are so buried in unnoticed, habitual spaces and routines that they are relatively resistant to the kinds of analyses undertaken by Barthes. I want to find a critical strategy that acknowledges this boredom in everyday life, rather than one that simply seeks to transform it through resourceful readings that strip away the veneer of what Barthes calls the 'falsely obvious' (1993: 11).

For Lefebvre, the structuralism of Barthes and other French theorists of the 1950s and 1960s overestimates the role of language in the construction of reality. Structuralism's 'fetishism of signification', its desire to pin phenomena down to a textual meaning, is ill-equipped to deal with the blankness and boredom of daily life (Lefebvre 2002: 276). The everyday cannot simply be read like a literary text, because it is lived out in spaces and practices as much as in language and discourse:

When codes worked up from literary spaces are applied to spaces – to urban spaces, say – we remain . . . on the purely descriptive level. Any attempt to use such codes as a means of deciphering social space must surely reduce that space itself to the status of a 'message', and the inhabiting of it to the status of a 'reading'.

(Lefebvre 1991b: 7)

In the postwar period, Lefebvre argues, these social spaces have become even more difficult to 'read' as they increasingly form part of illegible technocratic systems, what he calls 'blind fields' (2003b: 29). The everyday can be read only in isolated 'moments' or 'rhythms', which fleetingly reveal the dynamic historical forces that underpin it (Lefebvre 2004). In his essay 'Seen from the Window', Lefebvre describes looking from the balcony of his Parisian apartment onto a busy intersection over a period of several hours. After a while he begins to notice patterns in this apparently chaotic street scene: the rhythm of the traffic-light cycle, the stop-start movements of cars and pedestrians, the contrast between moments of feverish activity and relative calm. He concludes that the everyday needs to be understood as a series of shifting, interconnecting elements that resist the modern notion that sight offers intelligibility: 'No camera, no image or sequence of images can show these rhythms. One needs equally attentive eyes and ears, a head, a memory, a heart' (Lefebvre 1996: 227).

Certeau's notion of reading as 'poaching', although it has tended to be appropriated in cultural studies as a model for the semiotic inventiveness of the consumer, also seeks to engage with these barely legible aspects of quotidian life. Much of his work is based on an opposition between *writing* as a cumulative activity attached to things or places (books, offices, libraries) and *reading* as an inarticulable experience lacking a specific place (Certeau 1984: 174). Certeau understands reading not as the deciphering of a pre-existing signifying system but as an anti-hermeneutics that fastens on slippery, non-discursive practices. In this sense, the textual reader's aimless 'drift across the page' mirrors the 'ephemeral dance' of those who participate in everyday practices (1984: xxi). Like Lefebvre, Certeau suggests that the 'imaginary totalizations produced by the eye', in a modern culture of insistent visuality, have largely erased these invisible, mobile practices (1984: 93). For all their political and theoretical differences, Certeau and Lefebvre both see the everyday as an elusive category, stretched out invisibly across urban space, incorporating wordless activities, and caught up in the nameless, indefinable feelings of alienation experienced in the relative comfort of Western consumer societies. At times, the 'everyday' in their work can seem almost unreadable, forever escaping analysis or interpretation, its structural relationships graspable only in disconnected fragments.[7]

In his *Theory of Film* (1960), Siegfried Kracauer suggests a different approach, which shares Certeau's and Lefebvre's scepticism about conventional social-scientific approaches to everyday life but focuses on a sphere that they tend to regard as inimical to the quotidian: the visual. When other social theorists were stressing the city's restless energy and phantasmagoric modernity, Kracauer wrote about the empty, purposeless moments that permeate the urban everyday, and that are filled with commuting, queuing and other forms of waiting.[8] He argues that the specific properties of film and photography can open up new ways of reading this mundane daily life that combine ethnographic investigation with careful textual analysis. Kracauer outlines a history of film in which the exploitation of its narrative potential leads to the progressive neglect of its mechanical possibilities. He shows how these contrasting creative directions were prefigured in cinema's earliest years in the work of two French directors, Louis Lumière and Georges Méliès. Lumière's short films, such as *Lunch Hour at the Lumière Factory* and *Arrival of a Train* (both 1895), recorded everyday happenings in public places that would still have taken place in the absence of the filmmaker. Méliès's films, such as *A Trip to the Moon* (1902) and *An Impossible Voyage* (1904), pioneered the use of the film studio and created a series of dramatic tableaux with the help of painted backdrops and special effects (Kracauer 1960: 30–3).

Hollywood filmmakers, who increasingly dominated the world film industry after the First World War, followed Méliès's studio model. The cinema closed itself off from the commonplace events of the everyday, staging instead an elaborate fantasy world of illusionism and escapism, in a way that was symptomatic of a more general tendency in popular culture to offer a short-lived fix of the needs and desires that quotidian life ignores:

> The more monotony holds sway over the working day, the further away you must be transported once work ends. . . . The true counterstroke against the office machine . . . is the world vibrant with colour. The world not as it is, but as it appears in popular hits. A world every last corner of which is cleansed, as though with a vacuum cleaner, of the dust of everyday existence.
>
> (Kracauer 1998: 92–3)

Kracauer sees the hegemony of Hollywood cinema as a particular tragedy because of film's potential affinity with the unstaged 'flow of life' (1960: 71). The mechanical automatism of the camera allows it to capture those everyday phenomena that we might prefer to ignore, or that we simply overlook because they are 'part of us like our skin, and because we know them by heart we do not know them with the eye' (1960: 55). In modern filmmaking, the use of continuity editing directs the viewer along a narrative line, and the close-up focalizes the narrative around its leading characters. But when film is reduced to its basic mechanical characteristics, such as in stationary or slow tracking shots, it has a unique capacity to reveal the anonymous, collective routines of daily life. Although Kracauer is often described as a realist, he actually argues that film engages with the everyday not when it attempts to be true to 'reality' but when it draws on its own unique qualities as a medium (1960: 12).[9]

In his final, unfinished book, *History: The Last Things Before the Last*, Kracauer suggests that his life's work is reducible to a single aim: 'the rehabilitation of objectives and modes of being which still lack a name and hence are over-looked or misjudged', and which 'despite all that has been written about them are still largely *terra incognita*' (1995b: 4). For Kracauer, the discipline of history is particularly suited to this task not only because it often deals with disregarded aspects of life but because it is a necessarily tentative mode of inquiry lying somewhere between the abstractions of philosophy and the 'pseudo-scientific methodological strictness' of social science (1995b: 214). He argues that, rather than relying on the controlled situations of the empir-ical researcher, the historian draws promiscuously on a range of sources, the meaning or significance of which cannot always be anticipated prior to exam-ining them. The historian should not strive for scientific objectivity but a kind of 'estrangement' or 'active passivity' in relation to these materials, allowing her to draw out relationships that do not simply 'freeze into a more or less rigid pattern of trends, cross-currents, majority and minority attitudes, and the like' (1995b: 84, 86). Kracauer compares examining historical evidence with looking at old photographs, in that they both have a kind of obdurate reality that must be acknowledged, but they also suggest endless-ness, that our knowledge of the past can never be complete (1995b: 58–9). He suggests that photography and history are both 'anteroom areas' where we find provisional truths rather than fixed meanings. Photographs

> help us to think *through* things, not above them . . . the photographic media make it much easier for us to incorporate the transient phe-nomena of the outer world, thereby redeeming them from oblivion. Something of this kind will also have to be said of history.
>
> (Kracauer 1995b: 192)

In the following chapters, I have taken these insights as a starting point for some of my own readings of the everyday. Like Kracauer's historian, I focus on a wide variety of texts – films, television programmes and per-formance works; webcam images, photographs, postcards and artwork; government reports, planning documents and codes of practice; professional and trade journals; newspaper and magazine articles; public information films; architecture, street furniture and material culture; and urban myths, stereo-types and rules of everyday etiquette – which have all been produced in different contexts for varying reasons that are not directly related to my own research. Kracauer's idea of the partially 'estranged' historian sifting through disparate sources to make previously unconsidered connections offers a way of acknowledging the difficulties of reading the everyday – as both overlooked, habitual reality and concealed metaphor for endless tedium and unexamined ordinariness – without necessarily yielding to its *un*readability.[10]

This approach might help to denaturalize a quotidian time that so often seems continuous and interminable. In daily life, as Maurice Blanchot puts it, 'we are neither born nor do we die: hence the weight and the enigmatic force of everyday truth' (1987: 20). My book aims to show that the spaces and practices of modern daily life were not always boringly routine but were, in the recent past, sites of leisure, consumption and tourism; standard-bearers of technological innovation, urban regeneration and modernist aesthetics; and sources of political controversy and popular protest. Unearthing these historical traces subverts what Certeau calls 'the modern mutation of time into a quantifiable and regulatable space', revealing 'a sort of anti-museum' that is 'not localizable . . . Objects and words also have hollow places in which a past sleeps, as in the everyday acts of walking, eating, going to bed, in which ancient revolutions slumber' (1984: 89, 108). When the study of daily life is historically contextualized, it points to the reality of uneven develop-ment, the co-existence of innovation, inertia and obsolescence in modern capitalist societies. As such, it can offer a way of re-opening what Richard Johnson sees as the interrupted dialogue between the various forms of radical cultural history emerging since the 1960s, which have emphasized the import-ance of 'history from below' and *Alltagsgeschichte* (the history of everyday life), and a cultural studies that has more usually emphasized the innovative and emergent in contemporary media cultures (Johnson 2001; Johnson *et al.* 2004: 123).[11]

I want to give an example of what I mean by returning to the experi-ence with which I began this chapter: waiting for a bus. Tom Wood's series of photographs taken from bus windows in Liverpool, collected in *All Zones Off Peak* (1998) and *Bus Odyssey* (2001), reveals how the political nature of bus travel is often buried in the ignored routines of daily life (Figure 1.2). Since the years in which Wood's photographs were taken (1979–97) exactly coincide with an unbroken period of Conservative government, they could be read as politically motivated studies of the disenfranchised of the northern inner cities in these years. His bus journeys visually connect the regenerated areas of the city with more neglected, peripheral spaces: the declining high streets, areas of wasteland, cleared slums and abandoned houses of the inner-ring suburbs. But what is really interesting about Wood's project is not the *punctum* of the individual images but the slow-burning, cumulative effect of the series as a whole, a small selection taken from over 3,000 rolls of film and 100,000 photographs. These photographs seek not so much to

Figure 1.2 Stockbridge Village (Cantrill Farm), 1988.
From Tom Wood, *All Zones Off Peak*, London: Dewi Lewis, 1998. © Tom Wood, reproduced by permission.

capture specific moments but rather to elaborate on the endlessly repeated routines and minimal, wordless communities produced by bus journeys. In Kracauer's terms, they fully exploit the visual possibilities of their particular medium, allowing the patient viewer to re-examine the overlooked surfaces of quotidian life.

Wood used a Leica camera with a quiet shutter and shot from the chest, allowing him to take photographs unobtrusively, in the manner of Walker Evans's secretly taken New York subway portraits (1938–41). Rather than catching his subjects unawares, though, Wood reveals them in that semi-introspective, blank-faced mode adopted in routine public spaces. The principal tension in these photographs is between these unnamed people, absent-mindedly following their fixed timetables and prescribed routes, and the minute changes to the physical environment picked up by the camera over time – an incongruity that shows how the temporality of the everyday is, in Susan Stewart's evocative phrase, 'drowned out by the silence of the ordinary' (1993: 14). Wood's images reveal historical and political contexts that are never acknowledged as such, obscured as they are behind the apparent inertia of daily routine. Their subject is what Georges Perec calls 'background noise', 'the infra-ordinary', the sphere of existence that lies beneath notice or comment, and within which 'we sleep through our lives in a dreamless sleep' (1999: 21, 50, 210). Wood's photographs aim to capture these events, which take up so many hours of our lives but are rarely the source of cultural anxiety or contestation. As the following chapters aim to show, this is what makes 'reading the everyday' so methodologically problematic but also potentially rewarding.

Chapter 2

WORKSPACE
Office life and commuting

IN THE NEO-LIBERAL ECONOMIC and political climate of the last few decades, work and its related activities have undergone seismic changes. Perhaps more than any other area of quotidian life, workspace throughout Europe, America and the rest of the world has become increasingly standardized as it is subsumed into a global corporate culture reaching far beyond the world of commerce into many areas of working life. While this kind of workspace is used by growing numbers of people throughout the world, its burdens and rewards are distributed unequally. This tension between globalized sameness and local inequality is evident in new, homogeneous types of working environment (open-plan offices, out-of-town call centres, business parks and industrial estates); in the pervasive 'consultative' ethos of managerial culture that seeks to conceal its harsher realities; and in complex patterns of mass commuting that reflect the dynamics of work culture. This chapter explores some of these issues with reference to theories and representations of office life and commuting. In their different ways, these discourses explore a particular problem: how to locate the reality of social change in the habitual acts of working life, which remain resistant to narrative representation, ethnographic investigation and political critique.

This chapter is divided into five parts. First, it applies Siegfried Kracauer's work on 'the salaried masses', with its meticulous examination of the minutiae of office life, to a reading of the modern-day call centre. Second, it explores the motivational rhetoric and spatial politics of corporate culture through an analysis of the film *Office Space*. Third, it shows how the television comedy *The Office* conveys the inertia and boredom of office life in its reworking of the narrative conventions of sitcom and docusoap. Fourth, it discusses the uses of ethnography as a way of thinking about the commute as a distinctive form of 'workspace', particularly in relation to Marc Augé's research on the Paris Métro. Finally, it employs some of these insights in an investigation of the rules, technologies, architecture and politics of the London Underground.

The rise of the *Angestellten*

In *The Salaried Masses*, his pioneering analysis of office life published in 1930, Siegfried Kracauer argues that his fellow Weimar intellectuals have underestimated the significance of the most ordinary experiences of daily life:

> We must rid ourselves of the delusion that it is major events which most determine a person. He is more deeply and lastingly influenced by the tiny catastrophes of which everyday existence is made up, and his fate is certainly linked predominantly to the sequence of these miniature occurrences. . . . The radicalism of these radicals would have more weight if it really penetrated the structure of reality, instead of issuing its decrees from on high. How is everyday life to change, if even those whose vocation is to stir it up pay it no attention?
>
> (Kracauer 1998: 62, 101)

In the last days of the Weimar Republic, as the country lurched from one financial or political crisis to another, this position was certainly counter-intuitive. For Kracauer, though, the notion of history as a sweeping, macro-force that punctuates the everyday with crises and disasters was precisely the problem. It made historical events seem capricious in the way that they influenced people's lives without changing their underlying conditions. Kracauer wanted to show instead how historical change emerged and consol-idated itself in the daily existence of new social groups, such as the white-collar workers who were increasingly populating large German cities such as Berlin and Frankfurt.

These *Angestellten* (salaried workers), particularly those of lower status such as stenographers, ledger clerks and switchboard operators, were prolif-erating as large firms and the expanding public sector acquired unprecedented levels of bureaucracy. With their monthly salaries, special insurance rights and the optimistic definition of their work as 'intellectual' labour, the new white-collar workers were encouraged to see themselves as an emergent middle class. After the First World War, though, the huge growth in white-collar work, and the migration of assembly-line techniques from factories to offices, meant that the salariat was actually increasingly proletarianized. Kracauer's argument about the link between routine lives and historical change proved prophetic. With just enough investment in the status quo to feel insecure about losing what little benefits they had, the office workers were courted by German political elites as a bulwark against communism, and later provided a key support base for Nazism (Mülder-Bach 1997: 45).

Kracauer's book was not translated into English until 1998, and is less well-known than more empirical sociologies of office life, such as C. Wright Mills's *White Collar* (1951) and David Lockwood's *The Blackcoated Worker* (1958). *The Salaried Masses* shares with these texts an interest in the declining class-consciousness and growing status anxiety of white-collar workers. Kracauer's work is unusual, though, in its attempt to understand office life in relation to a new type of quotidian existence experienced in modern cities, with its moments of tedious waiting, ephemeral community and nameless anxiety contained not only in the office but in cheap lodgings, commuting trains and city bars. Kracauer suggests that office life requires a new kind of research to make sense of it, because its political realities are obscured behind mundane tasks and vague, inarticulable feelings of alienation. His salaried employees, undertaking repetitive work that could easily be done by others, experience both the boredom of routine and the fear that even this impoverished existence, and its increasingly hollow claims to privileged status, might come to an end. Deprived of a career structure, they are pushed back into the trivia of their daily lives, either the clockwatching of the office or the fleeting distractions of city nightlife. This after-hours 'flight of images' is 'a flight from revolution and from death' (Kracauer 1998: 94), a culture of short-term escapism that distracts workers from the unproductive time of the office and lives frittered away in hourly segments.

For Kracauer, office life reproduces itself not so much through ideological indoctrination as through daily routines that come to seem inexorable and unchallengeable. The lives of the new salariat are like the purloined letter in Edgar Allen Poe's story: invisible by virtue of being so clearly on display (Kracauer 1998: 29). In the face of this methodological problem, Kracauer seeks to carve out a new kind of intellectual space somewhere between the rigours of social science and the more descriptive style of journalistic reportage. His methodology is distinct from that of the traditional ethnographer, who aims to provide an insider's account of an unfamiliar culture through observation, interviews and discourse analysis. Instead, Kracauer focuses on what he calls the 'inconspicuous surface-level expressions' (1995c: 75) of everyday life, seeking to re-examine the obvious rather than excavate buried meanings. Much of *The Salaried Masses* appeared first in the *feuilleton* section of the *Frankfurter Zeitung*, where writers sought to combine the topicality, vividness and quotidian detail of newspaper journalism with more in-depth analysis. But Kracauer also acknowledges that 'reality is a construction' that cannot simply be found in 'the more or less random observational results of reportage'. Reportage, he argues, merely 'photographs life' in a way that fails to examine how everyday phenomena are the product of particular

31

historical moments (1998: 32). His aim is to show how these 'minute details' of office life taken together 'characterize the economic life that spawns them' (1998: 62).

Kracauer assembles what he calls a 'mosaic' (1998: 32) of office life from interviews with workers, employers and union reps; overheard conversations in offices, labour exchanges and after-work hangouts; and quotations from company bulletins, news stories and classified ads. His book relies less on a carefully developed, linear argument than the cumulative effect of telling details – such as the young man who has to change his job from skilled metal-worker to unskilled bank messenger in order to gain his girlfriend's father's consent to their marriage (1998: 85); the official in the Berlin job centre who says that people with grey hair or a limp are harder to place (1998: 38); the chief executive who uses light signals to let employees standing outside his office know whether they should enter, wait or go away (1998: 40); and the office manager who talks about providing his women punch-card operators with 'short breaks for ventilation' (1998: 41). Kracauer shows how these small acts betray hidden tensions and incongruities: the gap between the inflated status of office work and its actual meniality; the superficial concern with appearance that lies behind the rhetoric of 'scientific' selection processes; the unaccountability of an executive that boasts of its informality and paternalism; and the tendency of employers to treat their workers like mechanical objects in need of servicing.

While Kracauer's book clearly belongs to a specific historical moment, it has many resonances with the modern workplace. On the one hand, the injustices and exploitations of the office life he examines are concrete and obvious; on the other hand, they are insubstantial and ethereal, concealed behind the dullness of routine and the unclear relationship between work tasks and their end results. Kracauer's method of painstaking attention to the boring and routine may be a useful way of thinking about how the tensions in post-Thatcherite working environments are lived out in what he calls 'the imperceptible dreadfulness of normal existence' (1998: 101).

Consider an increasingly familiar manifestation of the office: the call centre. The monotonous, poorly paid lot of the telephone operative is real enough, and the proliferation of call centres in recent years has led to a number of concerned press articles about the rise of these new 'dark satanic mills', 'phone farms' and 'sweatshops' (see Poulter 2000; Boggan 2001), supported by a more considered sociological literature (see Taylor et al. 2002). But the call centre is also a virtual space, founded on unseen relationships between workers and consumers. Ulrich Beck argues that one of the characteristics of the new kind of 'flexible, pluralized underemployment' in liberal economies is that its dynamics are increasingly hidden: 'The place of the *visible* character of work, concentrated in factory halls and tall buildings, is taken by an invisible organization of the firm' (1992: 129, 142). City centre offices often function as a brand statement, flaunting the status and prestige of the company with their high-rise towers, mirror-glass walls, and imposing atria for important visitors. Call centres, though, are largely unnoticed features of the peri-urban landscape. They are typically found in anonymous warehouses or sheds in out-of-town office parks surrounded by parking lots and security barriers, without even a logo outside identifying the company. The technology of the call centre allows for flexibility over location, so they can be built in areas where land and labour are cheap, such as the north-east, Merseyside and the 'Celtic fringe' in the UK, or the Midwest in America. British and American companies are also increasingly relocating their call centres to parts of the English-speaking developing world, such as the West Indies, Malaysia and, especially, India.

In a few short years, the exasperating experience of phoning a call centre – being guided through the elaborate menu options by a recorded voice, put on hold with insipid muzak, and then connected to a relatively unskilled operative who may not be able to deal with complicated queries – has become a stock feature of Western daily life. This process obscures the stretching of capitalist relations across global space, relations that are experienced only as a deracinated accent on the other end of the line, with state-of-the-art fibre optics erasing any telltale fuzziness that might reveal the true distance between workers and customers.

In fact, the call-centre conversation is the clearest example of the application of queuing theory, an amalgam of applied mathematics and management science increasingly used in workplaces and other everyday situations such as traffic jams, supermarket queues and the rotation of beds in hospital wards. Queuing theory tries to manage systems in which customers arrive in so-called 'poisson distribution': in unpredictable numbers, at variable intervals, and requiring different periods of service. Agner Krarup Erlang, an engineer who worked for the Danish Telephone Company in Copenhagen, published the first paper on queuing theory in 1909. Erlang was trying to determine the optimum number of telephone switchboards required to serve a given population. The installation of more than the optimum would mean unnecessary expense, while less would mean unacceptable delays in connecting callers. The application of queuing theory would allow the company to offer a 'good enough' service while cutting down on the number of switchboard operators (Gross and Harris 1974: 10–11).

Modern queuing theory follows the same principles by reducing customers and workers to mathematical configurations. Its aim is to design a system at minimum cost by cutting down on server 'idle time' without inducing too much 'balking' (customers deciding not to join a queue if they think it will take them too long to be served) or 'reneging' (customers leaving the queue if they feel they have waited too long). The call centre applies queuing theory through the use of computer technologies such as IVR (interactive voice response, where the caller selects options from a menu using tone-dialling or simple verbal responses), ACD (automatic call distribution, which distributes the incoming calls to operators using a queuing system) and CTI (computer telephony integration, which allows workers to deal with customers by finding their details onscreen).

As Robin Leidner argues, the behaviour required of call-centre workers is similar to that required at McDonald's – 'a very stripped-down kind of interactive style, with some pseudo-*Gemeinschaft* thrown in' (1993: 183). Leidner notes a comment made, without apparent irony, by a member of the training staff at McDonald's Hamburger University: 'We want to treat each customer as an individual, in sixty seconds, or less' (1993: 178). Call-centre workers have to follow scripts when talking to clients, in order to get the customer served and off the line as quickly as possible. Deborah Cameron has shown this in her discourse analysis of call-centre workers' phone talk, which includes the repeating of numbers and addresses to eliminate errors, scripted familiarities (introducing themselves by their first name and using the name of the customer at the beginning and end of the conversation), polite 'fillers' ('just searching for you . . . sorry to keep you waiting') and listening noises (2000: 96–104).

Leidner suggests that companies find this routinization of service work useful because it helps to standardize the behaviour of customers as well as employees. The caller is not likely to bother the call-centre worker with time-wasting requests or clarifications, because she suspects that the worker is not trained or authorized to deal with them (Leidner 1993: 32). As Kracauer recognized in *The Salaried Masses*, this system is sustained by something more deep-rooted than ideological mystification. The phrases used to keep the customer on the line ('your call is important to us') are empty words that fool no one. As newly trained, youthful employees field calls from often irate, baffled customers, with more senior staff undertaking only the role of super-vision and surveillance, the call-centre conversation reveals much about the nature of workspace in contemporary capitalism. Kracauer's assessment of the office still seems apt:

> The summit of the hierarchy is lost in the dark skies of finance capital. The high-ups have withdrawn so far that they are no longer touched by life down below and can make their decisions purely on the basis of economic considerations.
>
> (Kracauer 1998: 48)

The multimedia stage production, *Alladeen*, which toured the world from 2003 to 2005, explores some of these issues.[1] *Alladeen* is set principally in Bangalore, the call-centre destination of choice for many Western companies because of its particular reputation for IT expertise. *Alladeen* follows a group of call-centre workers as they go through their training. They learn to watch out for 'mother-tongue interference', the unconscious lapsing into their own accents, and attend 'culture-sensitization' modules, where they are taught the rules of touchdown in American football and the names of sitcom characters, so they can identify more easily with their callers. As in *The Salaried Masses*, the reality of the call-centre workers' lives in *Alladeen* is captured in apparently inconsequential details that subtly reveal the abasement of their own culture. In the opening scene, for example, a group of sari-clad Indian women adopt the personae of *Friends* characters: 'This is Phoebe. How can I help you today?' Later on, when a caller says he is from Chicago, the Bangalore worker cries cheerily: 'My kind of town!'

Alladeen shows how these virtual lives as super-friendly, disembodied telephone voices clash with the money and family problems of the workers' own daily lives. As they have to work from 3am to noon to fit in with the working days of those thousands of miles away, virtual relationships serve as a poor substitute for a social life. In one scene, a female operative flirts with an Indian Silicon Valley whizz-kid who is trying to book a flight home to Delhi for a wedding. Having used her Rachel-from-*Friends* persona, she cannot reveal her true identity. As its title suggests, *Alladeen* sees its characters as modern-day Aladdins, searching vainly for personal transformation and wish fulfilment in a technology that only further entraps them in their mundane lives. For young Indian graduates, working in a call centre is a 'good' job with relatively high status. The characters in *Alladeen* suffer the double bind of the *Angestellten*, caught between these frustratingly abstract pretensions to professionalism and the depressingly concrete nature of their actual working conditions. *Alladeen* explores the hidden politics of the call centre by juxtaposing visibility and invisibility. A big screen hanging above the stage relays computer graphics, documentary footage of a real Bangalore call centre, snatches of Bollywood movies and Hollywood versions of Aladdin films. While it explores the theatrical possibilities of technology in this way, though, *Alladeen* makes some of the scenes that take place in the call centre invisible to the audience – which, of course, is exactly what Indian call-centre workers are to Western callers.

In showing how politics intrudes into the most routine operations of working life, *Alladeen* suggests that the call centre, far from being an inevitable effect of technological advance, is produced by specific historical contexts. Indeed, it is no coincidence that Britain and America have led the way in the development of call centres. Their proliferation since the late 1980s has been made possible by the deregulated labour markets in these two countries, and was given added impetus by the 'shareholder revolution', which meant that management policies were increasingly dictated by the search for short-term profits to boost stock prices. One of the effects of deregulation and shareholder power has been the creation of what is euphemistically known as 'flexible' labour markets in the white-collar sector, where temporary, casualized work is increasingly common. When New Labour came to power, it was particularly supportive of call centres because they connected with its overall aims of technological innovation, deregulated markets and the regeneration of depressed areas. This post-Thatcherite political culture is essentially fatalistic in its assumption that governments simply have to accept and adapt to the inexorable demands of global capitalism. When asked in December 2003 about the growing trend for offshoring, in which British companies were relocating their call centres to the developing world, Tony Blair tellingly replied that it was just 'the way the world is today . . . We have not tried to pretend to people that we can stop what is happening in the global economy' (Treanor 2003).

Exploring office space

Contemporary office life is closely bound up with the development of new types of space. The term 'the office' describes both a building and a particular form of work culture, and the two are increasingly interrelated. This new kind of designated workspace is epitomized in the science or business park – a site of high-quality offices in parkland on the edge of a big city, often near a motorway intersection and airport. The land is cheaper here than in city-centre locations, so there is more space for parking and large, open-plan offices wired up for computer terminals and other technologies. Business parks boomed in America in the 1970s, and were increasingly exported to Europe and the rest of the world in the 1980s and 1990s. The larger business parks have achieved a critical mass that allows them to offer sophisticated amenities (Phillips 1993: 12). Stockley Park near Heathrow Airport is one of the biggest and best European examples: 350 acres of ex-landfill converted into low-rise office buildings surrounded by greenery, lakes, weirs and ample parking, and equipped with wine bars, shops, banks, a swimming pool, a golf course and an equestrian centre. The amount of money invested in these environments, though, means that they tend to be reserved for multinational corporations and relatively high-status graduate workers.

The nature of this new kind of workspace, and the ideology of consultative managerialism that seeks to conceal its resilient hierarchies, are the subject of Mike Judge's film, *Office Space* (1999).[2] Unlike many other films about the white-collar workplace, such as *Nine-to-Five* (1980), *Working Girl* (1988) and *What Women Want* (2000), Judge's film does not simply use the office as a backdrop for conventional plot intrigue between the characters, or the comic implications of contemporary gender politics. In the first part of *Office Space*, the film focuses on the iterations of daily life rather than the unique events normally expected in mainstream film narrative. We hear a telephonist call countless times, in a grating voice, 'Corporate accounts payable, Nina speaking', and the central character, Peter Gibbons (Ron Livingston), is admonished on several occasions with the stock phrase: 'Sounds like someone has a case of the Mondays'. Gibbons's actual job is seminally pointless. In a prescient piece of plotting for a film made in 1999, he is working on updating bank software in preparation for what turned out to be a phantom problem: the Y2K bug.

Gibbons's workplace, Initech, which does something unspecified with computers, is located in an out-of-town business park. Filmed near Austin, Texas, *Office Space*'s flat, generic landscape – single-storey box buildings identifiable only by their clean corporate logos, endless parking spaces, and insipid landscaping made up of grass verges, concrete paving and symmetrical rows of newly planted trees – could be almost anywhere in the developed world. The slow pace of the early part of the film allows it to rest on the mundane generica of office life: the panelled ceilings, pencil cups, desk tidies, mouse pads, motivational pictures and artificial plants that are an increasingly uniform feature of working life as office supplies are monopolized by multinationals such as Office World and Corporate Express. Initech's open-plan workplace is dominated, though, by cubicles, those quasi-offices assembled from partition panels that were first made by the American company Herman Miller in the late 1960s as part of its 'Action Office System' and that have since become what Andrew Ross calls 'the signature footprint of alienation' for white-collar workers (2003: 59). The cubicles are often filmed from above to highlight their boxy uniformity and the proximity they enforce between co-workers.

Office Space is primarily about the tension between an assertive managerialism and the consultative rhetoric that seeks both to explain and to implement it. There is nothing particularly new about the 'libertarian' school of management theory, despite its self-presentation as groundbreaking and revolutionary. In the mid-1950s, William H. Whyte was already noting the rise of a management style that sought moral legitimacy through its emphasis on the employee's 'personality' and 'soul' (1960: 8–18). In the 1980s and 1990s, though, this school of management took on an increasingly evangelical tone, reflected in the work of bestselling authors such as Charles Handy, Tom Peters and Peter Senge and the huge amounts of money spent by firms on outside consultants, training programmes, motivational speakers and life coaches.

In a period of declining union power and reduced government intervention, in which executives wield tremendous power and command ever-rising salaries, management theorists increasingly emphasize the importance of employee 'consultation' and 'empowerment'. Thomas Frank explores this paradox in his discussion of 'market populism', the belief that unregulated markets are fundamentally democratic and consensual, serving to sweep away outdated hierarchies and inefficient bureaucracy. Frank sees libertarian management theory as part of this wider belief system: it is a form of public relations for an increasingly deregulated working environment, acclimatizing people to the exciting challenges of 'discontinuous change' (2001: 180). For Frank, the touchy-feely emphasis on flexibility and self-management serves mainly to sugar the pill of downsizing and outsourcing. His argument is echoed in Luc Boltanski and Ève Chiapello's discussion of 'the new spirit of capitalism', which, they argue, has accommodated elements of the 'artistic critique' of capitalism emerging in bohemian urban cultures in the nineteenth century. Their survey of 1990s management literature argues that this new 'connexionist' capitalism, which emphasizes flexible practices, flattened hierarchies and teamwork, has significant parallels with the libertarian left's critique of everyday life of the late 1960s, which similarly valued self-expression and self-management over bureaucratic conformity. For Boltanski and Chiapello, the acceptance of this 'artistic critique' has undercut the 'social critique' of capitalism, creating a society in which injustices and inequalities are simply an accepted part of daily life (1999).

The libertarian school of management is both egalitarian and proselytizing: employees must be consulted and empowered, but also well led and well motivated. The entire workforce, including the most poorly paid temps, has to be on-message, familiar with mission statements and benchmark standards, working towards the same, pre-determined ends of increased 'customer satisfaction' and 'shareholder value'. At the middle and lower levels of office life, the hyperbole of management theory translates into the duplication of tasks and the proliferation of meetings. The mainly deskbound job of Whyte's 'Organization Man' has been supplemented by the time-consuming activity of consensus-building, encapsulated in stock phrases such as 'none of us is as smart as all of us' and 'there's no "I" in team'. Despite all the predictions about the imminent arrival of the paperless office, paperwork has actually increased (Sellen and Harper 2002). The never-ending search for 'total quality' creates a daily life drowning in memos, newsletters, reports and timesheets. At the beginning of *Office Space*, there is an extended sequence in which a small mistake by Gibbons – forgetting to include the cover sheet on his 'TPS report', despite receiving a memo reminding him to do this – is corrected by two bosses, and then by his colleagues. This repetitive sequence suggests that memos in this new 'quality culture' are less about communication than about protecting the sender, offloading responsibility and generating unnecessary labour for everyone.

In *Office Space*, the non-confrontational style of the Divisional Vice-President, Bill Lumbergh ('Uh, great, yeah, listen, I'm going to have to go ahead and ask you to . . .'), masks the reality of management coercion. His supposedly enlightened rule epitomizes what Kracauer calls 'refined informality', where the rationalized workplace undermines normal human relationships and then seeks to manufacture them after the fact through common rooms, sports events and day trips (1998: 75). After announcing a consultation programme that is going to make many of them redundant, Lumbergh reminds his employees that 'next Friday is Hawaiian shirt day'. In this environment in which bland euphemisms conceal the true nature of corporate power, ruthless rationalization is described as 'housecleaning', and firing people on a Friday so they will not cause an incident is 'standard operating procedure'.

Office Space's romantic subplot, instead of offering light relief from the oppressiveness of the workplace, points to the spatial pervasiveness of corporate culture. Gibbons begins a relationship with Joanna (Jennifer Aniston) who works as a waitress in a nearby restaurant, Tchotchke's. Like the other serving staff, Joanna has to wear at least 15 jokey accessories or 'pieces of flair' on her braces, but is 'encouraged' to wear more. A circular conversation with her supervisor reveals the unacknowledged dynamics of this relationship. When her supervisor hints that she should be wearing more pieces of flair, Joanna asks why he does not simply raise the minimum number. Her supervisor asks what she thinks of someone who just does the 'bare minimum': 'We want you to express yourself . . . you *do* want to express yourself, don't you?' It is not enough for Joanna to do as she is told; she must actually *want* to do it and let everybody else know about it. Her predicament mirrors that of the menial Initech workers who are simultaneously deskilled and encouraged to feel a deep emotional attachment to their work. In a scene in which Gibbons hides from Lumbergh in the vain hope that he will not be asked to come in at the weekend, *Office Space* shows that the decline of formal hierarchies comes at a cost of increased uncertainty about where work begins and ends. As Ross argues, the laid-back offices of so-called 'no-collar' work – the first-name etiquette, relaxed dress codes and flexible working hours – tend to blur the distinctions between the office and other areas of social life, reframing work as an 'existential challenge' and enlisting 'employees' freest thoughts and impulses in the services of salaried time' (2003: 51, 19). When the search for quality is 'total', and improvement is always 'continuous', work is potentially endless.

The plotless first part of *Office Space* ends when Gibbons goes to see an occupational hypnotherapist. The hypnotherapist keels over and dies in mid-session, leaving Gibbons stuck in the relaxation stage. Shortly after this, two 'efficiency experts' arrive at Initech. They interview all the employees and ask them to explain what they do, as a prelude to firing some of them so they can 'bring in some entry-level graduates, farm some work out to Singapore, that's the usual deal'. When they ask Gibbons to walk them through a typical day, he cheerfully tells them that he comes in late through the side door, 'spaces out' for an hour and then stares at his desk to make it look as though he is working. The efficiency experts conclude that Gibbons is a repressed creative, 'a straight shooter with upper management written all over him'. Gibbons starts behaving more strangely, turning up for work in Bermuda shorts, parking in Lumbergh's reserved space, playing Tetris and dismantling his cubicle.

When he realizes that his two friends, Michael and Samir, are about to be fired, Gibbons comes out of his hypnotic trance and undergoes a political awakening:

> It's not just about me and my dream of doing nothing. It's about all of us together . . . Human beings were not meant to sit in little cubicles, staring at computer screens all day, filling out useless forms. And listening to eight different bosses drone on about mission statements . . . For five years now you've worked your ass off at Initech hoping for a promotion or some kind of profit-sharing or something . . . And you're gonna go in tomorrow and they're gonna throw you out on the street. You know why? So that Bill Lumbergh's stock will go up *a quarter of a point*.

Corporate culture often precludes critique by presuming to exist in a political vacuum. Refuseniks are simply seen as being in denial, not pulling together as part of a team, not responding to the inevitable realities of a globalized economy, 'not "with it", not with the movement that justifies its own existence merely by moving' (Lefebvre 1995a: 1). *Office Space* critiques these assumptions by pointing to the divide between the cubicle-dwelling wage slaves and the executives who have a real reason to be 'motivated': stock options and equity-sharing programmes.

The three friends hatch a plot to siphon cash from the company accounts, in tiny fractions of a cent that will not be noticed. This goes badly wrong when the computer program they have devised steals thousands of dollars from the company, making discovery inevitable. As Gibbons faces the prospect of jail, he has a heart-to-heart with Joanna, who tells him: 'Most people don't like their jobs, but you go out there and you find something that makes you happy.' Having brought its central character to an uneasy accommodation with his dull life, *Office Space* ends with a magical resolution. Another disaffected employee burns the Initech building to the ground, removing all trace of the three friends' wrongdoing.

Office Space thus seems to lose its political nerve and turns into a revenge fantasy. At the end of the film, Gibbons leaves his job and ends up happily working in the construction industry like his condo neighbour, Lawrence: This plot resolution suggests that the white-collar worker can escape the rat race by moving out of the physical confines of the office and acquiring a hardhat. Joanna has also left her job and we hear her say over the credits: 'I'm working at Hooter's [presumably another fast-food restaurant] now, it's really cool.' Michael and Samir seem happier with their very similar jobs at another firm, Intertrobe. Given that much of the earlier part of the film is about the intrusion of corporate culture into all aspects of everyday life, this partial escape seems like an evasion of more troublesome issues about the workplace. At its close, *Office Space* reproduces mainstream Hollywood conventions: lives are charmed, problems resolved and ambitions achieved. But in its earlier scenes, it subverts narrative expectations, and simply holds in tension the paradoxes of modern office life: the endless search for 'excellence', which produces only meaningless paper chases; the emphasis on the 'happy family' of the workplace, which denies its political realities; the celebration of risk-taking and free-thinking, which actually encourages pre-approved responses and groupthink; and the ethos of transparency and accountability, which makes everything opaque and leaves no one accountable.

The fall of the middle manager

Ricky Gervais and Stephen Merchant's sitcom, *The Office*[3] pays subtle homage to *Office Space*, through an absent ex-employee called Pete Gibbons who is mentioned in two of the episodes. But *The Office* follows a different narrative logic that does not transcend the circularity of office life through plot twists and unexpected resolutions. It is set on the Slough Trading Estate, the first of its kind when it was built in the 1920s, and still one of the largest in Europe. Trading estates are earlier, less prestigious incarnations of business parks, given over to warehouse and back-office functions. Slough also occupies a particular place in the English imagination. It is one of the unplanned new towns that developed between the wars along the main arterial roads leading out of west London. In the 1930s, the prosperity of towns such as Slough contrasted markedly with northern towns such as Jarrow and Wigan where declining industries were leading to mass unemployment (Hall 2002: 57). George Orwell saw Slough as one of the places to look for 'the germs of the future England', as the growth of low-grade white-collar work and light industry created an expanding, if downwardly mobile, middle class (1970: 98). Perhaps because of this 'classlessness', it became a byword for dreary subtopia, a reputation consolidated by John Betjeman's famous poem, 'Slough', which the central character in *The Office* reads aloud in one episode.

In more recent years, Slough has become part of the high-tech 'edge cities', reminiscent of New Jersey or California, which have developed in south-east England along the main motorways out of London. Despite being in the centre of Britain's own Silicon Valley of technology and communications industries, Slough has never quite shaken off its boring reputation. Over *The Office*'s opening credits, we are shown grim shots of the town under an overcast sky, with various signifiers of its daily life: a road sign, a large traffic roundabout, a bus station and a drab 1960s office block raised on pilotis. Gervais says that he picked Slough because 'it's middle-earning, middle-aged and middle-management. It's grey. The Slough thing isn't important, but it had to be summing up normalness and averageness' (Hann 2001). While Initech in *Office Space* could be in any out-of-town business park in the Western world, the Slough Trading Estate is both inescapably global and quintessentially English. The workers in *The Office* are both somewhere and nowhere, stuck in a notoriously dull place that is often the butt of their lame jokes but controlled by wider economic forces that they can neither influence nor understand.

The Office mimics the docusoap format that flourished on British television in the late 1990s and early 2000s in that it purports to be the work of a documentary production team granted access to a branch office of Wernham-Hogg paper merchants. Its use of the visual codes of reality TV – wobbly handheld cameras, dizzy panning, disjointed editing, clumsy fades – creates a sense of both intimacy and distance. The self-consciously amateurish camerawork might suggest that it is conveying the reality of office life in a spontaneous, unmediated way, but it also shows that the office is an intermediate, public–private space in which much remains unsaid. The camera captures stilted small talk, clandestine chats, private meetings taking place behind half-drawn blinds, knowing glances to the camera and surreptitiously linked hands. Unlike most docusoaps, there is no post-production voiceover providing commentary on what is happening. Even in the interviews to camera that interrupt the action, the characters are still in presentational work mode. *The Office* does not deal with inner states, and the various attempts at self-insight peter out into inarticulacies and obfuscations.

Almost all the action of *The Office* takes place within the claustrophobic reality of the Slough branch itself, with little backstory about the lives of the characters outside work. Indeed, they do not seem to *have* much of a life outside work. The episodes are simply made up of the universal rituals of office life: 'meet and greets' at which people drink cheap wine from plastic cups, fire drills, health and safety demonstrations, training days, staff meetings, flipchart brainstorming sessions, coffee breaks and, in the last episode, the Christmas party. The narrative pace of *The Office* is much slower than is usual in sitcoms or docusoaps, and the bridging shots are longer and more frequent. Employees yawn, feed paper into shredders, twiddle their pencils, leave messages on voicemail and field wrong numbers. There is a repeated shot of a mechanical collator sorting paper, its rhythmic movements marking out the slow passage of time. These apparently redundant shots convey the boredom of office life in a way that silently subverts the motivational rhetoric of corporate culture.

The slow pace of *The Office* also means that, like *Office Space*, it foregrounds the physical arrangement of the workplace. In the frequent, mid-range shots of the office itself, the lack of anything dramatic to look at means that the viewer's eye is drawn to standard-issue objects such as shelving

units, filing cabinets and water coolers. The Wernham-Hogg office is a variation on *Bürolandschaft* (office landscaping), a concept developed in the late
1950s by the German management consultants, Quickborner, and popular-
ized in English-speaking countries in the 1960s by the architect and designer
Francis Duffy. *Bürolandschaft* aimed to create pleasant, cooperative working
environments through the grouping of desks in 'islands', the use of shoulder-
high acoustic screens rather than partition walls, and the addition of foliage
and décor. But the standardization of office furniture and the tendency for
British and American offices to be built speculatively for unknown clients
mean that office landscaping has simply become 'open-plan with added plants'
(Baldry 1997: 370). In managerial theory, the 'borderless office' has been
almost evangelically associated with informality, egalitarianism and creativity.
But it also serves more pragmatic ends by saving on space and reducing rent
costs, flattening middle-management hierarchies and simplifying work flow-
lines. In *The Office*, the open plan creates an environment with no hiding place,
where strained relationships and personality clashes are exposed. It produces
an aimless territoriality where colleagues argue with each other about desk
space, and build walls of box files so they do not have to look at each other.
It also makes for an easily surveyable and navigable environment in which no
one can escape the hovering neediness of Wernham-Hogg's regional manager,
David Brent (Gervais).

The problem with Brent is not that he is a tyrant or bully, but that he
sees himself, with chronic self-delusion, as 'a friend first, boss second, and
probably an entertainer third'. He constantly boasts about his office being a
'madhouse' where the workers bring in funny mascots, moonwalk across the
floor or break into renditions of television theme tunes. But when several
workers from Swindon are relocated to Slough as the company is downsized,
and they fail to respond to his sense of humour, it becomes clear that this
easy-going environment is actually a subtle form of duress. After his jokey
speech of welcome falls flat, he calls them together in an impromptu huddle:
'You've got to chill out, yeah? Trust me. This is what I do. . . . You'll never
have another boss like me, someone who's basically a chilled-out entertainer.'
This perfectly captures the confused signals of motivational management
theory. You've *got* to chill out – that's an order. And yet when the joke is
turned on Brent as he learns that 'the Swindon lot' have given him unflat-
tering nicknames, he clumsily seeks to reassert his authority. In the absence
of a clear chain of command, the right to joke and the compulsion to find
something funny mark out the invisible hierarchies of the office. Brent may
claim that he has a 'chill out let's get to know each other vibe', but he is still
the boss.

In *The Salaried Masses*, Kracauer noted that the office manager was
emerging as a key figure in the new white-collar workplace. As companies
grew in size, and the connection between different elements of the firm

became more abstract, the office manager became the sole personification of authority to his subordinates, although that authority might be more symbolic than real (Kracauer 1998: 48). In the workplace revolution of the 1980s and 1990s, middle managers were given an increasingly important symbolic role while their actual authority was diminished. They were now charged with the task of 'making meaning', communicating management initiatives to baffled employees, and passing on bad news about redundancies (Ciulla 2000: xv). At the same time, middle managers were the most likely employees to be sacked because of their relative expense and expendability.

The threat of redundancy hangs over *The Office* from beginning to end. In the first episode, Brent's line manager tells him that the company can no longer justify two branches, and his office will close unless he proves it is more efficient than the Swindon branch. The real movers and shakers, the senior partners and board members, are largely absent in *The Office*; we never get to know why Wernham-Hogg is being downsized. In this context, it is interesting that the series is set in a paper merchant's office, because this industry has fared particularly badly as a result of the shareholder revolution. While its output and sales are bigger than ever, its stock valuation has declined in recent years, because investors no longer believe in its long-term future in a digital age (Sellen and Harper 2002: 9–10). When tough managerial decisions need to be made in this new work culture, it is easy to blame abstractions: the need to maintain stock price, the impact of new technologies, the unbuckable global markets. Squeezed from all sides in this environment, middle managers are nominally authoritative but actually insecure figures. A running joke from the first series has Gareth introduce himself as 'Assistant Regional Manager' and Brent correct him: 'Assistant *to* the Regional Manager'. Unlike the share-optioned Lumbergh in *Office Space*, Brent's authority in this de-layered environment is precarious, hence his passive-aggressive need to bolster it by maintaining his own little status-markers. He sees himself as a corporate rebel, boasting about not living by 'the rules'. In fact, his leadership style chimes perfectly with management theory's voguish flirtation with soft skills. In one scene, Brent parrots the stock phrase, 'the employees are our most important commodity', while his receptionist is crying quietly in the background.

In the modern workplace, power is exercised not through direct coercion but through a rhetorical fluency that conceals the contradictions of office life. Brent's problem is that he is a chronically inarticulate man who cannot survive without a script, whether it is his beloved comedy catchphrases or the vacuous soundbites that he culls from mind-body-spirit books and passes off as his own. While he claims to loathe management-speak, Brent's sentences are littered with inept variations on it: made-up portmanteau terms ('team individuality'), meaningless lists of abstract nouns ('trust, encouragement, reward, loyalty . . . satisfaction'), shaky metaphors ('you're not looking at the whole pie'), empty platitudes ('nothing ever changes by staying the same') and patronizing aphorisms ('never assume, it makes an ass out of u and me'). Brent often accompanies these phrases with hand movements, such as weaving his fingers together or miming inverted commas. Towards the end of the second series, as his failure as a manager is increasingly exposed, he runs out of words altogether. When he tries to define his work methods by simply moving his hands outwards, his new line manager, Neil, says impatiently: 'David, some words would be useful here.' Forced to address concrete issues without the protection of managerial platitudes, Brent is rendered speechless.

As Kracauer suggests, office conventions reproduce themselves less by explicit ideological reinforcement than by inertia. The employees in *The Office* can see through Brent, just as they can see through the vacuity of management theory when it filters through to them in the form of tedious training sessions on 'customer care' and 'team building', during which they are shown poorly made, fading videos from the 1980s, fronted by minor no-longer-celebrities. The problem is not that they are lulled into false consciousness but that their workplace routines seem so entrenched and unchangeable. Office procedures become unexamined nounal phrases ('take it out of petty cash', 'it's against health and safety'), mundane objects such as staplers and hole punches turn into status symbols, and work tasks simply regenerate themselves without reference to value or meaning.

The episode in which Brent conducts the staff appraisals shows how he exposes these tired conventions of office life by performing them so ineptly. A common criticism of appraisals or 'performance reviews', now a near-universal feature of the workplace, is that their rhetoric of employee empowerment simply legitimizes management surveillance. In *The Office*, though, Brent makes it clear that the appraisals are not a 'witch hunt', and he is right: their rationale is more subtle and insidious. Like the psychotherapeutic relationship that they mimic, appraisals conflate issues of agency and inevitability so that, as the business saying goes, 'the only thing that can hurt you is your resistance to change'. They encourage employees to reflect on and take control of their own working lives, but only by working within the hierarchical constraints of the organization. More fundamental changes in work cultures cannot even be conceptualized, let alone achieved. The appraisals that Brent conducts are a classic case of workers being required to manage 'change' in this environment. Some of his employees mistakenly see them as a way of discussing life-changing opportunities. But Brent summarily dismisses Tim's aim of going to university ('no point') and Dawn's ambition to be a children's illustrator ('keep up the doodling . . . pipe dreams are good in a way'). Without any useful function, the appraisal simply becomes a vehicle for Brent's own self-promotion, as he recites words of wisdom from a book hidden under his desk and tries to get the appraisee to describe him as a role model so that he can put it on the form.

In one scene, Brent helps the catatonic Keith to complete his appraisal form. Keith responds to the exploratory questions with a stonewalling literalism, listing his strengths as 'accounts' and his weaknesses as 'eczema'. He is then asked questions about the training and skills he needs to do his job effectively, using the familiar sliding scale designed by Rensis Likert in *New Patterns of Management* (1961) ('Not at all', 'to some extent', 'very much so', 'don't know'). Keith answers 'don't know' to every question and then, when he is asked to pick a different response, has forgotten the questions. Brent repeats the various options continually, his obvious impatience exposing the process as a charade. Without the opportunity to flatter his own ego, he simply wants the form to be completed. This scene points not to the hidden coerciveness of consultative managerialism, but to its dishonesty. It wastes our *time* because it insists on the formulation of 'strategic goals' for the most routine tasks, and refuses to be open about the inequalities of the workplace.

Along with the soap opera, the sitcom is the television genre particularly concerned with the representation of the everyday. In its classic British incarnations, such as *Porridge*, *Steptoe and Son*, *Dad's Army* and *Only Fools and Horses*, the characters experience a series of bathetic defeats in the course of their daily lives, and grudgingly have to accept an existence made up of boredom, irritation and incompetence. *The Office* is firmly within this tradition of the sitcom based around entrapment in a particular situation, with the characters learning to live with frustrated desires by reconciling themselves reluctantly with the social sphere. The theme of entrapment is reinforced after the closing music and end credits of each episode, when there is a final shot of one of the characters, often doing what he or she usually does: typing away at a workstation, speaking on the phone or sitting behind a reception desk.

Traditional sitcoms, though, provide the audience with a reassuring sense of distance from the pathos of entrapment. The tendency to caricature the central characters, the release of tension in the movement of each episode to narrative closure and the laughter of the studio audience all suggest that what is happening on screen is not quite like life. These sitcoms follow a classical narrative structure in which there is a disruption to a stable situation and a return to this stability at the end (rather than, as in a film, the achievement of a new kind of equilibrium). The traditional sitcom offers a way of incorporating potential change and crises into the rhythms and routines of everyday life (Neale and Krutnik 1990: 234–5).

The Office is unusual in that it erases this comfort zone, partly because of its hybrid status as a soap-cum-sitcom. Although the individual episodes seem fairly unstructured, they have the temporal development of serial narrative when viewed in sequence. There are two main plot strands: the development, thwarting and final consummation of Dawn and Tim's relationship, and Brent's encounter with his nemesis – the more popular and successful Neil, who makes him redundant at the end of the second series. When Brent loses his job, he expects there to be a staff mutiny, but people respond instead with boredom and indifference. The tragic last episode of the second series has him handing out homemade business cards as office life continues around him, oblivious to his leaving. This scene is all the more poignant because it is not primarily about Brent's unpopularity. It is about the forgetfulness of office life, the way that its impersonal procedures do not acknowledge the finite trajectory of individual lives, despite the leaving dos and retirement parties that lamely suggest otherwise. (This theme is reinforced in the final special, when it emerges that one employee thinks that Dawn still works behind the reception desk, even though she left two years before.) Throughout *The Office*, Brent is obsessed with not looking his age and with 'chillin' out' while he is young. At the end of the second series, though, he is cruelly exposed as a middle-aged man without a future.

Ray Carney suggests that we normally laugh at characters in comedies on the assumption that nothing really awful will happen to them. Brent's decline and fall is a kind of betrayal of this compact between the sitcom and its audience. *The Office* tricks the viewer into letting down her guard, and laughing at something that turns out to be rather tragic (Carney 2000: 93). In the first series, Brent is often a kind of wise fool who inadvertently speaks the truth about the bleaker aspects of office life:

> You grow up, you work half a century, you get a golden handshake, you rest a couple of years and you're dead. And the only thing that makes that crazy ride worthwhile is, 'Did I enjoy it? What did I learn? What was the point?' That's where I come in.

Brent's self-image as a guru who lightens the load of his workers prevents him absorbing the true impact of his words. As the second series develops, though, his carapace of smugness is gradually stripped away. There are progressively more awkward silences, and shots of Brent in his office, staring into space. In the painful last scene of the second series in which he begs for his job back, he turns out to be not a grotesque but a rather vulnerable, tragic figure. Asked by an interviewer if the crucial ingredient in a sitcom is people being stuck in a situation, Gervais replied: 'It's not just being stuck, it's knowing you're stuck' (Thompson 2004: 13). While most of the characters are aware of this from the beginning, Brent's tragedy is that he only realizes it at the end.

There is a strange semi-redemption, though, in the final two specials of *The Office*. Brent is now working as a sales rep, moving solitarily between cheap motels, service stations and lay-bys. When he keeps coming back to the Slough office out of loneliness, Neil effectively bans him: 'You don't work here and you can't keep coming in for a natter. . . . This is a place of business, not a social club.' Neil's point is partially disproved at the office Christmas party, a largely British tradition associated with drunken debauchery and fumbled seductions. Brent, allowed to attend on sufferance, has a successful date with a woman he meets through a dating agency, and *The Office* ends with his ex-colleagues laughing at his jokes in a spirit of reconciliation. For all its dysfunctional qualities, the office emerges as a vital place of social connection.

Tim and Dawn's relationship also comes to a head at the end of the second special. Unlike Peter and Joanna in *Office Space*, Tim does not tell his bosses where to stick their job. He is clearly the most able employee but, while he constantly talks about leaving, the risk and uncertainty of a future outside the office continually hold him back. At the end of the second series, Tim talks to camera, with unusual eloquence, about the human relationships that are all the more important for taking place within a working environment indifferent to intimacy:

> The people you work with are people you were just thrown together with. You don't know them, it wasn't your choice. And yet you spend more time with them than you do your friends or your family. But probably all you've got in common is the fact you walk around on the same bit of carpet for eight hours a day. And so obviously, when someone comes in who you . . . you have a connection with, yeah . . . and Dawn was a ray of sunshine in my life and it meant a lot.

Tim and Dawn come together unexpectedly through 'Secret Santa', a recent workplace innovation in which employees pick the names of colleagues out of a hat and buy them an anonymous Christmas present. Tim picks Dawn's name out and in the taxi home she opens up his present, which alludes to her long-deferred ambition to become a children's illustrator: a box of paints and a message written on Wernham-Hogg stationery, 'Never Give Up'. What follows, as Dawn stops the cab and makes her way back to the party to claim her man, seems like a deliberate subversion of Tim's earlier fatalism ('I don't know what a happy ending *is*. Life isn't about endings, is it? It's a series of moments'). Unlike in *Office Space*, though, this 'happy ending' is not about romantic love transcending the brutalizing aspects of work. It is about ordinary people trying to carve out a small amount of happiness within the constraints of a work culture that, despite all its protestations to the contrary, lets them know every day that they count for nothing.

Ethnographies of commuting

The capacity of work cultures to create new kinds of space, such as the out-of-town estate inhabited by the workers in *The Office*, means that the daily activity of reaching that space becomes part of work itself. Workers are commuting longer distances than ever, partly because they are employed by a smaller number of large corporations that increasingly relocate their workers to new sites for reasons of economic efficiency (Franklin and Crang 2001: 10). New portable technologies have also created what Jill Andresky Fraser calls 'job spill' (2001: 24). Mobile phones, pagers, personal digital assistants and portable fax machines allow for new forms of mobile office work that turn commuting into a form of multi-tasking (see also Laurier 2004). The commute has become part of 'workspace'.

The symbiotic relationship between work and commuting has been part of the critique of everyday life since the Situationist attack on the reconstruction of Paris and the dispersal of workers into suburbs in the 1950s and 1960s. For the Situationists, the commute was an expanding but largely unrepresented space in modern life, a product of capitalist societies that divided time between alienating work and commodified leisure. But the Situationist notion of commuting time as worthless, unpaid labour led to a certain condescension towards the straphanging masses, whose stultifying routines tragically separated them from their more authentic needs and desires. In *The Revolution of Everyday Life*, Raoul Vaneigem wonders how much humanity can remain in people who are 'dragged out of sleep at six every morning, jolted about in suburban trains' and 'tossed out at the end of the day into the entrance halls of railway stations, those cathedrals of departure for the hell of weekdays and the nugatory paradise of weekends, where the crowd communes in a brutish weariness' (1994: 52). The Situationist practice of *dérive* (drifting) was partly imagined as an inversion of the daily grind of *métro-boulot-dodo* (commuting-working-sleeping). Unlike the commute, the *dérive* emphasized chance, unconstrained movements rather than habitual, restricted ones; open-ended rather than restrictive time; and travel as pleasure rather than simply an adjunct to work.

In his work on the Paris Métro, the ethnographer Marc Augé offers a more developed analysis that imagines the subway as an archetypal space of quotidian life. As a practical way of moving large numbers of people across urban space, subway systems are a growing and increasingly global phenomenon, a crucial part of the infrastructure of almost every major world city. Although not of course used exclusively by commuters, their 'double-peak' distribution of traffic – heavy crowds inbound in the morning and outbound in the evening with a relatively slack period in between – is intimately linked to the rhythms of work. Congested subway systems show the continuing importance of city centres as working environments, despite the proliferation of out-of-town offices, call centres and business parks. The problems of mass transit in London, for example, partly reflect the long-term failure of governments to relocate jobs out of the capital, despite this being the professed aim of organizations such as the Location of Offices Bureau (1963–79). The

Thatcher revolution, as with the neo-liberal economic transformation of other Western countries, increased the importance of cities, and particularly London, as financial centres. London's population stopped falling in the mid-1980s, and has benefited from the almost continuous growth of the economy since then (Wolmar 2002: 2). The Underground, which was losing passengers two decades ago, is now busier than ever, with over three million passenger journeys a day (Transport for London 2004a).

Augé began his career as an ethnographer of tribal societies on the west coast of Africa, and his analysis of the Paris Métro is part of what he calls a 'reverse ethnology' that challenges the traditional idea of anthropology as the study of small-scale, geographically remote societies (1998: 23). He argues that anthropology should respond to 'the death of exoticism', the discrediting of its traditionally hierarchical relationship to a primitive 'other', by finding new areas of ethnographic investigation and reflecting on different types of 'otherness' (1998: 122). For Augé, social practices such as commuting show how ideas of community have been transformed by the new status of the individual in contemporary society. Commuting produces new forms of collectively experienced solitude that demand innovative ways of thinking and theorizing about them.

Augé's book on the Métro can be usefully contrasted with work within cultural studies that has also applied ethnographic theories and methodologies to modern Western societies. This body of work tends to deal with distinctive subcultural groups, as in, for example, the work of the Birmingham CCCS on youth cultures such as bikers, mods and punks. By contrast, Augé examines widely practised activities such as the daily commute, which incorporate difference and diversity within their common rhythms and routines. He sees the Métro as a particularly fruitful area for ethnography, because it brings together highly paid professionals and people on the fringes of society, such as impoverished artists, buskers, homeless people using the concourses for warmth and shelter, and more active beggars patrolling the carriages with children in tow. On the Métro we meet 'proximal others', who are not so different from us that they can be reassuringly exoticized, but who still force us to reflect on the extent and limits of community (Augé 2002: 48).

Discussions of commuting spaces in cultural studies have tended to focus on how individuals or subcultures can subvert the institutions that define and limit them. For example, Iain Chambers cites the self-proclaimed 'can man', a black man on the New York subway who sells artwork carved out of beer cans with a pocket knife, as evidence of an 'urban black aesthetic' that 'secretly undermine[s] the presumptions of a monolithic or homogeneous culture' (1994: 36–7); Michael Bull sees the Walkman as a way of negotiating the relationship between public and private space, transforming the unproductive time spent in the 'no man's land' between work and home into pleasurable activity (2000: 188); and Nancy Macdonald explores the attempts by subway graffiti artists to win symbolic capital in their fraternity by getting one over transit officials and the police, and leaving their personal tags on the moving canvas of the train, which spreads their notoriety throughout the city (2001: 83).

Augé explicitly distinguishes his approach from this emphasis on 'arts de faire', which he associates primarily with the work of Michel de Certeau, who describes the graffiti on New York subway trains as 'the fleeting images, yellowish-green and metallic blue calligraphies that howl without raising their voices and emblazon themselves on the subterranean passages of the city' (Certeau 1984: 102). Augé does discuss the activities undertaken by individual Métro travellers, such as knitting, reading and doing crossword puzzles, as well as more subversive behaviour such as petty theft, ticket-dodging and begging (2002: 34–5, 45–7). But he does not treat these activities as markers of otherness or resistance. Instead, he is interested in the ways that they reveal the subway as a space of both multiple solitudes and minimal communality. Augé argues that the really definitive experience of the Métro is the low-intensity, ephemeral interaction of strangers with little else in common. On the Métro, we are simply required to contribute to that 'minimum of collective identity through which a community is defined' (2002: 30).[4]

Augé's discussion of the Métro makes use of the notion of the 'total social fact', a term employed by Marcel Mauss to describe collective rituals such as gift-giving that penetrate the whole political, economic, legal and religious life of a culture, and show that society is a single, interconnected system (Mauss 1970: 78–81). More specifically, Augé draws on Claude Lévi-Strauss's interpretation of this notion to suggest its essentially subjective, unstated dimension. For Lévi-Strauss, the total social fact manifests itself ultimately in the individual mind:

> The proof of the social cannot be other than mental. . . . We can never be sure of having reached the meaning and the function of an institution, if we are not in a position to relive its impact on an individual consciousness.
>
> (Lévi-Strauss 1987: 28)

Like Lévi-Strauss, Augé sees the total social fact as both sociological and psychological, combining observable behaviour with less tangible ideas, feelings and memories. The Métro journey can function as a 'total social fact' precisely because its qualities are never stated or defined, allowing different subjectivities to co-exist within it (Augé 2002: 42–3). If the fundamental quality of the Métro is its ordered and contractual nature, this is found not simply in its explicit rules (the ban on smoking, for example, or the regulation of travel through ticket types) but in its 'collective morality', the complex etiquette necessitated by its cramped and warren-like environments. Although it is true that certain people remain indifferent to these rules, Augé suggests that what is 'most astonishing is that there are not more of them' (2002: 30).

Augé's analysis of Métro behaviour thus tends to focus on what Erving Goffman refers to as 'civil inattention' (Goffman 1971: 209–10), the forms of social interaction in which strangers nominally acknowledge or block out each other's presence in public places, a perennial concern of urban theorists from Georg Simmel onwards. Augé notes, for example, the ways in which commuters exchange fleeting glances, or the flickers of emotion that can sometimes be detected behind the apparently blank faces of daydreamers (2002: 6, 35). These silent acts show how much the Métro is based on both peaceful co-existence and the impossibility of knowing anything substantive about the lives of one's fellow passengers. In similar vein, Augé focuses less on conscious acts of resistance by commuters and more on their 'virtuosity tied to habit' (2002: 8). The movements of regular Métro passengers, he suggests, have the balletic economy of endlessly repeated actions, with no unnecessary or redundant effort. They will get set and be on their marks before departing from a carriage; they will know whether or not to quicken their pace based on the noise of a train whooshing through the tunnels; or they will stand on the platform at the exact spot at which the train doors will open, and which will deposit them near their exit on the destination platform (2002: 7, 31).

For Augé, the instinctive routines of subway travel mean that history on the Métro tends to be 'impregnated' rather than actively commemorated. While the names of Métro stations often refer to famous battles or historical figures, commuters simply see in these names 'the more or less rapid flow of their individual duration, estimated only in terms of being ahead of or behind schedule' (2002: 18). Augé adopts a kind of quasi-Proustian methodology in which brief, unbidden moments disrupt the apparent eternality of this system, which appears to obey 'the commands of a mysterious director, the god-architect of this subterranean universe' (2002: 53). Every day on the Métro, he points out, we may see someone who is taking their first trip and someone else their last (2002: 59). By drawing us into 'quotidian humanity', commuting spaces make us more aware that we are moving away from the world and will eventually leave it behind (2002: 14–15). While Augé's work could be criticized for its unscientific reliance on personal memories, eidetic images, snatches of poetry and song lyrics, this impressionistic quality also usefully foregrounds the methodological problems faced by ethnographers of the quotidian.[5]

Augé's book is not, strictly speaking, an ethnography but a series of three essays concluding with a brief discussion of how an ethnologist on the Métro should proceed. He argues that traditional social-scientific methods such as interviews with informants, surveys or polls cannot account for the Métro's rudimentary, non-ritualistic forms of community. Its daily routines produce a kind of 'shattered sacrality' (2002: 24), a wordless melding of the collective and the subjective that individual passengers would not necessarily be able to articulate. An ethnography of the Métro needs to begin instead with 'a methodical description of place', of the platforms, corridors, escalators and advertising posters, in order to determine how this controlled environment dictates collective behaviours (2002: 60, 37). Augé's approach is distinct from that of Clifford Geertz, who similarly critiques the quasi-scientific ambitions of ethnography, but in the name of a 'thick description' that tries to unravel 'a stratified hierarchy of meaningful structures' (Geertz 1973: 7). Unlike Geertz, Augé does not deal with the unfamiliar practices of distant societies, but with the excessively familiar, banal routines of quotidian life in the West. In a sense, he produces a deliberately 'thin description' that, as in Kracauer's analysis of office life, explores the unnoticed surfaces of daily experience.

On the Underground

Even more than the Paris Métro, the London Underground is a rule-driven and standardized environment. The Tube is full of what Joe Hermer and Alan Hunt call 'the official graffiti of the everyday': prohibitory or advisory signs that stand in for 'absent experts' who tell us how to act and behave, an increasingly pervasive form of governance that appears normal because of its penetration into daily life (1996: 478). Among other things, Tube passengers are told to 'mind the gap' between train and platform by a white-painted sign on the ground; to pass along the platform to prevent bottlenecks; to keep hold of the handrail on the escalator; and to make sure that the carriage doors are clear of baggage. Aural as well as visual cues add to this sense of the pervasive authority of invisible legislators. The PA systems, for example, use the voices of professional actors, digitally recorded and stored on computer. The computer pieces together words and phrases spoken by the actors when the required message is typed in. The operator can programme the computer to play several different messages ('Stand clear of the train doors please . . .', 'Please remember to keep all your belongings with you . . .', 'London Underground wishes to apologize . . .') at pre-set intervals in any location throughout the station.

As Hermer and Hunt point out, though, the purpose of these injunctions is not simply Foucauldian surveillance but the interpellation of the reader or listener as a 'customer' or 'passenger' (1996: 476). Their aim is to 'responsibilize' members of the public, urging them to 'accept responsibility for their conduct by reference to some asserted social or ethical value' (1996: 468). There is a series of bylaws that operate on the Tube, some of which are unsurprising (laws against walking on the track or carrying a gun, for example), and others of which are minute interventions into everyday lives (laws against spitting, using obscene language, entering a train before any person leaving by that door has done so, soiling any part of the railway with dirty clothing, refusing to queue when asked to do so by a member of staff, and travelling the wrong way on an escalator) (Transport for London 2004a). Although these bylaws are largely unknown to passengers, they tend to overlap with well-known rules of Tube etiquette, which exist in both written and unwritten form. These suggest, for example, that people should stick to the right on the escalators to allow those in a hurry to pass; give up the priority seating by the carriage doors to elderly people and parents with young children; and move down the carriage in order to let new passengers on.

Although there are, of course, individual dissidents, it is remarkable how much these rules of the Underground are obeyed. The usefulness of Augé's work on the Métro, I would suggest, is that it provides a way of thinking about this collectively agreed behaviour in a way that moves beyond the emphasis in ethnographic cultural studies on the divergence between social prescriptions and actual practices. In an Underground train in the rush hour, the opportunities for an individualized micropolitics could be said to be limited. On an anecdotal level, this was brought home to me quite starkly during one Tube journey, when I saw a passenger angrily accuse another of using his back as a bookrest. Even the humblest London office workers have air-conditioning, water coolers and a reasonable amount of desk space. But a Tube train on one of the deep-level lines can squeeze up to 1,600 passengers through tunnels less than twelve feet in diameter (James 2001: n.p.). Indeed, the transport of live animals within the EU is subject to rules about minimum space and maximum temperature that would be the envy of most rush-hour Tube passengers in the height of summer (Dowling 2002). A television advert in early 2004 for the new tabloid version of *The Times* exploited this problem of engaging in individual activity in such a crowded environment. It showed a series of standing Tube commuters trying to fold back broadsheet news-papers, and saying 'sorry' to clearly annoyed fellow passengers as they bumped against them. The camera eventually rested on a serenely peaceful, straphanging commuter holding her tabloid copy of *The Times* with one hand. The pay-off line was: 'The new compact *Times*. Buy it. You won't be sorry.'

The minimal acknowledgement of fellow passengers, identified by Augé as the definitive experience of the Métro, is also evident on the Tube. One example is what Goffman calls 'dead-eyeing', in which two individuals accidentally exchange eye contact but 'do not ratify the exchange of lookings with the ritual of "social recognition"' (1971: 71). There are unspoken interdictions against talking to and even looking at one's fellow passengers on the Tube. The rule about looking exists in spite of, and is perhaps a product of, the fact that the layout of the carriages, with longitudinal rather than transverse seating as in most mainline trains, actually encourages staring. A Tube passenger who inadvertently exchanges glances with another person will often stare briefly at other people in the carriage as well, in order to make it clear that the initial look was not specifically directed. Accomplished Tube travellers also practise the kind of nonchalant virtuosity noted by Augé. They will push their iron-oxide coated tickets through the slot, or place their rechargeable plastic Oyster cards on the electronic reader, and walk straight through the automatic barriers in one fluent movement, knowing the exact moment at which they will open, so their stride is not broken; they will respond to the beeping sound that precedes the closing of the train doors by instinctively contorting their bodies to fit into the carriage; they will undertake complex manoeuvres while reading newspapers or talking on mobile phones, pulled along by force of habit and the momentum of other moving bodies.

The routines of the London Underground serve effectively to blank out meaning and present its operations as timeless and inexorable. There is not enough room on the trains, tracks and platforms to undertake essential daily maintenance and repairs when the trains are running. So it is in the middle of the night that delivery people refill the chocolate machines; cleaners sweep the platforms and remove the 15 tons of rubbish left by passengers every day; bill stickers change the large posters lining the tunnels opposite the platforms; the heavy-duty, heavily-used escalators are serviced; and a train nicknamed the 'big yellow duster' sweeps the tunnels of daily debris such as dust, hair, skin cells and particles of brake lining deposited by passing trains (Halliday 2001: 195). The invisibility of these practices makes Underground passengers less inclined to reflect on the practical realities that underpin their daily routines. The absence of published train times – there is a 'metro service', which means that (hopefully) trains turn up too regularly to warrant a timetable – reinforces this impression of eternal sameness. The principal indicators of time on the platforms are the dot-matrix information displays hung from the ceiling, which tell people how many minutes they will have to wait for the next train. But these minutes are a notoriously contractable or (more usually) expandable resource, because their accuracy depends on incomplete signalling information and boarding delays on stations further up the line (Heath *et al.* 1999: 570). There is an urban myth that London Underground 'minutes' are decimalized to last 100 seconds, but in fact they frequently last even longer than this.

The highly predictable layout and design of the Underground system adds to this sense of timeless routine. The design of Underground stations tends to be more uniform than other railway stations, because the huge practical problems of tunnelling meant that civil engineers rather than architects determined their construction (Edwards 1997: 105). (The comparative variety of the station designs on the Jubilee Line Extension is partly due to the development of new tunnelling methods.) The design of Tube stations is also relatively homogeneous because the London Underground has been a pioneer of corporate branding since 1907, when the different train companies decided to promote themselves jointly under one name. This house style was fully established in the 1920s and 1930s, when the London Underground chief executive, Frank Pick, and the architect, Charles Holden, unified the system through an integrated architectural approach incorporating not just the station facades but the interiors, furniture and signage. As London's area rapidly expanded in the interwar years, and the Underground lines extended deep into the home counties, the Tube's distinctive look came to define the city limits. This house style remains today, and confronts commuters with a whole series of visual familiars, such as the red, blue and silver corporate livery of the trains; the seat moquettes associated with particular lines; and the famous roundel, the red circle crossed by a blue bar which is one of the oldest surviving corporate images, and now a ubiquitous feature on documents and signage.

Perhaps the most significant form of corporate branding on the Underground is Harry Beck's Tube map, a classic of 1930s design, which famously bears little relation to the street-level city. Beck's creation is not, in fact, a map but a linear cartogram that shows only the different routes and the relative positions of the stations along horizontal, vertical and diagonal lines. Apart from an approximate representation of the river Thames, the map omits all information about overground location so that the reader can focus her attention on routes and intersections. As well as being found in every Tube station, it is reproduced in the London A–Z, Filofaxes, diaries and many other products. Other than for a few aficionados who know its history, the Underground map seems to be authorless and anonymous, arriving from nowhere and existing eternally. This apparent eternality obscures the minute changes that have been made to Beck's map over the years, through which the developing history of London commuting can be traced: proposed routes are written in dotted lines, peak-hours-only shadings introduced and defunct stations omitted. The map is a highly successful branding exercise that simplifies the labyrinthine maze of Underground lines, and the complicated institutional context of their daily running. The Tube map tends to inspire indifference or even affection among commuters, for whom it is simply part of the timeless visual logic of the Underground.[6]

Transport infrastructure is a notoriously 'lumpy' development, requiring a huge initial investment of time and money, taking a long time to construct, and likely to be outdated as soon as it is finished (Jarvis et al. 2001: 14). The bulk of London's Underground system was built over a century ago. Adding new elements to the system, such as the Victoria Line (1968–71), the Jubilee Line (1979) and the Jubilee Line Extension (1999) is always costly, disruptive and politically contentious. Of three proposed routes in the late 1980s, for example, the Jubilee Line Extension was the least necessary in reducing commuter congestion (Wolmar 2002: 79–80). It was given the go-ahead largely because of the construction of the Canary Wharf office development on the London Docklands, which won the enthusiastic support of Margaret Thatcher, who saw it as a version of La Défense, the business area to the west of Paris, which she greatly admired (Murray 2001: 6). The arrival of new transport links such as the Jubilee Line Extension and the Docklands Light Railway have led to the rapid gentrification of certain parts of east London. Areas of London south of the Thames, such as Peckham and Camberwell, meanwhile, have suffered from the absence of a Tube link. From the opening up of the outer suburbs to the middle classes in the interwar period through to more recent links between Tube extensions and urban regeneration, the Underground has helped to create new social divisions and new relationships between home and workplace. The predictability of the Tube's architecture, design and corporate packaging tends to obscure these important issues of class, money and power.

This reflects a more general difficulty in thinking critically about the spaces and practices of commuting. In Britain, commuting is represented in the media in several contrasting ways. First, it is seen as a claustrophobic, tiresome experience that simply has to be endured. The overcrowding and unreliability of the London Underground, in particular, have become significant ways in which people who live and work in the capital think about its everyday life. The delays on certain lines, particularly the infamous Northern ('misery') Line, are a word-of-mouth legend; London newspapers such as the *Evening Standard* and *Metro* refer frequently in headlines to 'commuter misery' and 'rush hour hell'; and news programmes illustrate stories about the Underground with library footage of sweat-soaked commuters crammed into carriages. The adverts placed above people's heads in the Tube carriages often buy into this negative mythology, providing a barbed counterpoint to them: 'You are here. You should be here' [with arrow pointing to a picture of a beach]. 'Scotland by Air. 1½ hours from this poster.' 'After a hard day's work, I love to ride the tube' [an advert promoting tourism in south-west England with a photo of a bronzed surfer riding a tubular wave]. These representations are essentially fatalistic, suggesting that it does not really matter who is running the Underground; it will always be a hellish place from which we are desperate to escape.

Second, commuting is seen as an increasingly elastic and even outdated phenomenon. Adverts for networked laptops, cellphones and home offices, also often displayed in Tube carriages, suggest that workers can dodge the dreaded commute by being mobile, adaptable and technologically available; and there has been a recent trend in broadsheet newspapers and television documentaries for human interest stories about downshifters who cash in the equity on their town houses and happily do their jobs from converted barns in remote places. This idea of the commute as residual, the preserve of unfortunate souls still chained to a desk from nine to five, is unmistakably class-inflected. Flexibility over time and space tends to be limited to those working in the relatively high-status knowledge economies, while the more lowly – shop assistants, clerical staff, contract workers – are more restricted in their work patterns. Even for more privileged workers, as the National Travel Survey indicates, these media representations overestimate the potential for flexibility (Department for Transport 2004: 3).

Third, commuting is represented as democratic and egalitarian. British politicians are often accused by journalists, and other politicians, of escaping the misery of commuting by relying on their chauffeur-driven, ministerial limousines – hence the media sobriquet of the deputy prime minister, John Prescott ('Two Jags'). Ministers will sometimes undertake a highly staged journey on the Tube in order to respond implicitly to this criticism, by signifying their commitment to public transport and their ability to stay in touch with ordinary citizens. In December 1999, for example, the prime minister, Tony Blair, pointedly purchased his own ticket at Waterloo and journeyed on the newly opened Jubilee Line Extension to the soon-to-be-opened Millennium Dome. Surrounded by police, advisers, Underground officials and press photographers, travelling on a specially cleaned train and walking through strangely spotless and empty platforms, Blair could hardly be described as a typical commuter. In fact, his journey was a political act, because the need to finish the Jubilee Line Extension in time for the immovable deadline of the opening of the ill-fated Dome, which his government had authorized, had hugely inflated the costs (Wolmar 2002: 78). But the prime minister's manufactured encounter with the general public was presented as purely routine, in a way that specifically erased these questions about political accountability.

After finding a seat, Blair made the fateful decision to turn to the young, black woman sat next to him and strike up a conversation. Gesturing to the various minders and photographers, he said: 'Hi. Sorry about this.' The woman completely ignored him, though, preferring to listen to music on her headphones. By the end of the ride, the silence had become so awkward that Blair had resorted to standing up in the carriage and shuffling his papers. Newspaper journalists gleefully reported the prime minister's embarrassment. Within a day, they had identified the woman as Georgina Leketi-Solomon, a secretary for an accountancy firm. She was invited to Downing Street for a cup of tea and a chat in order to clear up what Blair called their 'misunderstanding'. He told reporters: 'We did actually say "hello" to each other. It's one of the good things to do on the Tube, to listen to a Walkman or read' (MacAskill 1999).

Other politicians have come unstuck when they have declined to engage in similarly synthetic rituals. Explaining the appeal of the car over public transport in February 1995, the transport minister Steven Norris said: 'You have your own company, your own temperature control, your own music – and you don't have to put up with the dreadful human beings sitting alongside you' (Deans 1995). After this comment provoked a media furore, Norris did public penance on a train journey from London to Manchester by giving up his first-class seat to travel in a second-class carriage. He described his travelling companions as

> fine, delightful. . . . I very much enjoy meeting people I don't know on buses and trains. Only last night I had a most interesting conversation with a passenger on the District Line who recognized me and said: 'I see you were having a bit of fun in the House this morning.'
>
> (Wainwright 1995)

Norris's discomfort echoed a similar incident three years earlier, when the transport minister, Roger Freeman, expressed the hope that railway privatization might produce 'a cheap and cheerful service at one moment of the day for the typists and perhaps a more luxurious service for civil servants and businessmen who might travel at a slightly different time' (Fogg 1992). Freeman was forced to retract his remarks and, the next day, symbolically abandoned his chauffeur-driven ministerial Sierra in order to travel to work on the Circle Line. Accompanied by a newspaper journalist and photographer, he carried three boxes of chocolates for his secretaries, each bearing a card that read: 'Typists are not second class. They are first class' (Travis 1992).

These self-abasing gestures, played out in scripted, choreographed ways in the mass media, are full of political symbolism. Both Norris and Freeman sought to make amends for their 'gaffes' by spuriously claiming an inoffensive identification with 'ordinary people'. This notion of the commute as a ritual of democratic belonging is essentially apolitical, ignoring more problematic issues about transport, work and public space. Indeed, there is little discussion of the *politics* of rail commuting in media and political discourse. Rail commuter pressure groups, and more general organizations that seek to improve public transport such as Transport 2000, do not have the same close links with the media as motoring groups such as the AA or RAC. London commuters are nominally represented by the London Transport Users Committee, an organization with a relatively low media profile (Gaber 2004: 13, 36). The traditionally high public subsidies for rail travel suggest that the disproportionately middle-class composition of rail commuters has influenced public policy even in the absence of these strong pressure groups, but these issues are not often publicly discussed.

The difficulty of thinking about the politics of commuting became clear in the early 2000s during the controversy over the Tube's transfer of ownership to a 'Public–Private Partnership' (PPP), a contract between the operator, Transport for London, and two privately owned infrastructure companies who maintain and upgrade the system in return for a monthly fee. PPP was heralded as a way for the London Underground to receive a steady income stream over a number of years and escape the curse of 'annuality', the inability to plan ahead because of the unpredictable release of funds in the Treasury's yearly spending round. But the creation of PPP was also underpinned by a series of political imperatives: the universally held belief among post-Thatcherite governments that private companies are more efficient than the public sector; the desire of the Treasury to take London Underground investment off the books by raising money through private finance rather than public borrowing, even though the former is more expensive in the long term; and the perceived political impossibility of raising funds through additional taxation.

PPP had the unusual effect of turning commuting into a political issue, as the future of the Underground dominated the 2000 London Mayoral election campaign. Opinion polls suggested that a large majority of Londoners was opposed to the introduction of PPP. When Ken Livingstone took the government to the law courts over the issue in July 2001, though, only a small group of protestors turned up on the Strand to protest about it (Glancey 2001: 6). The labyrinthine nature of the PPP contracts, which generated paperwork stretching to 135 volumes and over two million words (Wolmar 2002: 220, 117), may have contributed to the issue remaining below the surface of media and public debate. But this is also the effect of a more general problem of political literacy, of learning to think about the impact of wider social forces in a public culture that denies them. The introduction of PPP revealed the conflict in neo-liberal societies between an enterprise economy and flexible work culture that demand ever-greater mobility, and a deteriorating infrastructure that struggles to provide it. But the unremarked, repeated acts of commuting do not encourage us to reflect on their relationship to wider factors such as public policy, planning, investment and corporate culture – their location, in other words, within 'workspace'.

Chapter 3

URBAN SPACE

The myths and meanings of traffic

TRAFFIC CIRCULATION IS ONE of the most important activities in the everyday life of cities. In recent years, as the number of vehicles has dramatically increased, many Western cities have experienced severe traffic congestion. Local and national governments have responded with increasingly complex traffic management systems: one-way streets, parking restrictions, carefully phased traffic lights and now, in extreme cases, road pricing. The policy emphasis has shifted from supply-side solutions, such as providing new roads, to so-called 'travel demand management', which seeks to persuade or force drivers to behave in certain ways (Taylor *et al.* 1996: 3). These demand-side measures are inevitably less popular with drivers because their coercive impact is more apparent. As driving in the city has become more difficult, a series of highly politicized myths and representations of traffic has developed to make sense of this problem.

This chapter explores these myths in relation to the often fraught politics of traffic circulation and urban space. It interprets 'traffic' broadly to include stationary as well as moving cars and the movement of pedestrians as well as vehicles – partly because the myths I want to interrogate often see car driving as the norm, in a way that obscures this complex interaction between pedestrians, public transport and private vehicles. The chapter will focus primarily on London, a city whose chronic traffic problems have led policy-makers to adopt radical measures. With the exception of Singapore, a capitalist autocracy where the absence of political wrangling has allowed it to become a laboratory for intelligent transport systems and electronic toll collection (Baum 2001: 171–2), London is the traffic management capital of the world. The myths and meanings surrounding London traffic have developed in intensity in proportion to both its congestion problems and the growing number of policies designed to tackle them.

This chapter has five sections. First, it discusses a particular road, London's Westway, as a way of thinking about more general mythologies of driving and traffic. Second, it investigates the controversy over the London congestion charge in relation to popular ideas about political intervention in everyday problems. Third, it shows how this controversy can be linked to wider anxieties about traffic management. Fourth, it examines parking as a largely invisible but politically significant aspect of urban life. Finally, it investigates how the practice of walking in the city and its representation in closed circuit television (CCTV), street photography and film undermines some of these dominant traffic myths.

Myths of the road

The Westway is one of the most atypical but culturally resonant roads in London (see Figure 3.1). It is a raised urban motorway – the longest stretch of elevated road in Europe when it was completed in 1970 – that runs for two-and-a-half miles between the Edgware Road and White City, where it joins Western Avenue (the A40), an arterial road built in the interwar period as a fast route out of London into the embryonic suburbs. While largely unknown to tourists, it has inspired many artists, writers, musicians and film-makers. Chris Petit's road movie, *Radio On* (1979), includes some arresting images of driving along the Westway, and *Breaking Glass* (1980) and *Sammy and Rosie Get Laid* (1987) both set riot scenes under its concrete stilts. In *Leadville: A Biography of the A40* (2000), Edward Platt writes elegiacally of how the original dream of escape to suburbia in the 1920s and 1930s culminated in the brutalized landscape of the Westway. The road is pictured on several album covers, including The Jam's *This is the Modern World* (1977) and The Clash's eponymous debut album (1977). The Clash's lead singer, Joe Strummer, famously dubbed their music 'the sound of the Westway', implicitly linking its guttural, aggressive sound with the simultaneous boredom and exhilaration of inner-city life, and the road itself is name-checked in 'London's Burning' (1977).

The true laureate of the Westway, though, is J. G. Ballard, who has set two of his novels on and around the road. In *Crash* (1973), the dense network of roads between the Westway and Heathrow, where the flyovers 'overla[y] one another like copulating giants, immense legs straddling each other's backs' (Ballard 1995: 76), forms the backdrop to an exploration of the car crash as erotic act and transcendent experience. In *Concrete Island* (1974), an architect suffers a blowout while breaking the speed limit down the exit lane of the Westway and crashes his Jaguar through the safety barriers. Since none of the passing drivers is inclined or able to stop for him, he is stranded for weeks in the triangle of waste ground between three converging motorway routes.

Figure 3.1   The Westway, London.
Photograph by the author.

Ballard views the motorway with a passionate ambivalence, as a symbol of both the devastation wrought by the car and the timidity of much of the rest of urban planning in 'a city that rarely entered the twentieth century':

> Rising above the crowded nineteenth-century squares, this massive concrete-motion sculpture is an heroically isolated fragment of the modern city London might once have become. There are few surveillance cameras, and you can make your own arrangements with the speed limits. . . . As you hurtle along this concrete deck you become a citizen of a virtual city-state borne on a rush of radial tyres.
>
> (Adams 2001: 166–7)

Originally conceived in the early 1950s, the Westway began to be constructed in 1965 as part of an ambitious roadbuilding programme for inner London. But there was huge public opposition to it, and when the Conservative minister Michael Heseltine formally opened the road in July 1970 he was met by protestors armed with placards ('Ramps rape residents' repose', 'You can't fly over human lives') and a banner draped from the windows of houses on Acklam Road, only 20 feet from the carriageway: 'Get us out of this hell! Rehouse us now.' For years, the Westway's concrete stanchions have been a canvas for Situationist-style graffiti on alienated urban life. A line from William

Blake's *The Marriage of Heaven and Hell* ('The road of excess leads to the palace of wisdom') was rewritten as 'The road of excess leads to the palace of Willesden'.[1] A bleaker message, visible to commuters from the nearby London Underground line, offered a variation on the Parisian complaint of *métro-boulot-dodo*: 'Same thing day after day. Tube. Work. Diner [*sic*]. Work. Tube. Armchair. TV. Sleep. Tube. Work. How much more can you take. One in ten go mad. One in five cracks up' (Glinert 2003: 444).

It is not surprising that the Westway has inspired such graffiti because its uncompromising monumentality leaves it open to a particularly Parisian critique of urban life that emerged out of the dramatic transformation of the French capital in the postwar era. In his polemical work, *The Assassination of Paris*, Louis Chevalier notes a particular historical point at which the 'undrivability' of the capital became the subject of radio reports, newspaper editorials and municipal council discussion:

> It seems to me that around 1953–4, maybe a bit earlier, people began to speak more and more frequently, more and more strongly, more and more forthrightly, in a voice carrying real authority, as they say, of how difficult it was to drive in Paris.
>
> (Chevalier 1994: 52)

For Chevalier, the concern about congestion was a pretext for the destruction of old Paris by a cabal of politicians, planners and developers. The conservative Chevalier agreed with Lefebvre and the Situationists that Parisian planners have historically sought increased traffic circulation at the expense of other factors such as the aesthetics of urban space, vernacular traditions and housing for the poor. With its history of compulsory purchases and sweeping demolition of tenement buildings and terraced streets, the Westway lends itself to similar interpretations. Its separation of the deprived areas of North Kensington and Ladbroke Grove from the more affluent Holland Park and Notting Hill also suggested that, as with Baron Haussmann's rebuilding of Paris in the mid-nineteenth century, these aims of traffic management were combined with those of social control and class coercion.

In *All That is Solid Melts into Air*, Marshall Berman makes a similar argument about Robert Moses's Cross-Bronx Expressway in New York, built in the late 1950s and early 1960s. The Expressway removed 60,000 people from their homes, ploughed through vibrant neighbourhoods and 'made the Bronx, above all, a place to get out of' (Berman 1983: 290–1). The Westway's social and aesthetic impact, though, is more complex and much debated. It is true that it brought noise, pollution and declining residential property values in its wake. But the dead zone alongside and under the road, unsuitable for houses and offices, has slowly grown back to life, creating a netherworld of football pitches, cricket nets, roller-skating parks, wholefood markets and community centres. This is largely thanks to the tenants' associations in the late 1960s that campaigned for the space to be put to community use instead of being turned into a giant commuter car park as the Greater London Council (GLC) envisaged (McCreery 1996: 39). Unlike the Cross-Bronx Expressway, much of which is below ground level and closed off from its surroundings by high brick walls (Berman 1983: 291), the Westway offers drivers entering the city an impressively cinematic panorama of central London. The writer Will Self describes it hyperbolically as

> a road sweeping across the city's cubist scape; clean, shiny, slicing by block after block in elegantly plotted curve after curve. Then tantalizing with a final roller-coaster plunge over the Marylebone Flyover, before depositing you, dazed by the hubbub after the cool heights, in the bebop beat of Central London.
>
> (Self 1996: 249)

When traffic is flowing freely, the motorway represents an enticing fragment of the Americanized freeway system that the capital never built. It is often a pleasure to drive along, which cannot be said for many other London roads, and which may explain why filmmakers and writers have been both appalled and fascinated by it. A recent obituary of John Baxter, the chief engineer of the Westway, referred to him as 'the man who masterminded London's most hated road' (Mylius 2003). In truth, the Westway provokes conflicted emotions, commensurate with our cultural confusion about the relationship between the individual freedom of driving and the collective horror of traffic congestion.

The uncompromising modernity of the Westway makes it seem like a vision of the future from a bygone age, an incomplete transformation of the city's contorted, medieval street pattern. The army never acquired the influence over the British government that it had in other European countries, and municipal government in the capital was ad hoc until the formation of the London County Council in 1889. This meant that, in Lionel Esher's words, 'alone of European capitals, London failed to provide itself with a system of wide boulevards in the days when the victims still made no sound' (1981: 90). London did not construct anything like the long, straight thoroughfares of Paris or Berlin, built primarily to allow troops to move quickly to quell riots. The Westway was part of an attempt to address this historical deficiency, but it also marked the beginnings of the anti-roads campaign in Britain. After the controversy surrounding the building of the motorway, the GLC decided in April 1973 to scrap its 800-mile road programme for the capital, including the so-called 'motorway box' plan for an inner ring road, the abortive slip roads to which still lead off the western end of the Westway. Little new roadbuilding was undertaken in inner London after the construction of the

Westway, and funds were redirected towards the construction of the M25 Orbital motorway (discussed in chapter four) (Hall 1989: 18).

For all its associations with gritty urbanism, the Westway is primarily interesting as a kind of reverse image of less noticeable mythologies of everyday city life. It is striking, for instance, how much London's motorists, deprived of the visual language of a freeway system, make sense of the daily experience of driving through the often unthinking activity of *naming*. The names of frequently congested areas – the Hogarth Roundabout, the Hangar Lane Gyratory, the Blackwall Tunnel – have attained an almost mythological status by being endlessly repeated in everyday conversation or on radio traffic reports. There is a kind of grim humour about the frustration these places induce, as well as a widespread belief that certain groups, such as taxi and transit van drivers, have an arcane understanding of forgotten side streets that allows them to be evaded.[2] Not for nothing is the intimate awareness of London's streets required of its black-cab drivers by the Public Carriage Office referred to as 'the knowledge', the addition of the definite article implying cabbalistic as well as merely informational associations. The increasing perception of roads as traffic-clogged hellholes has reinforced this idea of the car as a mobile personal space within which individual drivers can feel emboldened or embattled. Driving involves motorists cooperating so as not to crash into each other, but it is also a quest for competitive advantage. There is much potential for confusion in the grey area between traffic law and the unwritten etiquette of the road, a problem exacerbated by the nature of driving as 'simultaneity without exchange, each element remaining enclosed in its own compartment, tucked away in its shell' (Lefebvre 1971: 100–1). These interpretive nuances are particularly significant in Britain, where there is a great deal of emphasis on defensive driving and good sense as supplements to legally enforceable rules. The Highway Code is simply that: a code, only some of which relates directly to statute law.

Congested roads require more of this kind of give-and-take from drivers. On a narrow street with parked cars on either side, motorists driving towards each other have to work out between themselves who goes first and who pulls over. In a traffic hold-up, they have to try to resist the temptation to jump the queue by racing up the outside lane and nudging in further up the line. On the shortest of urban journeys, they need a series of other drivers to let them through from side roads into main roads if they are to proceed. The low rate of traffic deaths in Britain compared to other European countries, particularly given its road density, suggests, among other things, that this code of civility generally works well (*Social Trends* 2004: 192). But road etiquette is, by its nature, improvised and implicit. For practical reasons no doubt, car indicators are meant to signal firm intention rather than suggestion, negotiation or apology. In ambiguous situations, drivers must make do with signals, such as flashing lights and raised arms, which are themselves ambiguous.

According to the Highway Code, flashing lights should simply warn other drivers that you are there, but this signal has developed to mean 'you go first'. On motorways, though, flashing lights have a more aggressive connotation ('I am moving faster than you: move into the inside lane so I can pass you').[3]

The mythologies surrounding driving tend to support Luc Boltanski's assertion that 'the race to appropriate road space is largely reducible to class conflict not perceived as such' (Ross 1995: 61). An obvious example is the reputation of 'white van man', a term coined in 1997 by Sarah Kennedy, a BBC Radio 2 DJ. White van men are the drivers of light goods vehicles, which are often white because they are sold in that colour and small firms do not want the expense of painting them. According to the negative stereotype, white van man is a relatively tame example of Stanley Cohen's 'folk devil' (2002): he is an aggressive driver who tailgates, never signals, overtakes on the left and harasses what he sees as his incompetent or hesitant fellow road-users. But white van man has also been hailed as the archetypal bloke-on-the-street, a symbol of doughtiness and independence. Between 1999 and 2003, *The Sun* newspaper ran a 'white van man of the week' column in which various transit van drivers could impart their wisdom about topical issues. Whether denigrated or celebrated, the white van man is defined not simply by gender but by social composition: he is a working-class, probably self-employed 'wheeler-dealer'. In 2003, the Social Issues Research Centre reported that white van man had become so iconic that he was influencing consumer choice. Older, self-employed workers were choosing vans in 'cosmic grey' rather than white to dissociate themselves from the stereotype (Social Issues Research Centre 2003).

In the congested streets of London, the national mythology of the white van man has been supplemented by myths about other types of driver that are inflected with issues of class, age and race. According to these myths, motorcycle courier riders are paid-by-the-mile, youthful yobs who weave dangerously between lanes; drivers of four-wheel-drive 'onroaders', also nick-named 'Chelsea tractors', are over-privileged hoggers of road space; cyclists are smugly eco-friendly 'lycra louts' who ignore red lights (a fairly recent representation, which dates from the proliferation of cycle lanes in the capital from the mid-1990s onwards); south London motorists, at least to their north London counterparts, are dangerous, inconsiderate drivers of uninsured rustheaps or souped-up old Mercedes with blacked-out windows; and minicab drivers are rude, incompetent crooks and potential rapists (a racialized construction, since many of them are recent immigrants from countries such as Afghanistan, Bangladesh and Iraq).

Perhaps the most ambiguous stereotype of a London driver is the 'school-run mum'. A significant cause of rush-hour congestion in British cities since the late 1980s has been the growing number of parents ferrying their children to and from school, and driving them longer distances in order to do so

(*Social Trends* 2004: 187). While this trend may be partly an effect of national, media-created perceptions about 'stranger danger', the figure of the 'school-run mum' is also disproportionately a London phenomenon, the product of a particular configuration of poorly performing state schools, gentrified areas and an ethos of 'parental choice' enshrined in government policy since the 1988 Education Act (Butler 2003: 69–70). The so-called 'school-run mum' is often mentioned in media discussions about rush-hour congestion in London, evoking sympathy as a harassed working mother trying to juggle career and home life, or censure as a middle-class parent driving her children beyond her immediate neighbourhood to fee-paying or grant-maintained schools (Sands 2003).[4] Whether heroized or demonized, the school-run mum is another example of how anxieties about congestion connect with broader questions about social class and difference. Whatever the empirically observable characteristics of different London drivers, these instant caricatures are a projection of particular fears and frustrations provoked by driving on busy roads.

The cost of congestion

The controversy over the introduction of the London congestion charge in February 2003 revealed the power and resilience of these mythologies. The congestion charge is a fee of £5 per day for driving a vehicle within a central zone between 7am and 6.30pm on weekdays. Drivers can pay in various ways including online, text message, vending machine and networked shop-till. To ensure compliance, street cameras take photographs of registration plates, computer systems check these details against databases of drivers who have paid the charge and DVLA (Driver and Vehicle Licensing Agency) records, and non-payers are sent fine notices. The lead-up to the introduction of the charge was characterized by vociferous media opposition to it, particularly in right-wing newspapers such as the London *Evening Standard*, *The Sun*, *The Times*, *The Daily Telegraph* and the *Daily Mail*. This campaign against the charge, encapsulated in the *Mail on Sunday*'s weekly feature, 'Countdown to chaos', largely took the form of grim predictions about what would happen when it was introduced.

It was claimed, for example, that there would be catastrophic overcrowding on the Tube and buses as commuters were forced out of their cars (Webster 2003a). New, congested rat-runs would be created around the perimeter of the charging zone, driving down house prices (Oakeshott 2003a). Householders in central London would have to pay more for home repairs as builders incorporated the cost of the charge into their bills (Oakeshott 2003b). The government would have to pay up to £500 million in rates rebates as businesses were hit by loss of trade (Williams and Wilkinson 2003). Crime would rise in the suburbs as offenders attempted to escape being caught on the CCTV cameras within the charging zone (Lydall 2003a). Speeding van drivers would cause accidents as they struggled to finish their deliveries before the start of the charging period (Webster 2003b). Thousands of motorists would endanger other road users by using their mobile phones while driving to pay the charge (Webster 2003c). Scooter and motorcycle accidents would rise as people took advantage of the exemption of these vehicles from the charge (Lydall 2003b). There would be a chronic labour shortage as low-paid workers would not be able to afford to get into the city centre (Pyke 2003). Shops within the charging zone would go out of business as they lost their commuter custom (Mount 2003). Children would be forced to walk on unsafe streets and busy roads as their parents abandoned the school run (D. Williams 2002). Central London schools would suffer a mass exodus of teachers, and would lose funding as parents removed their children *en masse* to avoid paying the charge (Compston and Nixson 2003). Women were more likely to be attacked as they would be forced to use unsafe public transport (Keeley 2003). Ambulance crews taking the sick and injured to hospitals would get caught in traffic jams on the perimeter of the zone (Hennessy 2002). Smithfield meat market might have to close because the charge would drive away both workers and customers (Prynn 2002). The computer system administering the charge would malfunction (Massey 2003). The call-centre telephone lines would crash and nobody would be able to pay (Arthur 2003). Snow, sunlight and mud would obscure car registration plates so they could not be photographed (Whitworth 2003). Dishonest motorists would buy false number plates or plate shields with LCD displays that would frost over the registration number as the car passed the cameras (Townsend 2003). The inaccuracy of DVLA records would mean that non-payment fines would be sent to the wrong people, including motorists who had never driven anywhere near London, the carless and the recently deceased (Walters and Harris 2002). A 'people's revolt', a mass programme of civil disobedience by motorists, including the sabotaging of cameras by vigilante groups, would immediately render the charge unworkable (Ludlow 2003).

This media opposition to the charge relied on what could be described as a neo-Poujadist construction of the 'ordinary' person who needed to be protected from the meddling of politicians and planners. Poujadism, an influential if short-lived movement of shopkeepers, craftworkers and small farmers in 1950s France, owed its appeal to its sympathetic construction of a 'little man' being threatened by the power of big business and big government.[5] News stories about the congestion charge tended to focus similarly on the little people who would suffer because of this act of political ineptitude: school-run mums, Smithfield market porters, West End restaurant staff and night-time charity volunteers. *The Sun* offered a series of variations on its favoured genre of 'funny old world' stories in which ordinary people are comically hampered by incompetent bureaucrats, with accounts of farmers who had been charged for allegedly driving through the zone in combine harvesters and crop sprayers (*Sun* 2003a, 2003b). The hero of the anti-congestion charge campaign was the beleaguered everyman, shackled by interfering politicians as he went about the unpleasant but unavoidable business of driving around the city.

The blind spot in this characterization was the very high proportion of London workers who use public transport, a much larger number than in most British cities (*Social Trends* 2004: 186). Despite this high usage, the anti-charge campaign included an implicit critique of this public sphere as marginal and residual. Before the charge was introduced, the London Mayor, Ken Livingstone, promised that there would be hundreds more buses to cater for the number of car drivers switching to public transport. Transport for London, a body of the new Greater London Authority formed in 2000, had already overseen a significant increase in bus travel. In an effort to improve the image of buses and the service for passengers, it introduced 'bendy buses' (a cuddlier name than 'articulated buses') and newer double-deckers to replace the old Routemasters, the famous London buses with the open back platforms and lopsided fronts.

As countless die-cast models, biscuit tins, moneyboxes and postcards in gift shops attest, the red double-decker bus is a tourist icon, as synonymous with London as Piccadilly Circus. But buses have been traditionally unpopular with middle-class Londoners, who tend to regard them as dirty, unreliable, slow and populated by undesirables. Anti-charge campaigners seized on this poor reputation to shore up support for their cause. Messages on the 'Sod-U-Ken' website, run by opponents of the charge, referred to buses as 'ghettos-on-wheels' inhabited by 'the underclass', which 'spew out more pollution than the Chernobyl nuclear reactor' (Sod-U-Ken 2003). Jeremy Clarkson, a presenter of television motoring programmes, used his weekly column in *The Sun* to rail against the 'anti-car Nazis' (2003). He told an audience on BBC1's *Question Time* on 16 January 2003 that he did not like sitting next to old people and students on buses, and that they should just be used as a 'safety net' for society's unfortunates. Stephen Bayley similarly argued that 'since buses favour the youthful and the elderly and other relatively unproductive elements, there are no good reasons for optimising London for their benefit alone' (2003: 70). These attacks on the London bus were characterized by a usually tacit, but sometimes explicit, assertion of social difference. Those who could afford to drive in central London should be able to continue doing so without interference; others would have to rely on the 'safety net' of public transport.

Traffic congestion is a contentious issue not just because it affects people unequally, but because it is unquantifiable. Being stuck in a jam is a frustratingly real event, but it is also a state of mind that can alter according to expectations and perceptions. One of Livingstone's main justifications for dealing with congestion was its negative economic impact on London, and in the run-up to the introduction of the charge the Greater London Authority produced a series of necessarily speculative statistics claiming to determine how much congestion 'cost' the capital's economy (Transport for London 2003: 147–73). The problem with this argument is that congestion is also an indicator of high employment and economic wellbeing, and it can actually benefit small businesses, such as shops on arterial roads. Whether you regard a road as congested depends on your ideas about how freely traffic should circulate, how much of a hurry you are in, and how much value you place on mobility and speed.[6] Traffic flow is affected by multiple factors and is, by definition, fluid and dynamic, so congestion is notoriously difficult to measure scientifically or subject to conventional cost-benefit analyses (Downs 1992: 1). In the absence of any broadly agreed framework for discussing the costs of congestion, much of the newspaper writing on the charge extrapolated the traffic problems of a whole city from personal experience. On the basis of their own daily journeys into London, journalists confidently asserted that the real causes of congestion were not cars at all, but malfunctioning traffic lights, underused buses, widened pavements, delivery vans parked on double yellow lines, anti-social cyclists and empty taxi cabs. These arguments implicitly reclaimed certain aspects of the city (for example, private car use) for an apolitical everyday life while dismissing others (for example, buses) as part of a residualized public sphere.

Few people on either side of the debate wondered why the need to ease traffic congestion had suddenly become such a pressing issue, or why a charge proposed decades earlier by figures of such different political persuasion as the free-market economist Milton Friedman (1996) and the urban geographer Peter Hall (1963: 109–14) was finally being implemented. Anyone who has tried to drive through the centre of London recently might regard this as a strange question, but it is still worth asking. Clearly, the introduction of the congestion charge was made possible by the development of interactive technologies that allow public services to be funded by individual user charges rather than general taxation. But the equipment used to record registration plates was very similar to that already used to catch speeding motorists, and some of the computerized payment methods were familiar from existing schemes such as the National Lottery. Despite the extraordinary collective pessimism about the capacity of this technology to actually work, it was hardly revolutionary.

The real impetus for the introduction of the charge was provided by the reform of London government, which led to the election of a London Mayor and the creation of the Greater London Authority in May 2000. For the previous 14 years, London had been virtually unique among major capital cities in having no citywide government (Thatcher abolished the Labour-controlled GLC, also led by Livingstone, in 1986). The direct election of the

Mayor encouraged the involvement of political outsiders with less allegiance to the mainstream political parties, which made them more likely to associate themselves with distinctive policy innovations. Livingstone's election manifesto included a firm pledge to introduce congestion charging. Despite the media campaign against it, opinion polls consistently suggested that a majority of Londoners was in favour of the charge. Other than the demonizing of 'Red Ken', though, the anti-charge campaign refused to address congestion as a problem for a democratic politics.

The congestion charge was a politically ambiguous innovation, based partly on environmentalist, left-leaning politics that sought to discourage car use in favour of walking, cycling and public transport and partly on a market-based rational choice theory, with its assumption that positive collective goals can be achieved through the pursuit of individual self-interest (in this case, the choice whether or not to pay to enter London). The campaign against the charge tended to ignore these political subtleties. While some journalists did criticize it as a 'poll tax on wheels' (*Independent* 2003), a flat-rate charge affecting poor people as well as rich, the overriding complaint was that it was a form of left-wing authoritarianism – a 'Soviet road scheme' (Amiel 2002) introduced by 'Lefties and eco-freaks' (Heffer 2003). Whatever the pros and cons of the charge, the campaign against it showed how easily traffic problems feed into mythologies of everyday life that conceal their political motivations behind the championing of 'ordinary people' and the aggressive assertion of 'common sense'.

The secret history of the traffic light

One of the striking features of the anti-charging campaign was its ignorance about the recent history of traffic management. As an alternative to the charge, many of its opponents suggested widening the roads, rephasing the traffic lights, installing 'smart' lights that could alter their timings according to the volume of traffic, and giving priority to buses at traffic signals (Clarkson 2003; Grayling 2002), apparently unaware that many of these policies had long been implemented. The science of traffic engineering, which emerged in the mid-1950s in America, began to influence transport policy in Britain from the early 1960s onwards, with the introduction of one-way systems, gyratories and complicated road markings. Traffic management is now a huge profession-cum-industry involving engineers, town planners, systems analysts and statisticians. It has a particularly significant role in cities, where traffic has increased enormously over the last few decades but there is little space for new roads. Traffic management is marked by its 'apolitical' emphasis on computer data-processing and engineering-based methodologies over more contentious issues about roads and roadbuilding. Congestion charging is the latest in a long series of traffic management policies stretching back several decades. London has traditionally been a 'shop window' for traffic engineering because of its particular congestion problems (Starkie 1982: 30). Its congestion charge has effectively been treated as a pilot scheme by other British and world cities with traffic-clogged roads, such as Edinburgh, Cardiff, Stockholm and Barcelona.

By far the most significant means of traffic management is the phasing and sequencing of traffic lights. The 'service rate' of the lights – how many cars can get through at any one time – is programmed to be sensitive to traffic. In congested areas, traffic engineers will aim to sequence a series of lights to allow drivers to move through them in a so-called 'green wave'. There are three main ways of controlling the sequencing: fixed time, variable time and manipulation by a traffic control centre. In fixed-time systems, the time allowed for green, red and amber lights is preset, using historical data about the traffic expected at that junction at particular times of the day and year. In variable-time systems, signal settings are constantly varied using a computer system such as SCOOT (split cycle time and offset optimization technique), which processes traffic-flow data with the aid of sensors placed on the approaches to junctions, calculates the optimum signal settings and then transmits the new timings to the individual traffic lights (Slinn *et al.* 1998: 82–5). Working in tandem with these systems, traffic control centre workers can alter the sequencing of lights as they monitor it using CCTV cameras. When long queues form at traffic lights but there is an empty road ahead, they can prolong the green to bring the backlog forward. When the city centre is congested, they can store traffic at lights on less busy roads.

In short, traffic lights are part of a highly planned system in which there is constant intervention by some kind of external (whether human or automated) regulator. As congestion worsens, this regulatory infrastructure expands. The introduction of the congestion charge coincided with Transport for London's inauguration of a London Traffic Control Centre (LTCC), a London Road Safety Unit (LRSU) and a Director of Traffic Management. The LTCC, staffed by Metropolitan Police and Transport for London staff, was opened in the month before the introduction of the charge. Its main task is to operate the 4,600 sets of traffic signals in London, the largest 'traffic adaptive' system in the world (Transport for London 2004b).

Lefebvre argues that the traffic light is symptomatic of the increasing preponderance of signals in everyday life. Signals are part of what he calls a 'dismantling [of] the semantic field', a 'triumph of redundancy' that closes off questions of interpretation and meaning. These kinds of signals were limited at first to controlled environments such as factories, where the klaxon marked the beginning and end of the working day. But then they were introduced into public spaces in the form of traffic lights and standardized street signs (Lefebvre 2002: 307, 300). Signals are powerful because, having no direct relationship to what is being stated or commanded, they are rarely questioned.

The particular colours used in traffic lights, for example, are not inherently meaningful but signify only through agreed conventions. The signal is defined by its anonymous eternality: 'The perfect signal is perfectly impersonal, it repeats itself indefinitely, even when there is no one in front of it . . . it is always in the same place, always reiterating its imperious command or interdiction, never beginning, never ending' (Lefebvre 2002: 279). For Lefebvre, the apparent blankness of the traffic light allows it to organize everyday life through a series of carefully delimited micro-situations, in a way that discourages reflection on broader structural processes. The growing number of signals points to the increasing colonization of everyday life by an abstract system that provides only for its own smooth running.

If we look at the history and development of traffic lights, Lefebvre's argument has some validity. As traffic signals have evolved, their operation has been gradually simplified and abstracted. The first traffic lights in Britain, developed in the late 1860s, were revolving gas lanterns manually operated by policemen. From the late 1920s onwards, these were replaced by fully automated electric lights. After the Second World War, the lights were further simplified by removing the words STOP and GO from the red and green light (Ogborn 2000: 262–3). Traffic lights now form part of complex technological and regulatory networks that are stretched, more or less invisibly, across urban space. The complexity of these networks means that they are, to use the technical term, 'black-boxed': they come to seem an automatic, intrinsic part of everyday life (Graham and Marvin 2001: 21).[7] Few drivers or pedestrians have more than a dim awareness of the intricate system of computers, traffic signals and cameras that manages traffic in London. The blankness of the traffic light both counters and exacerbates the frustration of the traffic jam. You may become angry with the hesitant driver in front but you can't jump a traffic light, at least not without breaking the law and putting your own life, and those of others, at risk.

But Lefebvre overestimates the capacity of the traffic light to blank out meaning. In certain parts of southern Europe and the developing world, red traffic lights are regarded by drivers, if not their governments, as advisory rather than compulsory. Even in heavily policed traffic systems such as Britain's, there is the potential for ambiguity and confusion in the intermediate amber light, or the green arrows that are increasingly used for filter lanes at complicated intersections. During the run-up to the 2001 general election, the Conservatives pledged to introduce a 'left on red' rule, a version of the North American 'right on red', which allows drivers stuck at traffic lights to turn right if the road is empty (Carr-Brown 2000). Although Labour won the election and the policy was never implemented, this does suggest that even in Britain the redness of a traffic light is open to negotiation, particularly when political parties wish to present themselves as the ally of the individual motorist against inflexible bureaucracy.

The congestion charge controversy brought these issues to the foreground, as part of more general concerns about the perceived coerciveness of traffic management. Anti-charge campaigners often accused Livingstone of engaging in dirty tricks to make the charge seem successful in reducing traffic, such as introducing the scheme during the half-term school holiday when traffic was lighter anyway, and suspending all roadworks. One *Daily Mail* journalist wrote on the day the charge was introduced: 'For years [Livingstone] has let bumbling contractors rearrange London's tarmac with the urgency of a world-weary sloth on a day off. Suddenly the cones are miraculously removed and the pneumatic drills fall silent. Fancy that!' (Hardman 2003).

The most serious accusation levelled at the Mayor, though, was that he had temporarily slowed down the sequencing of the lights in the run-up to the charge in order to make the traffic seem lighter once it was introduced. This claim, which surfaced first in the *Evening Standard* in March 2002, attributed to an unspecified source (D. Williams 2002), became a piece of London folklore, repeated by journalists, talk radio presenters and London cabbies ad infinitum (see Gaber 2004: 105–22). Transport for London did indeed 'tamper' with the lights in the run-up to the charge, adding pedestrian phases at certain junctions and extra sets of lights to replace Zebra with Pelican crossings, on the grounds that the former were less safe and caused traffic hold-ups. Whatever the political motivations for these actions, the really significant factor is the anger they produced. Although traffic lights are continually altered by planners, engineers and the police, motorists tend to believe that they should be free from political interference. As Ivor Gaber points out, one of the key arguments made by journalists to support the existence of a conspiracy was that extra sets of lights had been installed 'in secret' with 'no publicity' – which raises the question of whether the installation of new traffic lights should normally merit publicity (2004: 129). Two months after the introduction of the charge, a minister from the Department for Transport met with officials from Transport for London to discuss allegations that the traffic lights had been fixed, and told them to review the phasing of lights at the capital's busiest junctions (Clark 2003). The effect of the controversy, then, was to transform the traffic light from a relatively inconspicuous piece of street furniture into a recognized manifestation of legal and governmental authority.

The controversy over London's traffic lights needs to be seen in the context of wider anxieties about traffic control. These anxieties have crystallized around two of the most common phenomena of recent traffic management, road humps and speed cameras. As usual, London was at the centre of these controversies. Armed with new regulatory powers in the early 2000s, Transport for London installed more CCTV cameras in order to deter motorists from speeding or driving in bus lanes, and introduced many traffic-calming measures such as road humps and chicanes to cut speeds in residential areas, so-called 'home zones'.

Road humps, or 'sleeping policemen', have been around in Britain since the early 1970s but their usage was initially restricted. In the mid-1990s, though, the Department for Transport relaxed its guidelines to allow local authorities to put road humps virtually anywhere, and to construct different types of hump (such as speed tables, speed cushions and 'sinusoidal' humps) in addition to the classic roundtop (BBC Radio 4 2004). Road humps were initially popular with local authorities because they were a cheap form of traffic management. But there have been vociferous campaigns against them, including anti-hump marches and traffic go-slow protests, and certain councils have sought electoral popularity by adopting no-hump policies. In 2003, the Conservative council in the north London borough of Barnet began flattening its humps, which led to the Greater London Authority suspending some of its funding. The leader of the council retaliated by describing Transport for London as 'Transport for Lefties' (Clark 2004). In the same year, a builder from Oxford invited a television crew along to watch him dig up a road hump outside his house with a mechanical excavator because, he claimed, the noise from lorries hitting it was preventing him sleeping (Robbins 2003). The Home Secretary, David Blunkett, even told an interviewer that he had a 'great deal of sympathy' for this man (Morris 2003). This statement, which might seem odd coming from the minister with chief responsibility for law and order, in fact shows a keen political awareness. Tabloid newspapers with traditionally authoritarian views on law and order issues have tended to relax these views in the face of what they see as unreasonable interventions into the free movements of 'ordinary people'. Indeed, they have often implicitly endorsed civil disobedience over such issues as the congestion charge, road humps and – the most contentious traffic management innovation of all – speed cameras.

Speed cameras began to be introduced after the 1991 Road Traffic Act, one of the last acts initiated by the Thatcher government, which allowed courts to accept photographic evidence of speeding. The media representation of speed cameras has been overwhelmingly negative and has been based on several assumptions. First, they are seen as a cash cow for local authorities and the police, with *The Sun* routinely referring to them as 'greed cameras' (Whittingham and MacAdam 2003). In fact, although recent legislation allows police forces to retain a portion of the revenue raised by these machines to cover the costs of installation, any profit goes directly to the Treasury. Second, speed cameras are seen as being unable to exercise discretion and 'common sense', leading to prosecutions for drivers travelling just a few miles per hour above the speed limit at three o'clock in the morning. This complaint about the mechanical stupidity of the speed camera is part of a wider sense that speeding is a victimless crime, in which trivial breaches should be overlooked. In fact, the police do not operate the cameras at 'zero tolerance' levels and allow for margins of error, so it is unlikely a motorist would be prosecuted for such minor infringements. Third, opponents of speed cameras claim that they *cause* accidents by encouraging people to brake sharply at camera sites or look at their speedometers rather than the road (a belief unsupported by any empirical evidence). Finally, speed cameras are seen as an infringement of civil liberties because they capture drivers unawares or 'trick' them into thinking they are being watched through the use of dummy cameras. *The Sun* successfully campaigned for speed cameras to be painted a more visible yellow, and not to be 'sneakily' hidden behind trees or signs (*Sun* 2001).

The campaign against the congestion charge could therefore be seen as part of this wider resistance to the proliferation of traffic management measures. The common feature of this resistance, which tends to cut across political affiliations precisely because it is seen as apolitical, is its valuing of personal freedom over social cost: its overriding assumption is that, left to the well-meaning improvisations of the individual motorist, the traffic will sort itself out of its own accord. In this realm of the depoliticized everyday, in which individual costs are obvious but social benefits are diffuse and debatable, everyone can claim to be an expert. In short, the media representation of traffic has tended to exploit a methodological problem – the difficulty in complex, urban societies of measuring unseen costs accrued by a whole community, what economists call 'externalities' – in order to promote its own unexamined assumptions.[8] Lefebvre's work has such an investment in questioning the autocratic judgements of planners, developers and technocrats that it does not capture this confidence in vernacular expertise. This confidence has been reinforced in the last few decades by a growing emphasis in the media on neo-liberal notions of personal libertarianism and the freedom to escape an intrusive public sphere through privatized consumption.

The parking wars

A recent BBC documentary about the photographer Martin Parr showed him embarking on a project that involved photographing the last available space in car parks around the world. Explaining the motivation behind this project, Parr said: 'The one thing we're all looking for in life is somewhere to park the car' (BBC1 2003). Parr's light-hearted remark is deceptively profound. It is estimated that, in a typical city centre, almost a third of the traffic consists of people driving around looking for somewhere to park (MacAlister Hall 2004). But if parking is a consuming interest of motorists, particularly in urban areas where it is scarcest and most in demand, it is hardly ever registered as a political issue. The prohibitive cost of parking in central London was rarely mentioned by anti-congestion charge campaigners, for example, when they argued that the charge would penalize low-wage workers. Even the use of the word 'parking' shows how little the activity is subjected to close analysis. 'Parking' is most commonly a gerund, a verb form ending in 'ing' that functions as a noun, and there is often slippage between the activity (the process of leaving a vehicle in a car park) and the thing (the patch of ground or building where the vehicle is parked). Although parking is clearly a *practice* of everyday life that takes place in the context of other activities such as driving, working and shopping, it is often referred to unthinkingly as a thing, a commodity ('is there any parking around here?').

In the history of urban planning, parking facilities tended to be an improvised afterthought to the more general aim of encouraging traffic circulation. Since even a well-used car is parked for most of the time, this was an unfortunate oversight. In his study of Los Angeles as one of the first cities in the world where automobile circulation and parking influenced urban design, Richard Longstreth demonstrates the consequences of this neglect. As Downtown LA expanded in the 1920s, public agencies looked after the upgrading of roads, but left the parking problem to the private sector, so that interventions tended to be ad hoc and piecemeal. There was widespread aesthetic dislike for open parking lots, which were considered 'residue space . . . incidental voids . . . unsightly gaps in the urban matrix, exposing the unadorned side walls of adjacent buildings and enhancing the opportunities for outdoor advertisements' (Longstreth 1999: 5). The main problem, though, was that parking rarely produced the best rate of return for property owners. Cars took up a lot of space relative to the people they carried, and the greatest need for parking tended to be where real estate was most valuable.

By the 1920s, the parking business had become lucrative enough to justify demolishing small, unused buildings, but this was usually a temporary measure to gain revenue before the real estate could be properly developed, a kind of 'land banking' (Jakle and Sculle 2004: 9). Multistorey garages had more space for cars, but their complex layouts and reinforced structures made them expensive to build, and they did not generate as much revenue as office buildings, hotels or department stores (Longstreth 1997: 44–6). Retailers generally relied on others to provide parking for their customers, not realizing that the lack of it would eventually affect their trade. It was not until after the Second World War that municipal authorities in the US became involved in parking provision as a way of revitalizing downtown areas (Jakle and Sculle 2004: 74).

Longstreth sees the parking problem as a key factor in the long-term decline of downtown department stores and the proliferation of out-of-town shopping malls from the 1930s onwards (1999: 148). His work shows how the most basic everyday needs lag behind more dramatic transformations in the modern city, before reasserting their centrality in problematic ways. When there are ambiguities over property rights in capitalist societies, any gains to be made from more efficient allocation have to be weighed against the higher administrative and infrastructure costs needed to achieve them. Usage has to reach a critical point before more complex allocation systems can pay their own way (Epstein 2002: 518). This means that solutions to parking problems, such as the provision of car parks or permit systems, tend to be too little, too late.

In Britain, public agencies were involved in parking provision much earlier than in America, but if anything the problems were magnified because they emerged later on. The mass automobile industry developed in the United States in the early twentieth century at a time of rapid urbanization, so there was at least the opportunity to integrate parking more effectively into an evolving city plan. Developing later in Europe because of the impact of two world wars and the depression of the 1930s, the mass-produced car struggled to fit in with an existing urban infrastructure (Ross 1995: 53). In post-Second World War Britain, local councils sought to accommodate parking, but in an unsystematic way that failed to address the structural relationship between available parking space and traffic congestion. In the 1950s and 1960s, politicians and policy-makers were anxious not to restrict car use because it had become a symbol of the end of austerity and the promise of an affluent society (Plowden 1973: 341). Local councils prided themselves on the provision of multistorey or underground car parks, often free or cheap to use, as a symbol of their progressiveness and modernity.

Parking meters also made a late appearance in Britain. They were first used in Oklahoma in 1935, and had spread to almost 3,000 towns and cities by 1950 (Relph 1987: 82). But they were only introduced in London, already one of the most congested cities in the world, in 1958. Even then, they were not viewed as a useful way of controlling the number of cars driving into city centres. In fact, the 1956 Road Traffic Act stipulated that profit from meter revenues should be used to pay for more off-street parking (Starkie 1982: 50). It was not until the 1960s, with the publication of Colin Buchanan's report *Traffic in Towns* (Ministry of Transport 1963) and the planning bulletin *Parking in Town Centres* (Ministry of Housing and Local Government 1965) that governments recognized a clear link between controlling parking and reducing congestion. This historical failure to integrate parking into the urban fabric, while car use has grown largely unchecked, has had far-reaching consequences.

For all its importance, parking occupies a passive place in the urban landscape. While the moving car has retained its (albeit compromised) iconography of speed, status and wealth, there is no iconography of parking. Car parks are buried underground or hidden away on side roads rather than integrated into prominent streets. Multistorey car parks, many of them built in the 1960s in the stark lines and untreated concrete of the 'new brutalism', are some of the least-loved buildings in Britain. Space is at a premium in the multistorey, so turning circles are tight, bays small, floor heights minimal and stairwells dark. With their cramped conditions and open sides to allow car fumes to escape, they are a strange mixture of the subterranean and the exposed. In many film and TV thrillers, the car park is an ungovernable space, where shady deals are done and crimes go unpunished. In the cult gangster movie, *Get Carter* (1971), for example, the eponymous anti-hero (Michael Caine) throws one of his adversaries from the upper floor of a Gateshead multistorey.

The deserved reputation of car parks as dangerous and crime-ridden is closely connected with the poor status and scarcity of parking. When we buy a ticket to park, we are not purchasing a service but renting a small area of private land for a short period. The operator is not required to look after the vehicle or driver, and car parks will often display notices making this clear. Some car parks have security guards, CCTV cameras and panic buttons under a voluntary Secured Car Park Scheme introduced by the Home Office in 1992, but most do not. When car parks are working to capacity, there is no good economic reason to make them any better. Yet when the magazine *Parking Review* inaugurated the annual British Parking Awards to reward excellence among car park providers, it was the occasion for much media derision. This tongue-in-cheek report is typical:

> The nominees sat in silence as the judges delivered their verdict. Suddenly all the waiting was over. 'And the winner is . . . the 450-space Jubilee in Harrogate, North Yorks!' . . . The 300-strong crowd went wild as Harrogate was singled out for its stylish brick cladding and bright lighting.
>
> (White 2003)

It is a sign of our peculiarly ambivalent approach to parking that it can be simultaneously acknowledged as a daily, near-universal obsession and dismissed as a nerdish, minority interest.

One of the reasons parking generates strong feelings is that there is considerable uncertainty over its fair allocation. Parking laws contain even more nuances than driving laws. Erving Goffman has referred to environments such as parking spaces as 'situational', in that, unlike fixed territories such as houses, they 'are made available to the populace in the form of claimed goods while-in-use'. The temporariness of the occupancy raises questions about how much right one has to enter the space, when the occupancy should begin and end, and what sort of relationship one should have with others who share that space (Goffman 1971: 29). Even in cities where parking is rigorously controlled, drivers still have to rely on what Richard Epstein calls 'bottom-up systems' where they work out the rules of the game on the basis of unwritten precedents. In the unlikely event of a London driver finding a kerb-side parking space, for example, she is normally entitled to it according to the rule of 'first possession' (in other words, if she saw it first). So the individual who drives past a parking space in order to reverse into it would be understandably annoyed if the car behind entered the space front first. There is a clear logic to this piece of driver etiquette: motorists need an incentive to enter rear first, which is easier and safer. But when the stakes are high, such rules can be jettisoned, and there are places where it is unclear who has arrived first, such as in angled parking lots where two cars can arrive from different sides (Epstein 2002: 524).

Meter and permit systems also generate ambiguity. There are often restrictions on the amount of time you can park and the period of time before you can return, and even in no-parking zones the driver is allowed a limited amount of time to do certain activities: load, unload, deliver goods, or allow passengers to get in and out. There may also be exemptions for certain vehicles, such as hearses and removal lorries, or for certain types of people, such as doctors, traders and disabled people. There is clearly ample scope for disagreements: about how long a car has been parked, whether a permit has been clearly displayed, at what point a driver who spends a long time unloading can be deemed to have parked more permanently, and so on. The common, illegal practice of 'meter feeding' to restart the cycle shows how difficult it is to police a system based on time limits. These ambiguities have generated a number of urban myths about parking, such as the belief that only the wheels of a car need to be within the parking bay and the bodywork does not count (it does) or that a parker has a few minutes' grace to get change for the meter (they do not) (Macalister Hall 2004).

The politics of parking became particularly fraught after the passing of the 1991 Road Traffic Act. At the time, London drivers were widely flouting parking regulations because of inadequate numbers of wardens and traffic police, and the act responded with a familiarly Thatcherite solution: contracting the process out to private companies. It gave local authorities the right to take over parking enforcement from the police and keep any money they earned, providing they spent it on transport improvements. The 33 London boroughs were the first to implement the provisions of the new act, during 1993–4, and they have since been followed by many councils outside London. The local authorities typically outsource their parking operations to private companies such as NCP and APCOA. Parking management is one of Britain's fastest growing industries, with millions to be made from meters, penalty tickets, clamping and tow-away charges. In the financial year 2002–3, for example, the borough of Kensington and Chelsea paid APCOA £6 million to manage its on-street parking, and still made a profit of £21.4 million (Macalister Hall 2004). Parking is a multinational industry, with all the main British operators forming part of huge European or American parent companies. But it is a largely invisible part of the economy, with none of the brand identities associated with other aspects of road culture such as petrol and service stations (Jakle and Sculle 2004: 54). Who cares who runs the car park, as long as there's a space?

The decriminalization of parking might appear to be a liberalizing move, because when a vehicle is parked where it should not be, it is no longer breaking the law but is 'in contravention of the regulations'. But the actual effect of the act has been to make parking policy more draconian. While the police are normally concerned with obstructive parking and can use their discretion about other violations, the private parking companies are revenue-motivated. Local authorities usually issue them with an annual quota for tickets, clamps and removals. If the quota is not met they are fined; if it is exceeded they are rewarded. In his ethnographic study of traffic wardens conducted in 1969 and 1970, Joel Richman found that they practised a subtle form of 'streetcraft', a series of tacit understandings that allowed them to let known locals or naïve out-of-towners off with a friendly warning, give people a small amount of additional meter time, and make allowances for women drivers perceived to be less endowed with 'natural' road sense (1983: 59, 134). Richman found that the wardens averaged under two-and-a-half tickets a day (1983: 53). The situation is now markedly different: the new, profit-making parking attendants often work on incentives, on top of a low hourly rate, and are basically urged to issue any ticket they can.

One of the main results of the much less forgiving climate produced by the 1991 act has been a further decline in the already low public reputation of traffic wardens and clampers, with unions such as UNISON reporting increasing levels of violence and abuse against them (Robbins and Brooke 1999). Wardens now patrol the streets in virtual combat gear, with padded waistcoats designed to protect them from stabbings. The reputation of wardens in the parking battleground of central London is particularly poor. This cheery thought from the *Evening Standard* is extreme in expression but typical in sentiment: 'On my first day in charge [as President in a British Republic], all traffic wardens and wheel clampers will be shot through the head and cremated, and their ashes used to fill in the dreadful potholes in our roads' (Lewis-Smith 2003). A 1998 BBC docusoap, *The Clampers*, made public hate figures of Ray Brown and Mike Greenidge, two zealous wardens for Southwark Council. One Sunday tabloid, taking exception to Greenidge's boast that he had ticketed 108 cars on the first day of a new parking zone, claimed: 'The place for this rat is on the dole' (*The People* 1998).

The poor reputation of wardens stems largely from a perceived conflict of interest between law enforcement and revenue-raising. A popular genre of tabloid story tells of the bounty hunters who slap parking tickets on funeral hearses, fire engines and buses waiting at bus stops (Riches 2003). A complementary genre tells of the heroic resistance fighters who foil the wardens, such as the London driver who escaped a fine by performing the seemingly impossible feat of unlocking a car clamp with a matchstick (Loudon 2000). Like the controversies over the congestion charge, speed cameras and other forms of traffic management, these narratives denote a crisis in the representation of political authority in neo-liberal systems. As public services are increasingly contracted out to private companies, enforcement is more likely to be seen not as the legitimate exercise of democratically elected authority but as a form of legalized racketeering.

The politics of parking have become increasingly complex, as local authorities struggle to make the best use of limited road space. Municipal car parks, for example, now use a sliding tariff structure to encourage short-stay drivers (shoppers: good) and discourage long-stay ones (commuters: bad) (Betts 2003). There have been bitter local struggles over issues such as levies on workplace parking as a surrogate form of road pricing, and the introduction of controlled zones where parking is restricted to residents with paid-for permits. The relative cost and availability of parking in certain areas has an obvious correlation with geographical iniquities of class and wealth. In 2004, for example, parking for 24 hours in an NCP multistorey in the centre of Liverpool cost £6, and a yearly ticket cost £1,110. By contrast, parking for 24 hours in an NCP multistorey in Soho cost £36, and a yearly season ticket cost £7,740, roughly seven times more than in Liverpool. In the case of highly coveted permanent parking spaces, these disparities are equally marked. Parking bays, or even more valuable lock-up garages, in central residential areas of London will fetch as much as luxurious detached houses in the north of England, and are often bulk-purchased by developers at property auctions as investments (Macalister Hall 2004). Parking foregrounds these issues in a particularly stark way because it is such a primitive form of real estate. A parking space is simply a small area with hardstanding for a car, the value of which will be entirely commensurate with its location and, less importantly, the time of day. Parking is one of the most obvious, but least analysed, examples of how political questions about power, resources and money operate in the routine, unnoticed landscapes of everyday life.

Watching the pedestrians

In its original sense, the word 'traffic' refers to general street movement, involving pedestrians as well as cars. The gradual shift in meaning to refer exclusively to vehicles reflects the marginalization of the pedestrian in urban life. The reasons for this are well documented. First, the motorist, in charge of several tons of speeding metal, has natural precedence over the fleshy, unprotected pedestrian. Second, traffic engineering has historically been a car-centred discipline, with pedestrians largely treated as impediments to traffic flow. Third, commercial vehicles and individual motorists are represented by powerful pressure groups and consumer organizations, but pedestrians have little political clout. Few people complain, for example, that traffic lights are rigged against pedestrians, even though 'green time' is invariably longer on major city streets, where walkers outnumber motorists. Since pedestrians are disproportionately women, children, the poor and the old, this marginalization reflects existing power inequalities in society.

In more recent years, though, architects, property developers and politicians have emphasized the importance of pedestrian schemes and traffic-free zones. Transport for London's traffic management schemes have been partly aimed at redressing the balance in favour of those on foot by rephasing traffic lights, pedestrianizing certain areas, and replacing underpasses and footbridges with surface crossings. Livingstone's professed aim was to turn the capital into a European city of tree-lined boulevards, pavement cafes and Barcelona-style ramblas. The semi-pedestrianization of Trafalgar Square, he claimed, would make it more 'like the great piazzas in Italy' (Grimston 2003). In part, this growing emphasis on 'walkability' is to do with the increasing influence of tourism on public policy, and the designation of city centres as sites of leisure, culture and consumption. While traffic congestion is seen as an obstruction to everyday trade, pedestrians are seen as economically useful if they are tourists rather than if they are people going about their daily business.

One of the reasons why the routine movements of pedestrians are a largely unnoticed element of urban life is that they are not seen as problematic. In recent years there has been some media discussion of 'pedlock', a term that originated in the US in the 1980s to describe conditions so crowded that they impede pedestrian movement. But there has been no serious policy attempt to coerce pedestrians into moving in certain ways. In December 2000, a group of businesses lodged plans with Westminster city council for a pedestrian management scheme for London's Oxford Street. Their campaign proposed a pedestrian fast lane, with a minimum speed limit of 3 mph, where people would be forbidden to dawdle, read maps, talk on mobile phones, carry bulky shopping bags, listen to personal stereos or walk in the 'wrong' direction. The street would be patrolled by marshals, with speed cameras used to catch offenders, who would be liable for a £10 on-the-spot fine. The proposals were lodged as part of 'Pavement Rage Awareness Week', and included a survey of pedestrians in Oxford Street that found that nine out of ten had experienced some form of pavement rage, with more than half suffering daily. But the proposals were thrown out by the council; although they received a great deal of press coverage, journalists largely dismissed the proposals as bizarre and unworkable – 'a solution in search of a problem' (Sutcliffe 2000).

Compared to driving a vehicle, pedestrian movement in Britain is uncontrolled and unpoliced. The Highway Code contains several pages of instructions for pedestrians, but they are unenforceable in law. Town planners may attempt to deter pedestrians from jaywalking through the use of barriers and pedestrian crossings, but they can ignore these without fear of prosecution. This is in stark contrast to large parts of North America and western Europe, where there are hefty fines for errant pedestrians. There have been various abortive attempts to police the movement of pedestrians in Britain, including an experiment in London in 1966 with red lines painted along the kerb and £20 fines for jaywalkers. As many as 5,000 people were warned in the first month but no one was fined, and the police dropped the scheme three months later, claiming it was unworkable (Wainwright 1986). Although drink-driving limits are strictly enforced in Britain, there is no similar law against drink-walking, even though, among people killed on the roads in the UK, pedestrians have significantly higher average blood alcohol levels than any other group (Department for Transport 2003).

But this widespread perception of walking as unproblematic has also meant that there is little discussion about, or public opposition to, infringement of pedestrians' liberties. While there has been a concerted media campaign against the increasing electronic surveillance of motorists, the increasing surveillance of pedestrians over the last decade has gone largely unmentioned. Traffic management schemes such as congestion charging, road humps and speed cameras aim to treat all drivers equally, using universally applied systems to ensure compliance. Pedestrians, however, tend to be watched for individual signs of 'deviance'.

Surveillance cameras were introduced to Britain in the 1950s to control the movement of vehicles, and were first used in shops to deter thieves in the 1960s. But their employment in open public spaces did not seriously begin until the mid-1990s, when the Home Office handed out millions of pounds in grants to police forces and local authorities to allow them to install CCTV systems in the belief that they would prevent crime. Many of these CCTV systems have been part-funded with businesses, which therefore have a say in their operation (Norris and Armstrong 1999: 37). They are often used in city centres not so much to prevent crime as to target social undesirables such as teenage gangs, drunks and beggars, and to create a pleasant environment for shopping and nightlife. The growing use of CCTV can be seen as part of a shift away from formal, regulated systems of crime control towards what Clive Norris and Gary Armstrong call 'actuarial justice', based on the 'legal abandonment of individualised suspicion' (1999: 26). Britain has a higher density of surveillance cameras than any other country and accounts for one-fifth of all CCTV systems worldwide. The centre of London is the most watched area in the world with, for example, 35 cameras trained on Oxford Street, 1,800 covering the main railway stations, and 500 on the Central Line alone (O'Hagan 2003: 5). But there is only minimal regulation of the use of cameras in public places, and no general right of privacy as there is in many European countries (Norris and Armstrong 1999: 26–7).

As the term suggests, closed circuit television consists of images that are recorded but rarely broadcast. In Britain, under the Data Protection Act of 1998, there is a CCTV Code of Practice, which says that signs must be posted informing people that they are being filmed, and giving them details of whom to contact if they wish to access footage of their own image (Information Commissioner 2000: 8), but these guidelines are widely ignored. CCTV images tend to be released to the public in fragmented ways, as part of anti-crime campaigns or as hybrid forms of 'infotainment'. Depending on the storage capacity of the system, and according to the Code of Practice, which suggests that images must not be kept longer than necessary, most CCTV footage is erased after a day, a week or at most a month. There is a sense in which the images that we see, simply because they are being broadcast, have been rescued from the vast, unseen residue of surveillance footage that deals only with the boredom and routine of everyday life.

As a result, we tend to read CCTV pictures in the anticipation of an unfolding narrative. We expect to be watching an unusual event, such as the last moments in the lives of abducted children, their indistinct images picked out of crowds by identifying haloes. We strain to pick out detail in the fuzzy, low-definition film that, in an age of computer-generated images and digital retouching, suggests authenticity and veracity. The telltale digits in the corner of the screen revealing the date and time convey not the reality of round-the-clock surveillance but the specific moment at which an extraordinary event happened or was about to happen. The carefully prescribed way in which we look at CCTV footage tends to gloss over the more problematic aspects of surveillance, by focusing on dramatic moments and thus implicitly endorsing the stated aim of crime prevention.

Web trafficams and metrocams, which (unlike CCTV footage) are available for general viewing, show more clearly how these 'ambient' technologies can produce new understandings of street movement and urban life. While some webcam images are now in full-stream motion video, many of them are still fairly primitive, jumpily updating every few seconds or even minutes.[9] Unlike CCTV footage, we tend to watch them in real or only slightly delayed time. The impossibility of editing or controlling the image forces the viewer to focus on the banal routines of quotidian life. Webcams show groups of people stopping at traffic lights and then moving forward in columns, passing each other silently on street corners, pouring out of Tube stations, congregating at bus shelters and queuing outside telephone boxes. The grainy image of the webcam foregrounds the sociality of street life, making out pedestrians as abstracted smudges and specks, identifiable not by their individual characteristics but their collective movements.

It is striking how much recent street photography and film draws, whether consciously or not, on a kind of aesthetic of the surveillance camera in its interest in what Walter Benjamin called the 'unconscious optics' of the camera, its ability to capture normally unnoticed aspects of the everyday (1979: 256). Tom Phillips's '20 sites n years' (Figure 3.2), for example, is an ongoing photographic project begun in 1973, which seeks to mirror the recurrences of daily life by working incrementally according to specific rules and procedures.[10] Every year, on a day between 24 May and 2 June, Phillips takes photographs of the same twenty locations around Camberwell and Peckham in south London. These locations are situated on the closest walkable route to a circle

Figure 3.2 Tom Phillips, '20 Sites *n* years': Site 18, Jones & Higgins, *c.*5.00pm, 1973, 1989 and 1992.

© Tom Phillips 2003. All rights reserved, DACS.

half a mile in radius from the central point of his former house. Between 10.20am and 5.30pm on the designated day, he walks the circumference of the circle, stopping at the various sites at regular intervals, which are thus photographed at the same time of day each year. He marks each spot with a cross using a car spray aerosol, so that the pictures are always taken from exactly the same position and angle.

Phillips's sites are chosen more or less at random, and are simply ordinary streets with shops, pubs, cafes, car parks and houses. Camberwell and Peckham are relatively deprived boroughs, usually excluded from London guidebooks, and not serviced by the Underground, with all the improved access to jobs, education and leisure that this provides. But even though it mimics the form of the longitudinal study, Phillips's project is not a socio-logical investigation of urban decline. Instead, he uses the relative absence of any visual evidence of gentrification in order to reflect on the slower trans-formations of urban landscapes. Since he has used the same type of colour slide film throughout the project, even stipulating in his project rubric that it should be stockpiled if it seems in danger of being discontinued, his project tends to avoid the aura of pastness and nostalgia that attaches to old black-and-white or early colour photographs.

'20 Sites' instead reveals the hidden temporality of the everyday by regis-tering infinitesimal changes. A milkman delivers bottles in 1981, soon to become a historical curiosity; Giles Gilbert Scott's red telephone box morphs into the more functional glass kiosk of the 1980s; satellite dishes sprout from roofs, and then shrink or disappear as newer technologies make them redun-dant; the Peckham Odeon is knocked down, under pressure from the multiplexes. Some of these changes show the intrusion of market values into everyday spaces, but many of them are not so easily attributable. When change occurs within the project, it often seems pointless, as if, in Phillips's words, 'there are spots in suburbia where the world feels an itch and needs to scratch itself' (1992: 140). Benches, paving stones and flowerbeds disappear and then return in slightly different places, while some streets seem to be used as prac-tice areas for road diggers or sign erectors. Phillips's project tracks the persistence and tenacity of this unnoticed civic life.

The real subjects of '20 Sites', though, are the pedestrians who interact unthinkingly with this constantly shifting environment. Phillips's work is a rejection of the 'decisive moment' school of street photography inaugurated by Henri Cartier-Bresson and later developed by Robert Doisneau, William Klein, Garry Winogrand and others.[11] This snapshot aesthetic, made possible by the introduction of faster film speeds and lighter cameras such as the Leica in the 1920s, aimed to capsulize urban life, focusing on the pieces of impromptu street theatre that interrupted the banality of the quotidian. But Phillips's photographs rely less on the compositional skills of the photogra-pher than the quieter insights gained from the automatism of film. As such, they break some of the cardinal rules of 'good' photography. Pedestrians are often looking out of rather than into the picture, their bodies bisected by passing cars, slightly out of focus or elongated by motion blur. Their presence in the frame is determined simply by the rhythms and rituals of the day, as an elderly woman walks her dog in mid-morning; a man strolls past at lunchtime eating a burger; a boy returns from school in mid-afternoon; and groups of men and women file home at the end of the working day.

In this sense, Phillips's photographs are reminiscent of the work of a much earlier street photographer, Eugène Atget, who used large-format view cameras that, even after the arrival of the dry plate in the 1870s, were extremely cumbersome. Atget took many of his photographs during the early hours of the morning, because his equipment was not able to capture fast action. In some of these pictures, one can see blurred images, ghostly apparitions of people who moved through the frame during the long exposure the camera needed (Westerbeck and Meyerowitz 2001: 105, 110). With their images of pedestrians walking out of shot in pursuit of their daily routines, Phillips's photographs similarly point to the disparity between the persistence of the city's mundane life and the brief lives of individual city-dwellers.

The same interest in the unnoticed choreography of pedestrian movement is evident in John Smith's *The Girl Chewing Gum* (1976), an 11-minute film consisting almost entirely of a single continuous shot of Stamford Road in Dalston Junction, a downbeat area of east London (Figure 3.3). The camera is mostly trained on the offices of a plate glass company at the corner of the street, and records passers-by as they go about their business. The principal and often very funny conceit of the film is that everything that moves or appears within shot – pedestrians, cars, pigeons, even clocks – is following the instructions of an omnipotent director who appears to be behind the camera: 'Now I want the man with white hair and glasses to cross the road . . . come on, *quickly* [the man speeds up], look this way . . . now walk off to the left.' Pedestrians put cigarettes in their mouths, talk to each other, eat chips, take their glasses off, cast a glance behind them or look at the camera, all at the apparent behest of this offscreen director. The mostly fixed camera suggests a proscenium frame in which the pedestrians are actors waiting to come in from the wings of a stage set. This suggestion is reinforced when, instead of asking the camera operator to zoom in, tilt up and down or pan to the right and left, the director asks the world to do his bidding: 'I want everything to move down. . . . I want everything to move a bit further away.'

As the film progresses, though, this impression of directorial omnipotence is slowly undermined. The director's instructions become increasingly complex and his voiceover starts to lag behind what is happening onscreen. He cannot keep pace with the action, as people arrive in shot whom he has not mentioned, and events take place that he has not prescribed. He becomes breathless, coughs and stumbles over his words. He then changes tack and

Figure 3.3   From John Smith, *The Girl Chewing Gum*, 1976.
© John Smith, reproduced by permission.

begins to invent stories about some of the pedestrians – speculating, for example, that a young man moving across the screen has just robbed a post office, which seems to account for the burglar alarm we have been hearing in the background since the start of the film. At the end of the film, the sound-track of miscellaneous street sounds is silenced and the camera shifts slowly to the right to reveal a queue of people waiting to get into the Dalston Odeon to see a film, *The Land that Time Forgot*. The 'director' reveals himself not to be behind the camera at all, but shouting into a microphone at Letchmore Heath, fifteen miles from the scene we have been watching.

The Girl Chewing Gum was inspired by François Truffaut's *Day for Night* (1973), a film about the making of another film. Smith was particularly struck by a scene in which the director gives instructions to the extras as well as the main actors, and even tells a dog to piss up a lamppost (Smith 2002: 65). But *The Girl Chewing Gum* is not just an investigation into the power of the *auteur* and the nature of cinematic reality. It uses these issues to invite the viewer to look at daily routines in new ways. The pedestrians' movements in Smith's film – which have, of course, simply been filmed rather than directed – seem very strange when watched in this concentrated way. People do not just pass by: they stop, fold their arms and then walk back to where they came from;

they read newspapers while walking, oblivious to where they are going; they flap their arms about for no apparent reason. Watching Smith's film three decades after it was made reveals the historical unevenness of the everyday. The commonplace features of urban life, such as road markings, lampposts and 'No Waiting' signs, seem very familiar because they have changed little in the intervening years. But the strange fashions of the mid-1970s (tartan fleeces, collar-length hair, horn-rimmed National Health Service spectacles, flared trousers, sideburns and Afros) make the passers-by seem as if they belong to another era entirely. Like Phillips's project, Smith's film shows the relative inertia of the everyday when set against the trajectory of individual lives and more obvious examples of social change.

If *The Girl Chewing Gum* uses the long take to defamiliarize the everyday, Smith's more recent film, *Worst Case Scenario* (2002), achieves a similar effect with montage editing (Figure 3.4). For this 18-minute film, Smith transferred 4,000 photographs of daily life on a Vienna street corner, taken with a 35-millimetre camera, on to video. The photographs are simply of ordinary people going about their business – drinking in cafes, looking in shop windows, talking on mobile phones and taking their pets for a walk. The succession of black-and-white still images is sometimes interrupted by small movements (such as the looped image of a woman putting a piece of litter in a bin), splashes of colour (the blinking orange of a car indicator) or isolated sounds (a motorcycle revving up, a couple kissing, the famously irritating Nokia ring-tone). By electronically melding together events that took place within the same frame at different times, *Worst Case Scenario* works up to a chaotic climax in which it appears that cars are colliding with trams, a mother and her small child are run over, and another woman is about to be mugged. The film is composed entirely of top shots, which gives it a slightly sinister quality reminiscent of CCTV footage. We assume something out of the ordinary is about to happen because we tend to watch surveillance camera footage when there is something to see, such as a crime being committed. It is only at the end of *Worst Case Scenario* that we realize that, in fact, very little has happened at all. Even the film's title turns out not to be a comment on the action but a deliberately weak pun on two of the signs on the shop opposite: 'Wurst' and 'Käse' (sausage and cheese).

Although we expect to see people with cameras in tourist settings, both Phillips and Smith implicitly acknowledge that the etiquette of more mundane spaces does not permit prolonged looking. In *Worst Case Scenario*, the shots are taken from a hotel window without the knowledge of the participants. In *The Girl Chewing Gum*, several people acknowledge the camera with puzzlement or amusement, one boy even raising two fingers to it. In the commentary accompanying '20 Sites *n* years', Phillips notes that, while working on the project, he has several times been threatened with violence, been accused of being 'one of them' for photographing men coming out of public toilets, and

Figure 3.4   From John Smith, *Worst Case Scenario*, 2002.

© John Smith, reproduced by permission.

twice nearly captured a crime being committed, in one of these cases being offered a wad of notes in exchange for the film (1992: 140–3). The very ordinariness of what Phillips and Smith are filming specifically foregrounds issues about power and consent that the unnoticed proliferation of CCTV cameras and webcams in recent years has obscured.

In their patient investigation of the routine movements of the city, Phillips's and Smith's works are reminiscent of the 'Street Life' project of the 1970s and 1980s, in which William H. Whyte and his team of researchers set up cameras to see how New York's public spaces were used throughout the day. They found that, particularly at high pedestrian densities, people settle into a series of predictable manoeuvres, albeit ones that they would never be able to notice or explain. They discovered, for example, that pedestrians will form platoons at traffic lights and remain in them after crossing the road; will stop to talk at a particular point on the sidewalk when they see someone they know; will walk in a line behind a fast-moving pedestrian, taking advantage of the slip-stream; and will unconsciously follow a series of rules similar to traffic codes in order to avoid collision with each other (Whyte 1988: 56–67). Like Whyte and his team, Phillips and Smith suggest that the time-consuming, sedentary examination of particular places within the city can reveal unexpected patterns in routine behaviours.

Urban cultural theorists have often concentrated on walking as a radical act, a form of resistance to social control and surveillance, but they have tended to emphasize the more ludic, improvisatory movements of the individual walker: the *flâneur*, the *dériviste*, the psychogeographer.[12] Visual media such as photography, film, CCTV and webcams, though, can reveal the 'pedestrian' in both its main senses: the traveller on foot, or the prosaic and commonplace. They can focus on people who are largely unrepresented in mythologies of traffic and the city, what Certeau calls the 'multitude of quantified heroes who lose names and faces as they become the ciphered river of the streets' (1984: v). One wonders what Certeau would have made of the webcam, which so vividly captures what he sees as the unconscious, inter-subjective space-acts that constitute walking in the city. These images of pedestrian movement implicitly challenge those traffic myths that see the collective life of urban spaces as simply an affront to the free movement of the individual motorist. They show that our anxieties about traffic reflect more general issues about how we read the city itself – a space of personal excitement and freedom, but also of boredom and routine in which, whether we like it or not, we are forced to consider the political consequences of social interdependence.

Chapter 4

NON-PLACES

Supermodernity and the everyday

IN HIS 1995 BOOK, *Non-Places*, Marc Augé analyses a new kind of space produced by the accelerated movement of people and goods in advanced capitalist societies. For Augé, non-places are everyday sites such as supermarkets, chain hotels, airports and motorways, in which faceless, contractual obligations replace human interaction: 'get in lane', 'queue this side', 'sign on the dotted line', 'key in your personal number', 'have your boarding cards ready'. Like his work on the Paris Métro (discussed in chapter two), Augé's book forms part of what he calls an 'anthropology of the near' (1995: 7), which focuses on the routine landscapes of daily life in the Western world. His notion of the 'non-place' offers an extremely suggestive way of thinking about these commonplace environments, but it also raises a number of interesting problems and ambiguities. In this chapter, I want to suggest that the notion of the non-place, which Augé defines by its blank homogeneity, also needs to be understood as a site of cultural politics. I aim to explore this politics by examining two particular aspects of non-places: their underexplored histories, which complicate Augé's characterization of them as products of the acceleration of time and shrinkage of space in 'supermodernity' (1995: 110); and their cultural representation, which has often served to obscure their political meanings.[1]

This chapter has five main parts. First, it discusses London's M25 motorway, a place that is metonymically associated with the tedium of everyday life but that also has its own unique histories, technologies and landscapes. Second, it explores the political meanings of road culture, particularly in relation to the semi-mythical region of 'Middle England' and the stereotype of 'Mondeo Man'. Third, it discusses the cultural associations surrounding another archetypal non-place, the motorway service station. Fourth, it analyses the representation of new towns such as Milton Keynes and Basildon, arguing that their perceived marginality and placelessness represents a denial of their political importance. Finally, it examines how 'boring' postcards and photographs can help to open up questions of memory, politics and historical change in relation to these 'non-places'.

The road to nowhere

Britain's M25 motorway is the world's longest and busiest bypass. Its official name, the London Orbital, aptly conveys the unending circularity of the daily routines it impedes and assists. Covering a 117-mile circumference around the capital and carrying over 170,000 vehicles a day, it is often dubbed 'London's biggest car park' because of its chronic traffic problems. According to one AA survey, the most-asked question by motorists about the M25 is how to avoid it (Cusick 1996), a strange fate for a road that was designed to reduce congestion by allowing drivers to circumvent busy routes. When the Highways Agency issued a leaflet in April 2001 advising motorists that the best way of avoiding the jams was to stay off the M25 during the rush hour, it seemed a telling inversion of the motorway's original purpose (Highways Agency 2001). In Britain, the M25 has become a universal signifier of the horrors of daily commuting. A listener's poll on BBC Radio 4's *Today* programme in August 2002 voted this motorway top in a survey of the 'seven horrors of Britain', ahead of such other famously tedious places as Heathrow Airport, Birmingham New Street Railway Station and Manchester's Arndale Centre.

The cultural significance of the M25 is partly a product of the economic and political dominance of London, and its attendant transport problems. While the centre of the capital remains an important commuter destination, the London region now effectively encompasses the whole of the south-east. Commuting around London is an increasingly complex pattern of inward, outward and lateral movement (Buck *et al.* 2002: 5, 18), and congestion on the M25 is a product of these patterns. But London is also the centre of media power in Britain, and its orbital motorway is widely used by the kinds of people who help to determine which everyday experiences are seen as emblematic. There are other badly congested British roads, such as the M5/M6 interchange near Birmingham and the M62 between Manchester and Leeds, that have not acquired the same symbolic status.

The tedium of the M25 is real enough, then, but its legendary reputation helps to conceptualize this tedium. This anti-mythology reveals much about the shifting role and meanings of motorways since the Second World War. In the postwar era, both European and American governments invested a great deal of political and economic capital in the development of national highway systems. As car ownership ceased to be a middle-class luxury in

Britain, the motorways were seen as opening up a new era of mobility and opportunity. The absence of speed limits on the motorways, and the relatively light traffic, meant that they were often characterized as glamorous, thrilling spaces, particularly among the young. When the minister for transport, Ernest Marples, officially opened Britain's first inter-urban motorway, a 72-mile stretch of the M1, in November 1959, he described it as a 'magnificent' achievement opening up 'a new era in road travel . . . in keeping with the bold, exciting and scientific age in which we live' (Merriman 2003: 124). In its first few weeks, the average car speed was 80 miles per hour, dangerously fast for the time; day-trippers picnicked on bridges, verges and even the hard shoulder, to watch the speeding traffic; and London Transport arranged special bus trips to see the motorway (R. J. Williams 2002: 281; Merriman 2003: 127).

The contrast with the current reputation of the M25, and the British motorway system in general, is striking. At the heart of this contrast is a complex story of rising environmentalism, Nimbyism, traffic congestion and under-investment in an integrated transport system. It shows how roads have come to be seen as one of the intractable problems of everyday life, instead of a way of resolving those problems. Margaret Thatcher's championing of the M25 encapsulates these tensions. Her consistent support for what she called 'the great car economy' was based on a strong association between road-building and entrepreneurialism (Collins 1999). As she cut the ribbon at the final section of the Orbital near Watford, Thatcher hinted at the motorway's political contentiousness. As well as celebrating the M25 as 'a showpiece of British engineering skills, planning, design and construction', she was careful to link its completion with her strong leadership, pointing out that of the 117 miles of motorway, 98 had been built since her government took office. In response to those who were already arguing that the road was a congested nightmare, Thatcher said: 'I can't stand those who carp and criticize when they ought to be congratulating Britain on a magnificent achievement and beating the drum for Britain all over the world.' These criticisms of the M25 put her in mind of an old saying that 'nobody shops at Sainsbury's because of the queues'. The M25's popularity, she argued, was 'a mark of its success, not of its failure' (Collins 1999).

As will be clear from this speech, the Orbital never had the romance and glamour of the first motorways. In the face of rising concerns about the destruction of the natural landscape and the uprooting of communities by new roadbuilding, it was pushed through in an attempt to relieve London's chronically congested roads. Its conspicuous failure to do so represented perhaps the first realization that Britain could not simply build its way out of its traffic problem. But Thatcher's government continued to see roadbuilding as the dynamo of an enterprise economy in a White Paper of May 1989, *Roads for Prosperity*, which outlined thousands of miles of motorway widening and new bypasses. This ambitious project, coming soon after the opening of the Orbital, produced a huge backlash and the road programme had to be dramatically reduced. The evident failure of the M25 to tackle congestion may have provided an additional stimulus for the big anti-road campaigns of the 1990s over the M3 extension at Twyford Down, the Newbury bypass and the M11 Link Road out of London. This cultural politics has had a significant impact on the construction and management of the existing motorways.

Augé suggests that there is a particularly significant piece of outdoor furniture that turns the motorway into a 'non-place': the road sign. In Britain, as in other countries, the construction of the motorways was the primary impetus for the simplification and standardization of traffic signs. The 1949 Geneva Protocol on Road Signs and Signals had recommended an internationalized system with relatively uniform colours, shapes and symbols. The new British road signs, designed along these lines, were formalized in the Anderson report on motorway signage (1962) and extended to other roads through the Worboys report (1963). They were created by a team headed by Jock Kinneir, an unsung design hero whose templates were considered so successful that they have been exported throughout the world, and have changed remarkably little in the intervening years.

Kinneir's team drew on scientific research about reading signs at speed, which was stimulated by the postwar roadbuilding programmes in Britain, Europe and America. Kinneir based his designs on the principles that squarely proportioned letters with consistent stroke thickness could be read from a greater distance than condensed or elongated characters with stroke shading; that lower-case lettering with initial capitals was more legible than block capitals; and that a colour contrast between letters and their background made them more conspicuous. The motorway signs thus had a regulation format and placement: white lettering on a blue background with the lower-case lettering at least 12 inches tall, and the sign situated at such an angle and position that drivers did not have to divert their gaze more than 15 degrees (Ministry of Transport 1962: 3–9; Kinneir 1980: 66; Stallabrass 1996: 118–19).

The Anderson committee took five years to report its findings, and during this period the provisional designs generated considerable controversy and discussion, conducted in national newspapers and journals such as *Design*, *Architectural Review* and the *Geographical Magazine* (Merriman 2001: 213–15). The Council of Industrial Design sponsored a colloquium in 1959 to air these debates. The main disagreement was over the use of lower-case rather than block capital letters, which many designers believed would lead to unnecessarily large signs with little gain in public safety. One architect complained about 'these vast signs cutting holes in the landscape' (*Design* 1959: 28). Others accused the designers of undermining national identity by adopting soulless continental models (BBC Radio 4 2004). The fact that these debates now seem so immaterial shows how the signs have become part of the ubiquitous apparatus of traffic compliance, allowing us to register them quickly and act accordingly, never giving them a second glance. .

Augé's book, which is concerned with the supermodern rather than its origins, overlooks these historical contexts. The importance of the road sign in the non-place, for Augé, is that it allows places to be cursorily acknowledged without actually being passed through or even formally identified. This argument is partly inspired by the French tradition of placing pictorial signs every few kilometres, informing the driver of a nearby medieval abbey, vineyard or fortified village (Augé 1995: 97). Augé points out that, in the France of a few decades ago, long-haul drivers would have to travel on *routes nationales* and *département* roads, and would gain intimate insights into the daily life of small towns as they drove through them. On the *autoroutes*, though, the driver connects with her surroundings only through words – what Augé calls 'instructions for use' – or, increasingly, ideograms that convey information in a condensed, quickly understood way (1995: 96–8). Margaret Morse makes a similar argument about the American freeway system which, even more than the French *autoroute* network, tends to be cut off from the areas it intersects by walls and guardrails. Time on the freeway, she writes, is experienced as duration rather than chronology, 'a "drive time" guided by graphics in Helvetica, connoting a clean, homogeneous or unmarked publicness and a vague temporality' (Morse 1998: 109). In terms similar to Augé's, she describes the space occupied by freeway drivers as 'nonspace', which is 'not mysterious or strange to us, but rather the very haunt for creatures of habit. . . . This ground is without locus, a partially derealized realm from which a new quotidian fiction emanates' (1998: 102).

Like Augé's *autoroutes* and Morse's freeways, the M25 is a road that provides little sense of the environment it passes through except through its signage. This is, in part, a consequence of its difficult political birth. The Orbital cuts through huge swathes of the Green Belt and conservation areas such as the North Downs and Epping Forest, and was built in such a way as to do as little damage to this landscape as possible. Carefully built earth mounds, and trees planted at an average of 20,000 per mile, have screened the motorway from the surrounding landscape and reduced noise (Institution of Highways and Transportation 2003). Driving on the motorway is thus about as visually stimulating as moving through a tunnel. There are no real external points of reference for motorists, with the exception of the view from the Queen Elizabeth II Toll Bridge over the Thames at Dartford, so they often have little idea of precisely where they are. The Highways Agency gave particularly close consideration to the placement and content of signs on the M25 because heavy traffic, numerous intersections and the absence of other types of landmark meant that they needed to be clear and unambiguous.

Augé's discussion of non-places, though, conveys a sense of speed and transience that is conspicuously absent from the usual experience of driving on the M25. Along with pioneering aestheticians of car motion such as Kevin Lynch and Alison Smithson, Augé suggests that driving offers a kind of blurred perception, a semi-virtual encounter with a floating world (see Appleyard *et al.* 1964; Smithson 1983). The motorist travelling through the non-place experiences a particular feeling of solitude and distance, the 'rare and sometimes melancholy pleasure' of 'taking up a position' in relation to the shifting landscape, an experience intensified by the sweeping course of French *autoroutes* (Augé 1995: 87). For Augé, their stark contrast with winding *département* roads marks 'a change from intimist cinema to the big sky of Westerns' (1995: 97).

This account of the panoramic vista stretching out in front of the motorist, though, fails to capture the experience of driving on the M25 or, indeed, most British motorways. French *autoroutes* and *routes nationales* tend to be long and straight with few junctions. Britain's motorway network, by contrast, is a maze of bypasses, spurs, link roads and upgraded A-roads constructed incrementally over decades. The M25, a series of stuck-together bits of new motorway and pre-existing roads, exemplifies this residuality. The idea of a parkway encircling London had first been mooted in a Royal Commission on London Traffic in 1905, and was formally proposed in Abercrombie's Greater London Plan of 1944, which actually anticipated *five* ring roads within and around the capital (Simmons 1990: 67). By the time the M25 was actually completed after years of discussion and postponement, it was already obsolete, because the planners had greatly underestimated traffic flows.

In fact, the Orbital clearly shows how public perceptions of motorways have impacted on their development and running. Now viewed as a complete entity, it actually developed in tortuous fashion over fourteen years (1972–86), with each section having to be statutorily approved. There were 39 separate public inquiries before the M25 could be completed. As a sweetener to the locals who lived around the proposed motorway and had to be consulted in the Byzantine planning process, the Orbital provides lots of intersections with other roads. This obviously creates more jams and is one of the reasons given for the many accidents on the M25, because junction-hopping commuters have little time to get used to motorway driving. Augé's notion of the road sign as facilitating the transience of the non-place makes less sense in relation to the Orbital, with its complex intersections, temporary speed-limit signs and lane control signals.

Chris Petit and Iain Sinclair's film *London Orbital* (2002)[2] offers a different perspective on the idea of the M25 as 'non-place' by exploring the relationship between its real-life tedium and its penetration into the urban imaginary. The screen is split for much of the film, and on the left-hand side there is an almost continuous shot taken through the grimy windscreen of a car driving around the Orbital, sometimes accompanied by the rhythmic movements of windscreen wipers or pendulous mobiles. On the voiceover, Petit and Sinclair offer a series of reflections on the history and culture of the motorway. We also hear repetitive electronic music, traffic reports and a phone-in about the M25 on a local London station, in which callers complain about rush-hour jams, tailgating juggernauts and useless politicians.

At one point in Petit's commentary, he considers the relationship between the Orbital's circularity and the nature of filmmaking. On the M25, he argues, the conventional notion of editing to construct a narrative does not make sense: how do you even begin a film on a motorway without origin or end, where not even the place where Thatcher cut the ribbon is marked? After trawling through many hours of wasted footage in search of something to edit, Petit realizes that the 'negative space' and 'dead time' of the M25 are best conveyed by simply leaving the camera running, adopting the non-aesthetic of the CCTV cameras that line the route: 'It was those camera sentinels guarding the road which pointed the way. . . . What, other than a surveillance camera, would want to record its ceaseless, undramatic motion?' As well as including archive CCTV film taken around the motorway, *London Orbital* often itself mimics the grainy effect and disjointed motion of surveillance camera footage – particularly on the right-hand side of the screen where, as well as shots taken from a car driving along the motorway, there are blurred images of the M25's surrounding landscape: its grass verges, service stations, hotels, office buildings and bridges.

By filming in this way, *London Orbital* seeks to show that motorways are not simply virtual, transient spaces; they have their own distinctive topographies. As long ago as 1955, Ian Nairn identified the generic landscape of car factories, warehouses, depots, transport cafes and motels developing around British arterial roads as 'subtopia' (1955: 365–9). This interzone has since expanded greatly in size and complexity, particularly since the planning deregulation of the Thatcher years. A good example is London's Inner Orbital, the North Circular Road (A406), which is lined with hotels, supermarkets, malls and multiplexes. Motorways are less cluttered than A-roads because building restrictions are more stringent, but they still have their own landscapes and hinterlands. The main M25 intersections, in particular, have been a magnet for business parks, commuter housing estates and shopping malls such as Bluewater and Lakeside, especially on the Eastern side where governments have used these developments as a tool of regeneration.

London Orbital seems torn between the desire to map this adjacent landscape and to imagine the M25 as a kind of micro-universe with its own peculiar psychogeography. Sinclair's sections of the commentary, in particular, register the motorway as a place of violence and conspiracy, by referring to the Essex gangsters who use it to move contraband, drugs and illegal immigrants around the country; the grassy knolls, slip roads and anonymous buildings that are reminiscent of Dallas on the day President Kennedy was shot; the lorries carrying 'diseased animal carcasses' that end up in drive-in burger franchises and sanitized supermarkets; the Bluewater shopping mall which is 'populated by zombies and serviced by punishment colony androids . . . free-market capitalism's end-game'.

Petit's parts of the commentary are more likely to acknowledge the tedium of the M25, but it is not the tedium of the daily commute. He suggests that the motorist experiences the true essence of the M25 by driving round and round, in pursuit of nothing:

> More than other motorways, the M25 is designed to test thresholds of boredom. . . . It is mainline boredom, it is true boredom, a quest for transcendental boredom, a state that offers nothing except itself, resisting any promise of breakthrough or story. The road becomes a tunnelled landscape, a perfect kind of amnesia.

Petit acknowledges that the 'senseless repetition' of the M25 has scuppered his hope that 'viewing the overfamiliar as a form of alien landscape would transform it'. But the boredom itself, as he describes it, is an excessive, extreme experience. This is not commuter boredom: it is a 'transcendental' or 'mainline' boredom inducing a higher, trance-like state, the motorway as 'doorway to another reality'. In fact, the M25 in *London Orbital* is never in danger of being boring; it is an endlessly interesting, overdetermined signifier.

Mapping Mondeo land

Sinclair's book *London Orbital*, attempting a rather different project from the film of the same name, is a quest to map the M25's roadside environment more thoroughly. Avoiding the tunnel-like experience of driving on the motorway itself, he sets off on a walk around the Orbital's 'acoustic footsteps', the term used by engineers to describe the space around the motorway from which the sound of tyres on tarmac can be heard. Sinclair's book is in the tradition of François Maspero's *Roissy Express* (1994), which describes a journey along the RER (Réseau Express Regional) line running from Charles de Gaulle airport to the centre of Paris. Like Maspero, Sinclair produces a kind of quotidian travel writing, which treats a trip ordinarily taken by commuters as an intrepid adventure. He imagines the motorway not as a site of Augean 'supermodernity' but as a space where the high-tech and residual meet.

Sinclair notes that in the nineteenth century, the area now occupied by the M25 housed mental hospitals and sanatoriums, and represented the safe distance to which Victorians would remove contaminated parts of the city. Since the building of the motorway, this historical pattern has been reinforced as the river Thames has lost its traditional role as a channel for the city's waste. The decline of the working docks means that the banks of the river, at least in its metropolitan upper reaches, have been transformed into a heritage site, enterprise zone and gentrified residential area. For Sinclair, the M25 is now the main repository for the unglamorous everyday life of the capital, as the spread of settlement pushes these residues – freight traffic, landfill sites, scrapyards and retail parks – further out. The Orbital is 'a rage-inducing asteroid belt, debris bumping and farting and belching around a sealed-off city' (Sinclair 2002: 11).

Sinclair's journey also marks out a Lefebvrian tension between the everyday as overlooked and marginalized, and as ordinary and familiar. Alongside the post-industrial detritus and consumerist ephemera, he comes across picture-postcard villages with cricket squares, old pubs and thatched cottages, and generic high streets with chain stores, charity shops and estate agents. He notes a contrast between the older, more prosperous suburbs in Surrey and Kent and the 'neo-Suburbia' of 'slumber colonies', mainly in Essex: newly built housing estates with CCTV and secure parking for middle-income workers who cannot afford to live closer to the centre (Sinclair 2002: 221, 58). Sinclair implicitly suggests that this contrast reflects the contradictory role of the M25 within Thatcherite ideology. On the one hand, the motorway would protect the well-to-do suburbs nearer the centre, such as Thatcher's own constituency of Finchley, from contamination by 'nasty, dirty trade goods'; on the other hand, it would help to turn the lower-middle and upper-working classes into property-owning suburbanites, 'stakeholders' in the new enterprise economy (2002: 10, 71). These neo-suburbanites, though, would have to make do with a second-rate suburbia uncomfortably close to the motorway, their uPVC windows double-glazed against the noise. For Sinclair, the older and newer suburbs have one thing in common: their determinedly villagey appearance denies the existence of the motorway at the same time as they depend on it for daily commuting (2002: 310).

More than the film, then, Sinclair's book sees the M25 as political space, since he recognizes it as a distinctive and varied landscape rather than simply a transient 'non-place'. In fact, the electoral constituencies overlapping and surrounding the M25 have a crucial political significance because they are often thought to encapsulate that semi-fictional entity 'Middle England'. The archetypal resident of Middle England is 'Mondeo Man', a term that has its origins in a speech made by Tony Blair at the Labour Party conference in 1996. The future prime minister told the story of the moment that he knew Labour had lost the 1992 election, when he was canvassing on a suburban estate in Telford in the West Midlands:

> I met a man polishing his Ford Sierra. He was a self-employed electrician. His dad always voted Labour, he said. He used to vote Labour, too. But he'd bought his own house now. He'd set up his own business. He

was doing quite nicely. 'So I've become a Tory', he said. . . . In that moment, he crystallised for me the basis of our failure, the reason why a whole generation has grown up under the Tories. People judge us on their instincts about what they believe our instincts to be. His instincts were to get on in life. And he thought our instincts were to stop him.

(*Times* 1996)

The man Blair claimed to have met developed from this conference speech into 'Sierra Man', an ideotype of extraordinary resonance and adaptability. The significance of the Sierra was that it was a medium-sized family saloon car that during its peak years in the 1980s accounted for about 10 per cent of all new cars sold in Britain (Freeman 1993). It was the car of choice for the burgeoning middle classes of the Thatcher years.

The Sierra had stopped being manufactured in Britain in 1992, so the media quickly updated the term with another one inspired by the car that Ford built to replace it: 'Mondeo Man'. 'Mondeo' is a made-up word meant to sound like 'world' in several languages, and indeed it was one of the first cars to be conceived as a truly global product, developed by a multinational design team and sold in North America, Europe and Asia. Ford spent over a billion pounds developing it, and when it was launched in 1993 through its huge international dealer network and fleet business, it was an instant success. The Mondeo had its heyday in Britain in the mid-1990s, in the last days of Conservative rule, when it accounted for almost a quarter of British sales in its class (Smith 2000). Unlike the rest of Europe, where employees tend to buy their own cars and be paid a mileage rate by their employers, Britain is a company car culture, and the make and mark of a car are an important indicator of an employee's status within a firm. Half the Mondeo's sales are to fleet managers, and its design partly reflects its characterization as a 'repmobile', used by middle managers and sales executives.

The Mondeo's exterior is relatively anonymous – attractive and modern without being scarily futuristic, and painted in understated colours such as Panther Black, Ink Blue and Magnum Grey. Ford's innovative energies were expended instead on the interior's generous standard specification: ergonomically designed driving seats, a remote-control CD player, power steering, and a ventilation system with dust and pollen filter. Updated models have trip computers, cruise control, rain-sensing windscreen wipers, automatic temperature control and heated seats. With its driver, passenger and side-curtain airbags, side-impact door beams, pre-tensioner seatbelts and decoupling brake pedals, the Mondeo also set new safety standards within its class. It has to be a pleasant and safe car to drive because many of its owners spend much of their lives behind the wheel. (The average British company car travels more than twice the number of miles of a privately owned car (Department for Transport 2004: 49).) With its well-equipped cabin decorated in tasteful ebony or camel leather, the Mondeo creates a micro-environment that cocoons its occupants from the outside world. It is a comfortingly predictable 'non-place', in which the driver can commune wordlessly and effortlessly with the machinery, creating 'refined power and responsive performance . . . pleasure and confidence in equal measure' (Ford Motor Company 2003: 29). The implicitly solitary nature of the experience is reflected in one of the car's few downsides, the relative lack of legroom in the back seats.

The Mondeo's popularity can be seen as part of the broader success of the car industry in creating new mythologies to supplement its increasingly discredited ones about speed and mobility. In the 1950s, Roland Barthes was already noting this shift in his essay on the Citroën DS19, whose dashboard he described as 'more *homely*, more attuned to the sublimation of the utensil which one also finds in the design of contemporary household equipment'. But the new Citroën was still marketed as a streamlined, smooth-finned exterior, a beautiful object that, like a Goddess, seemed to have 'fallen from the sky' (in French, the initials DS sound like *Déesse*, the French for goddess) (Barthes 1993: 88–9). The Mondeo represents a much more advanced stage in the interiorization of car design. As Kristin Ross argues, this cultural shift is implicitly political because it re-imagines the car as a kind of escape from public into private space:

> The commute . . . has become the respite, the retreat. A miraculous object, the car can compensate for the destruction it has created. . . . In the later compensatory myths of the car it is its protected interior space that takes on value, its quasi-domestic (but also anti-domestic) function: a home away from home, a place for solitude or intimacy. . . . With the actual decline in mobility brought on by mass consumption, the inviolate shell of the car can still provide, though in a weakened form, the liberty from social constraint that speed once promised to provide.
>
> (Ross 1995: 55)

In this sense, the Mondeo's design reflects the way that 'Mondeo Man' has himself been caricatured, as someone who simply wants to retreat from the public sphere into the apolitical space of everyday life. According to this stereotype, Mondeo Man is an aspirational but insecure figure. He feels he has worked hard for his mid-range car, semi-detached suburban home and foreign holidays, and is keen to hold on to them by opposing excessive tax burdens and other forms of government interference into his life.[3]

The concept of 'Mondeo Man' needs to be understood in the context of Labour's fourth successive election defeat in 1992, a traumatic event for the party because it came in the middle of a recession when a change of government might have been expected. After this defeat, the Labour MP, Giles

Radice, wrote an influential Fabian Society pamphlet, *Southern Discomfort*, which identified the constituencies surrounding the M25, rather than the Midlands, as the heart of 'Middle England'. Radice argued that the key constituencies Labour needed to gain were in the south-east, in predominantly suburban areas with high homeownership and an above-average number of 'C1s' and 'C2s', the white-collar and skilled manual workers who now made up a majority of the electorate and were the crucial swing voters in any election (Radice 1992: 1–6). Radice conducted a survey of floating voters in five of the marginal south-east seats that Labour failed to win in 1992 – Gravesham, Harlow, Luton South, Slough and Stevenage, all situated near or around the M25. He found that these voters thought that Labour was likely to soak them with high taxes and did not understand those 'who wanted to better themselves' (1992: 5). Radice argued that 'in a "two thirds, one third" society in which the majority of people has a genuine stake in society', Labour could not afford to be just 'the party of the poor' (1992: 16). He concluded that Labour needed to appeal to voters in these south-east constituencies in order to gain power.

On the one hand, Radice was right: Labour won all five of these marginal seats in its landslide victories of 1997 and 2001 and repeated the pattern in other seats surrounding or overlapping the M25. Labour's increase in the share of the vote, while spread across almost every region and class, was largest in Greater London and the rest of the south-east (Butler and Kavanagh 1997: 244). On the other hand, Radice's argument obscures a complex relationship between the monitoring and anticipation of public opinion. 'Mondeo Man' may partly reflect a demographic reality, but he is also an invented (and gendered) construction, which may help to dissuade governments from taking difficult political decisions on controversial issues. Recent electoral surveys suggest that social attitudes can change quite sharply and, as the example of Thatcherism shows, can themselves be influenced by the successful implementation of initially unpopular policies. Heath *et al.* argue that the success of the Tories in the 1980s and New Labour in the 1990s had more to do with class dealignment (the establishment of a broad base of support across classes) than class realignment (the winning over of a particular class of voter, such as 'Mondeo Man') (2001: 123). There is little evidence, they argue, that key 'median electors' decide elections (2001: 166).

New Labour's changing policy on the roads, however, shows the persistence of the belief that median electors need to be tirelessly courted. In a 1998 White Paper, *A New Deal for Transport: Better for Everyone*, the government announced that it planned to cancel the Tories' road construction plans and cut traffic by taxing motorists more and providing extra funds for public transport. But the perceived importance of the motorist's vote made these radical plans difficult to implement. In July 2003, the transport secretary, Alistair Darling, announced an apparent U-turn: a £7.1 billion package of roadbuilding, including the widening of most of the remaining three-lane sections of the M25 to four lanes. The government has undoubtedly been influenced by the media discussion of transport policy, which tends to see mooted innovations such as road charging as a 'war on the motorist' (Hughes and Massey 1999). Tabloid newspapers routinely present road charging technologies as frightening, 'Big Brother'-style sci-fi (*Sun* 2003c). In fact, the technology for so-called 'smart highways' – satellite geopositioning systems, proximity radar and digital maps – has been available since the first Gulf War in 1991, when it was used to follow the movements of Iraqi tanks and troops (Baum 2001: 174). The main problem with electronic road pricing is not its technological ambition but its political contentiousness.

Augé's reading of the motorway as a non-place relies crucially on the fact that, in France as in some other European countries, the major roads are covered by toll systems. Since the tolls are now an accepted part of French everyday life, Augé's main concern is with their legal and economic operation rather than their broader political or historical context. He argues that 'the user of the non-place is always required to prove his innocence' (1995: 102), by paying by credit card, handing in her ticket or otherwise confirming her identity and good standing. (Augé's translator, John Howe, points out that the term *non-lieu* or 'non-place' in French is often used in a legal context to mean that someone is innocent and has 'no case to answer' (Augé 1995: 102).) This emphasis on the contractual nature of the operation neglects the often fierce political battles about how such non-places are funded and organized.

In Britain, there is no widespread toll system and motorway driving is minimally contractual: apart from the facts that motorists need to have passed their driving test to use them, and certain smaller vehicles are excluded, the motorways are open to all. Since a government-commissioned report on orbital traffic around London has recommended charging as the only long-term solution to congestion, some form of electronic road pricing seems inevitable in the future, but it remains politically contentious (Orbit 2002). In the meantime, Britain is following the example of the US, Australia and Canada in allowing private companies to build and operate toll roads, where drivers prepared to pay a surcharge can escape the congestion on public highways. In early 2004, illuminated advertising panels at motorway service stations promoted the new M6 toll road, which bypasses the most congested section of the country's busiest inter-urban motorway, with a picture of two indigestion pills and a tumbler of water above the words: 'Eases congestion: fast, effective relief from the M6.' With this telling metaphor, the motorist was invited to relieve the permanent dyspepsia of commuting by escaping into the private sphere. Like the cultural myths surrounding the M25 and the people who drive on it, this advert can be seen as a sublimated expression of the battle over the allocation of road space – an expensive, scarce and politically charged commodity.

Roadside cultures

In Michael Winterbottom's film, *Butterfly Kiss* (1994), Eunice (Amanda Plummer) roams the petrol station forecourts, transport cafes and service stations of the Lancashire A-roads and motorways in search of her ex-lover. She meets up with Miriam (Saskia Reeves) and they begin a passionate affair, which only intensifies when Miriam discovers that Eunice is a serial killer. On a deserted bridge walkway at a motorway service station, Eunice screams: 'God's forgotten me. He's forgotten me! I kill people and nothing happens!' With its use of the road as a metaphor for existential alienation and isolation, *Butterfly Kiss* feels strikingly un-British. It owes more to American movies (*Two-Lane Blacktop* (1971), *Thelma and Louise* (1991), *Roadkill* (2001)) in which gas stations, diners and motels are lawless places outside the city limits, or continental films (*The Vanishing* (1988), *A Strange Place to Meet* (1988), *Harry, He's Here to Help* (2000)) where service stations are *terrains vagues* in which abductions and strange liaisons occur.

British motorway service stations are known instead for their stultifying mundanity, and even their names have become part of this distinctively national mythology.[4] Augé argues that the incontestability of the non-place's name allows for the erasure of geographical specifics in a generic experience (1995: 85). It is true that, whether inappropriately bucolic (Clacket Lane, Pease Pottage, Hartshead Moor) or blandly functional (Birmingham North, London Gateway, Medway), the names of service stations take on significance because of their relative homogeneity as non-places: for many motorists, the name is the only way that they can tell the difference between them. These names often evoke an extremely imprecise geography. The phrase 'north of the Watford Gap' uses the name of a service station to connote the north of England, and it is sometimes employed semi-ironically by southerners to refer to a region of more primitive mores and culture. This is often abbreviated to 'north of Watford', suggesting some confusion between Watford, Northamptonshire, home of the service station, and the more famous Watford, Hertfordshire, just outside London.

But the names of service stations can also contain implicit meanings and associations, what Certeau calls a 'second, poetic geography' which insinuates itself into the functionalist logic of place names (1984: 105), a good example of which is the way they are used in song lyrics. In The Smiths' 'Is It Really So Strange?' (1986), Morrissey sings of a man chasing a lover up and down the M1 and losing his bag in Newport Pagnell. The song refers simply to the place name, but British listeners will associate it instantly with the service station, the first to be opened on the M1 (in 1960), rather than the small town that surrounds it. Roy Harper's song 'Watford Gap' (1977) is a more explicit attack on the greasy burgers, watery tea and alienating ambience of the service station — so explicit, in fact, that Watford Gap's owners sued his record label for defamation (Merriman 2004: 160). For British motorists, the mere names of these older service stations can instantly conjure up bathetic images of monotonous journeys, melancholic diners and bad food.

Augé argues that French service stations, which are often centres of regional culture, with local goods, souvenirs and maps, allow surrounding places to be fleetingly acknowledged without actually being visited (1995: 97–8). Motorists get a more impoverished version of this in British service station shops, where they can sometimes buy postcards of the town or area they are bypassing. The touristic pleasure being offered is necessarily vicarious, because highway regulations forbid drivers from leaving or entering the motorway system at a service station – rules that exist so that the local and trunk traffic will not mix, and the companies that run the service stations will not have to compete with off-the-motorway facilities. In fact, there has always been an unusual relationship between the touristic and quotidian in the service station, which is a product of both its cultural history and the changing nature of travel in increasingly mobile societies.

When the first motorways were built, the British government realized they would need more than the improvised arrangement of transport cafes and filling stations on the existing A-roads. The weight of traffic, the law against stopping and the difficulties of getting on and off the motorway meant that there would have to be 24-hour, planned services at regular intervals (Lawrence 1999: 15). Although they were commercial operations, the service stations were leased by the government and heavily regulated. This meant that, from the beginning, they were ambiguous environments. They had a public service ethos but were also glamorous, semi-touristic places embracing a consumerist, car-oriented culture. When they first opened, young people would drive to the service stations at high speeds to play pinball, drink coffee and eat ice cream, as a more alluring alternative to the only other all-night venue, the launderette (Lawrence 1999: 19). The early 1960s was the first great era of mass air travel. The service stations followed the example of the airlines by having uniformed staff greet customers (Lawrence 1999: 26), and marketing their services at different types of clientele. Along with the workaday facilities for truckers and other frequent users, there were more sophisticated restaurants for the 'gin and jag' brigade. As one early commentator put it, with more than a hint of class condescension, you could get 'a seven-course meal from a suave waiter or a double-decker motorburger from a dusky girl in a frilly apron' (Spurrier 1960: 418). Bridge restaurants were built over the motorways, so that patrons could practise what now seems a peculiar form of sightseeing: watching speeding traffic.

By the mid-1960s, though, the introduction of the motorway speed limit and the narcotizing effects of habit had taken some of the glamour out of the service station. A report, undertaken by the Bartlett School of Architecture for the Ministry of Transport in 1965, aimed to find out why the service areas were not as profitable as anticipated. The report concluded that the 'illusion of grandeur' and 'eye-catching' developments of some service areas did not add to business (Nutt 1967: 85). Motorists wanted simple meals and fast service, and the much trumpeted tower and bridge restaurants simply prevented them from getting in and out quickly. The example of countries with a longer motorway history, such as Germany and the US, showed that the novelty of 'motorway gazing' soon wore off (Nutt 1968: 190). The key factors affecting the percentage turn-in – the ratio of motorists stopping at the service station to those driving past it – were simply the location and the time of day, week and year (Nutt 1967: 84). Service stations also suffered from large-scale vandalism and theft, a problem exacerbated by their 24-hour operation. Motorists were stealing several thousands of pounds worth of cutlery every year, along with less obvious items, such as wooden trays, lavatory seats and chains, toilet-roll holders, mirrors and coat hooks (Hearn 1971: 84). From the late 1960s, the operators started to implement the policy of 'least commitment' recommended by the Bartlett advisers (Nutt 1967: 92). They concentrated on providing basic facilities, with less waiter-service, greater use of the vending machine and sliding tray, certain areas shut down in slack periods, and low-cost materials to solve the problem of theft (Lawrence 1999: 52). Truckers, who had previously had separate transport cafes at the service stations, started to refer disparagingly to these newly rudimentary spaces as 'plastic jungles': plastic cutlery, plastic crockery and plastic food (Lawrence 1999: 60).

In an article published in *New Society* in 1968, Reyner Banham saw the service station problem differently, arguing that they were not commercial or enterprising enough. He complained that

> our motorways and their ancillaries are the product of the way we are now: a mixed economy, a primarily preventive body of planning law, the arable-land-is-sacred lobby . . . a belief that advertising is inherently offensive, and a whole gamut of other Island Attitudes.
>
> (Banham 1968: 762)

For Banham, the real problem with the service station was that it was not allowed to contaminate the surrounding area, so that it could only be accessed by motorway drivers (1968: 762). A champion of the Los Angeles freeway system and American roadside culture, he saw the service station as a case study in the mean-spirited nature of British public services and the grudging acceptance of them as part of the human landscape.

Banham's article anticipated his later notion of 'non-plan'. Devised jointly with Paul Barker, Peter Hall and Cedric Price in 1969, this 'non-plan' manifesto was a reaction against the highly restrictive British planning system and its roots in a class-based, preservationist culture. Presented three years before

Robert Venturi and his colleagues wrote *Learning from Las Vegas* (1972), the 'non-plan' manifesto celebrated the improvised architecture of American out-of-town and strip retail development. It argued that, left to its own devices, the petrol station could become a locus of social and economic change, allowing mini-economies made up of fast-food outlets, post offices and shops to develop around it. But in Britain it was hard enough to get planning permission for a filling station, let alone to include anything else around it: 'Only in the motorway service areas (themselves damply overplanned) is there anything like this; and here the unfortunately not unique combination of incompetence and non-spontaneity kills the whole thing' (Banham *et al.* 1969: 436).

Ironically, these left-of-centre proponents of non-plan anticipated the thrust of Thatcherite planning policy from the early 1980s onwards.[5] Thatcher's support for new roads as engines of the new economy extended to her promotion of roadside environments, from retail parks to service stations. When she formally opened the first service station on the M25 at South Mimms, the weekend before her landslide victory in the 1987 election, she shared a platform with the founding figure of the motorway service industry. Charles Forte, the owner of South Mimms, referred to the prime minister as 'this wonderful woman that God sent from heaven', while she in turn declared 'how much I love the style of Lord Forte' (Collins 1999).

For all these effusive words, though, the development of service stations since the 1980s reveals the tensions in Thatcherite planning policy between preservationism and commercialism. Forte had to wait until John Major's government before service stations were officially deregulated, in August 1992, as part of the 'Citizen's Charter'. Major made much of his liking for what he quaintly called 'wayside taverns', such as Happy Eaters and Little Chefs, and was often filmed in these roadside cafes (*Independent* 2001: 3). He made a *tour de force* speech at the Conservative Party conference in October 1992, complaining about the scandalous lack of service stations on the M11:

> Take the bureaucratic controls, which mean Whitehall decides whether you have the chance to stop off the motorway. Every parent knows what I mean. Next services 54 miles – when your children can't make 10. . . . *They've* got to go, so *those rules* have got to go.
>
> (Nicholson-Lord 1992)

This little vignette encapsulates a classically neo-liberal notion: deregulation will make life better for 'ordinary people' by freeing them from the unreasonable restraints of faceless bureaucrats. Under the new system introduced by Major, the Department for Transport no longer selected and tendered sites for service stations; private developers simply had to get planning permission and build the facilities themselves, while the minimum-spacing requirement between stations was halved from 30 to 15 miles. In practice, though, this did not lead to many more service stations being built. Local authorities have been slow to grant the necessary planning permission, and the cost of building a site the size of a small village in the middle of nowhere tends to discourage all but the big players. There are now only three major motorway service chains in Britain – Moto, Roadchef and Welcome Break. The effects of Thatcherite deregulation have been felt less in the proliferation of new stations and companies and more in the diversification of provision within the stations themselves.

The look and feel of the service stations built since the 1990s suggests that they have simultaneously sought to follow commercial imperatives while appeasing conservationists. With one or two exceptions, such as Donington near the East Midlands Airport on the M1, they tend not to be architecturally innovative because they are built to blend in to the surrounding area. The confident, flat-roofed modernism of the early service stations (see Figure 4.1) has been replaced by the apologetic, ranch-style bungalow village: soft land-scaping, redbrick walls, clay-tiled, mansarded roofs, exposed wooden eaves, and weather vanes (see Figure 4.2).[6] Inside, though, the new service stations are light, open-plan spaces resembling shopping malls or airport concourses. Restaurants have been replaced by 'food courts' with different counters for

Figure 4.1 Newport Pagnell Service Station (Welcome Break), M1 motorway, opened 1960.

Photograph by the author.

Figure 4.2   Tibshelf Service Station (Roadchef), M1 motorway, opened 1999.
Photograph by the author.

franchises like McDonald's, KFC and Pizza Hut. The new service stations
also offer baby changing facilities, children's play areas, dog feeding stations
and workspaces where business people can use their laptops, send faxes and
recharge their mobile phones.

This diversification of service has led some operators to claim that their
flagship sites, like Donington, will become places that customers will seek
out – 'destination service stations' (Edwards 1999). There is one problem:
destination service stations are illegal. Government is opposed to them
being developed as destinations in themselves, on the grounds that this would
increase overcrowding on already congested motorways. The service stations
are still subject to strict political controls: they cannot offer more than 5,000
square feet of retail space, or provide facilities such as cinemas, bowling alleys,
sports centres, DIY outlets or supermarkets; they can only advertise themselves at particular points along the motorway; and they must provide the
unprofitable basics, such as free toilets, a picnic area and space for those
carrying out emergency repairs (Walton and Dixon 2000: 336).

The modern service station is thus a necessarily basic, functional space.
For most of its users, it offers what marketing people call the 'distress
purchase' and coach drivers call the 'comfort stop'. People turn in because
they have to relieve themselves, score a caffeine or nicotine hit, change drivers

or buy petrol. They stop for an average of only 20 minutes, and about half of them spend no money at all (Lawrence 1999: 103; Doward 1999). The service station's material culture suggests utilitarian, heavy-duty use: hardwearing carpet tiles or terrazzo flooring, plastic plants, tables and chairs bolted to the floor, toilet cubicles finished in textured laminate to discourage graffiti. This utilitarianism is also apparent in the new breed of 'value' (a word always preferred to 'budget') hotels such as Travelodges, Days Inns and Travel Inns that have adjoined the service stations since the mid-1980s. These hotels make a virtue of their no-frills service and unfussy accommodation ('no chandeliers, just comfy beds' in the words of Travelodge's website). Meals, including breakfast, are not included in the price, the on-site restaurant is usually a franchise, and payment is on check-in for 'a hassle-free departure'. There is nothing in the rooms, such as a telephone, mini-bar or TV with pay-per-view channels, that might require additional payment.

These standardized aspects of the service station and its adjoining buildings are clearly reminiscent of Augé's notion of the 'non-place'. But they also accommodate an activity he rarely discusses: waiting. Richard Longstreth explores this form of temporary rootedness in his examination of the range of outlets that developed from the simple filling station in Los Angeles from the 1910s onwards, such as auto-laundries, drive-in markets and retail malls. In the manner of the 'non-place', the lateral rather than vertical organization of these environments offered fast, unencumbered movement through aisles full of merchandise, and minimal contact with serving staff. But these out-of-town developments also relied crucially on the possibility of waiting. They were always surrounded by large areas of parking space, occupying more land than the building itself (Longstreth 1997: xiv).

Parking remains the key to out-of-town development. Developers who do not make provisions for enough parking will be unable to get finance for their projects because they will be dismissed as commercially unviable. Based on a rough approximation that the space drivers use to park their cars will be about one-and-a-half times bigger than the personal space they will occupy once in the building, the cheapest option is usually to construct a single-storey building covering 40 per cent of the ground, leaving 60 per cent for the parking lot. Taller buildings will need to house more people and thus require more parking, often of the more expensive kind such as multistorey garages or underground lots. This explains why a lot of out-of-town developments, including service stations, are single storey (Garreau 1991: 119–20). Without the ample provision of spaces in a surface-level parking lot, motorway service stations would obviously cease to function, and in Britain they are actually required by law to provide at least two hours' free parking.

The reality of waiting in the non-place opens it up to the kinds of questions about social difference that Augé's analysis seems to preclude. At the beginning of his book, he describes a day in the life of a hypothetical Parisian,

Pierre Dupont, as he sets out on an international business trip. Dupont stops at a cash dispenser on his way to his car, sails through the light Sunday morning traffic on the *autoroute*, pays at the Dourdan toll gate with his blue card, parks at the airport by purchasing a ticket, buys some duty-free goods and carefully retains the receipt for expenses, goes through the boarding procedure, and settles down in business class. One is struck by two aspects of this account: first, the smoothness of the transitions between one place and another (no malfunctioning ATMs, traffic jams or flight delays); and second, the way that this smoothness is made possible by the possession of certain requisite pieces of plastic that are not carried by everyone.

In his discussion of the international airport, Augé suggests that the non-place makes the traditional task of the anthropologist redundant. It is not possible to produce a Durkheimian analysis of the transit lounge at Roissy, he argues, because here the 'organically social' has been replaced by 'solitary contractuality' (Augé 1995: 94). Airports have signs and displays that produce and position the 'average man' (1995: 100), internationally standardized icons that invite us to surrender to the authority of people who check us in, take our baggage, usher us through security barriers and relieve us of identity and responsibility. Of course, this 'average man' tends to equate with the airlines' most frequent and valued customer: the white, male, middle-aged, business-class traveller. Even with the rise of cheap airfares, airports and aeroplanes are the last bastion of the old-fashioned hierarchies of commercial travel. Non-budget airlines ruthlessly segregate the flying elite from what is known disparagingly in the trade as 'zoo class', the economy fliers offered less facilities, less legroom and less oxygen. Business-class passengers who suffer flight delays or missed connections are given free meals, long-distance calls and hotel rooms. Economy-class passengers are lucky if they get a token for a cup of coffee. Airports are not always places of smooth contractuality, as Augé suggests, and the experience of waiting is itself differentiated.

Motorway service stations generate a different kind of waiting because our relationship to them is not so obviously contractual. They do not require the surrendering of tickets, credit card details or PIN numbers in order to enter them. Even if tolls are introduced, it seems likely that, for reasons of road safety, service stations will still need to provide free facilities at regular intervals along the motorway. The defining characteristic of service stations is not their contractuality but their inescapability. They are the most frequently visited public eating places in Britain (Lawrence 1999: 3), not because people want to eat in them but because they are the only places to stop on long motorway journeys. As non-hierarchical environments allowing for short periods of waiting, the service stations bring different classes of people together in a relatively unstructured way. From the beginning, the service stations were unusual in catering for all classes of people, and they still have an exceptionally diverse clientele. Although this offers a more democratic form of waiting than the airport, it may also help to account for their poor image. In A. A. Gill's novel *Starcrossed*, the two central characters, a glamorous actress and her social-climbing lover, visit a service station:

> Inside the canteen were the gormless, dispossessed drifting of England on the move. Fat women in sweat pants beating surly children; huddles of permed pensioners . . . humpy-backed youths phut-phutting at video machines . . . a few mired bikers . . . married men fishing for casual boys; lorry drivers with prison tattoos of women who'd got under their skin and then pissed off; root-faced, Northern ooh-ah lads . . . wanted men; unwanted men . . . fat-arsed women called Maureen and Doreen and Shirleen, starting again on hard shoulders. A great crusade of democracy, freedom, consumption, boredom and disappointment, a pervading sense of irritability and repressed violence.
>
> (Gill 2000: 55–6)

Although this description is unusually disdainful, it does suggest another dimension to the cultural dismissal of the service station. In 'Going, Going', his 1972 poem about the creeping growth of subtopia, Philip Larkin evokes a somewhat similar image of a service station, when he writes about kids 'screaming for more' in an M1 cafe, not just more food but 'more houses, more parking allowed, / More caravan sites, more pay' (1988: 189). For Augé, one of the positive aspects of the non-place's contractuality is that, although we are in the company of others, they make few demands on us. For Larkin, as for Gill, the opposite is true. The enforced consumption of the service station brings us into unavoidable proximity with these screaming kids, who are devouring land and resources and producing a world of 'concrete and tyres' (Larkin 1988: 190). These stigmatic images suggest that the unglamorous reputation of the service station is a product of residual class attitudes, provoked by the reality of ephemeral contact with otherwise avoidable others, as much as anxieties about placelessness. This buried class politics, which is symptomatic of the distinctively national ecology of British roadside culture, is even more apparent in representations of the new town.

Imagining the new town

Augé frames his theory of the 'non-place' in relation to a traditional anthropological notion of 'place': somewhere specific to a time and region that provides its inhabitants with a sense of identity, community and tradition. He argues that this notion of 'a founded, ceaselessly re-founding place' is based on a false assumption that the geographically remote, 'primitive' societies normally studied by ethnographers are static and homogeneous. This assumption combines 'the indigenous population's semi-fantasy' about its own unique identity with 'the ethnologist's illusion' that she can provide an authoritative and singular understanding of a particular tribe (Augé 1995: 46–7). But when Augé discusses the loss of local identity in French towns and villages since the Second World War, he seems to accept the existential importance of this sense of 'place'. He points out that the French new towns have been criticized for having failed to offer

> 'places for living', equivalent to those produced by an older, slower history: where individual itineraries can intersect and mingle, where a few words are exchanged and solitudes momentarily forgotten, on the church steps, in front of the town hall, at the café counter or in the baker's doorway.
>
> (Augé 1995: 66–7)

While Augé does not make it clear whether he shares this criticism, his comments certainly have a nostalgic tenor. The new town is an unusual kind of 'non-place', though, because its inhabitants have more than a transient relationship to it. The anonymous contractuality that might be liberating for users of toll roads and airport check-ins is potentially alienating for new town residents. When applied to the new town, Augé's idea of the non-place as a blank, supermodern environment (which arguably mirrors the notion of anthropological 'place' in its denial of historical unevenness and difference) implicitly sets up the 'place' as a site of lost plenitude.

Lefebvre's writings on the new town reveal a similar kind of drift between a critique of the spatial politics of capitalism and a nostalgic evocation of a lost community untainted by them. These writings, which were provoked by his dismay at the development in the late 1950s of a new town, Mourenx, near his birthplace in the Hautes Pyrénées, are particularly heartfelt. Lefebvre argues that the new town is a hyper-controlled place that brings together the worst aspects of technocratic urban planning. The gridplan layout of streets, the standardized street furniture and the sameness of the houses all suggest that life here is 'organized, neatly subdivided and programmed to fit a controlled, exact timetable' (Lefebvre 1971: 59). The overriding aim in Mourenx seems to be the smooth circulation of people and vehicles: although there are not yet many traffic lights in the town, the place is in fact 'nothing but traffic lights: do this, don't do that' (Lefebvre 1995b: 119).

In his essay, 'Notes on the new town' (1960), Lefebvre contrasts Mourenx with his birthplace, the nearby town of Navarrenx, which is like a seashell in the sense that 'a living creature has slowly secreted a structure', a delicate casing that has an organic relationship with its 'soft, slimy and shapeless' interior (1995b: 116). In the new town, this dynamic connection between a fluid everyday life and its manifestations in art, architecture and ritual is entirely absent. It is no longer possible to 'read' the everyday in terms of its symbolic expressions, because it has been 'written' in such a way as to antici- pate every potential reading. The new town satisfies clearly defined *needs* rather than more nebulous *desires* that cannot necessarily be named or categorized but are an essential part of being fully human. All the elements of the good life are there in Mourenx, but they remain unassimilated ingredients rather than an integrated, evolving whole:

> Boredom is pregnant with desires, frustrated frenzies, unrealized possi- bilities. A magnificent life is waiting just around the corner, and far, far away. It is waiting like the cake is waiting when there's butter, milk, flour and sugar. . . . Here man's magnificent power over nature has left him alone with himself, powerless. It is the boredom of youth without a future.
>
> (Lefebvre 1995b: 124)

For Lefebvre, time and history have come to an end in the new town, and an unnameable, interminable boredom has taken their place.

Lefebvre was writing in the 1950s and 1960s, when new towns were in their infancy. The sustained neo-liberal attack on centralized planning over the last few decades puts this work in historical perspective. In fact, it could be argued that the problem with the French new towns was not that they represented some nightmarish dystopia of hierarchical control but that they were *under*planned. Mourenx was unusual among these new towns in being built to serve the gas fields and petrochemical complex at nearby Lacq. Most of the French new towns were collections of rapidly built *grands ensembles* servicing Paris, situated closer to the capital than their British counterparts. Unlike the more integrated environments of the British new towns, they were essentially dormitory suburbs for workers excluded from the centre of Paris by redevelopment and rising rents. The later French new towns, constructed in the 1970s, were more carefully planned and managed, but they were still satellite towns for the capital, heavily reliant on the RER rail network.

Lefebvre's account of the new town as a series of blank signals and pre- programmed experiences seems to close off questions of historical context and cultural meaning. Long after they have been founded, new towns remain signifiers of what everyday life should or should not be like, and so it is diffi- cult to separate their origins and development from the mythologies that have surrounded them. Indeed, the characterization of the new town as a site of ahistorical sterility and boredom has been an important element in their cul- tural representation. As planned new towns have been built in more than 75 countries since the Second World War (Relph 1987: 155), they have come to be seen as the quintessence of modern placelessness. This is particularly the case in Britain, where new towns have long been the subject of throwaway insults in newspaper columns, TV programmes, stand-up comedy routines and everyday conversation. This unthinking dismissal of the new towns as non-places has obscured their more complex cultural politics.

The most notorious British new town is Milton Keynes, inaugurated in Buckinghamshire in 1967. Milton Keynes is characterized, often by people who have never been there, as 'the archetypal antiseptic new town – Teflon city, where individuality and character slide off its non-stick surface' (Cowie 1988). The symbolic life of Milton Keynes has been rather similar to Los Angeles, a place that is similarly depicted as an unreal or counterfeit city and with which it is often compared. Milton Keynes has its own iconic representation of this artificiality: the famous 'concrete cows' (actually made of waste materials and fibreglass) grazing in a field beside the railway line at Bancroft, which were donated to a local college in 1978 by Liz Leyh, a departing American artist-in-residence. These cows have assumed a mythological status that seems quite disproportionate to their modest, makeshift origins. They have been beheaded, kidnapped by students, painted with zebra and pyjama stripes, daubed with obscene graffiti and mounted by homemade papier-mâché bulls. Although they were not officially commissioned, they have been widely misrepresented as a misguided attempt by the authorities to imbue the new town with a spuriously bucolic effect.

It is difficult to decipher what lies behind these negative attitudes because they depend so much on the short-circuiting of meaning: new towns are simply synthetic non-places, devoid of identity, meaning or history. On closer reading, though, this idea of the new town as placeless accommodates unspoken, often contradictory political perspectives. First, it focalizes a contemporary prejudice against ambitiously planned public spaces, which are seen as both politically obsolete and unrecuperable by the heritage industry.[7] Second, it incorporates a sense that the new towns are stalled 'works in progress' that have failed to live up to the ambitions of their planners – partly a consequence of the fact that they phase development, so land is left vacant while the population catches up with the projections. It was this idea of Milton Keynes as a vast housing estate with few central amenities that contributed to its mythic reputation in the 1970s. Third, it feeds into anxieties about the increasing commercialization of public space, the development of an Americanized landscape of shopping malls, drive-in restaurants, ten-pin bowling alleys and multi-screens. These notions clearly speak to different stages in the development of Milton Keynes, and point to the difficulty of separating the lived reality of the town from its mythologies.

This tension between representation and practice is evident in the most notorious feature of Milton Keynes and many other new towns: its roads. Milton Keynes's road layout has been depicted as Los Angeles transplanted to Buckinghamshire, a maze of freeways in which the priorities of transit take precedence over habitation and community. A Christmas card on sale in the

1990s depicted three wise men in front of a Milton Keynes road sign, with one of them saying: 'I am sure I saw a star somewhere' (Bendixson and Platt 1992: 167). When the Japanese photographer Naoya Hatakeyama undertook a four-month residency in the town in 2001, he chose to photograph the city's sites as a blur through glass drenched with water, as if through a car window in the rain. Hatakeyama's images of Milton Keynes suggestively combine the perceived problems of orientation within an Americanized freeway system with a renowned phenomenon of British daily life: the unpredictable weather (Hatakeyama 2002).

This characterization of Milton Keynes as an automobile-dominated dystopia is simplistic, but is rooted in an observable reality. The road layout remains integral to any reading of the town for the same reason that Edward Soja regards Los Angeles as the 'quintessentially postmodern metropolis': not because it offers a doom-laden or utopian model of the future but because the relative lack of residual landscapes gives a clarity and transparency to its spatial development (Soja 1995: 128). From the beginnings of motor transport, urban planners sought to impose an order on the street pattern, distinguishing between trunk, distributor and access roads. In cities, the need to work with roads designed before the car tended to obscure these distinctions. In new towns, though, planners were largely able to maintain these road classifications.

Milton Keynes is famously laid out in an Americanized grid system of one-kilometre squares, with the main roads (identified by the letters H or V, for horizontal or vertical, and a number) located along the gridlines, and distributor and access roads within the squares. In fact, the reality is more complex than the image: it is actually a 'lazy grid' that takes account of topographical features and the layout of already existing towns and villages (Lock 1994: 87). There is also another aspect of the road system that is distinctly un-American. Like many other British new towns, Milton Keynes manages the transition between its different types of road through the provision of circular roads with inaccessible central islands. A former planning director for the Milton Keynes Development Corporation describes the town, with some justification, as 'the land of a thousand roundabouts' (Clapson et al. 1998: 28). There is even an urban myth that car tyres wear out quicker in Milton Keynes than anywhere else in the country, because locals drive round the roundabouts too fast (Brown 2003).

The roundabout is the landscape feature most associated with the British new towns in the popular imagination. In 2002, BB Print Digital, a company based in the Midlands new town of Redditch, produced a freebie calendar for its clients, *Roundabouts of Redditch*, which achieved unlikely cult status after being featured on a late-night Channel 4 talk show, *V Graham Norton*. Inundated with orders, the company went on to produce calendars of roundabouts in other new towns or unglamorous places such as Croydon, Swindon and, of course, Milton Keynes. The caption writers for the Milton Keynes 2004 calendar invite the viewer to laugh at their painstaking attention to roundabouts that are, by implication, all the same: the Bottledump roundabout is 'quite a cutie', the Denbigh Hall Drive roundabout a 'cheeky little blighter', and the Two Sisters roundabout 'breathtaking'.

The modern roundabout was invented in Britain in 1966, when a new law stipulated that vehicles approaching the roundabout had to give way to traffic already on it. This differentiated it from the more anarchic traffic circle, inaugurated in America and France in the early 1900s, where the constant weaving movements caused frequent hold-ups and accidents. Despite their poor reputation in Britain, roundabouts with offside priority have been a highly successful export. A series of studies of traffic flow at roundabouts conducted by the Road Research Laboratory in the late 1960s and early 1970s made the British the leading authorities in the field. In the last two decades, roundabouts have become increasingly common in the Commonwealth and Europe – especially France, which at one point in the 1990s was building them at a rate of about a thousand per year (Transportation Research Board 1998: 4). The case for roundabouts is compelling. They are less congested than signalled intersections, as they cut out unnecessary delays with stop signs or lights; they save on electricity and maintenance fees; they reduce fuel emissions because there is less stopping and starting; and they eliminate one of the most dangerous turning movements, right or left turn into oncoming traffic, with its potentially lethal side-on impacts.

It seems odd, then, that roundabouts should have become a pet hate of the British motorist in a way that signalled intersections have not. There are two elements to this dislike of roundabouts. First, they can seem like an over-directive form of social engineering because they force drivers to slow down and alter their path. In traffic engineering terms, driver delay at roundabouts has two components: 'geometric delay', which means the reduction of speed due to the physical attributes of the roundabout, and 'service time', which means the delay caused by other vehicles (Brown 1995: 88). Drivers find the high ratio of geometric delay to service time in uncongested areas frustrating, particularly when they encounter a number of roundabouts in succession. Writing about the roundabouts of Crawley new town, one *Guardian* writer complained that they seemed 'designed to deter people from trying to leave. No one gets out of Crawley quite quick enough' (Gibbons 1996). Augé makes a similar but less negative point in describing the roundabout as 'the revenge of the local on the global'. By forcing drivers on major roads to decelerate, it produces an egalitarian contractuality that 'imposes the same democracy of the road on the tractor coming from a country lane as it does on the limousine exiting the motorway' (Augé 2000: 207). Second, roundabouts symbolize the anonymous homogeneity of the non-place. Drivers get lost easily in road landscapes with successive roundabouts, a problem that

Milton Keynes has tried to solve by naming its roundabouts, introducing landscape features and allowing firms to sponsor them (Clapson *et al.* 1998: 29). It seems that, for British drivers, the roundabout carries the same symbolic weight as the traffic light in Lefebvre's description of the French new town: it is a byword for clinically planned environments in which more nebulous experiences and desires are erased. For one social historian, the construction of Milton Keynes as a network of roads connecting dispersed residential areas and workplaces produces 'an inevitable anonymity: a town which seem[s] more like a series of linked roundabouts rather than a living community' (Stevenson 1991: 102).

This idea of the new town as a non-place in which history has come to a standstill obscures perhaps its most important characteristic from a contemporary perspective: it is no longer new. Over the last few decades, the British new towns have often been lodestones for political and cultural change. They were inaugurated during a very particular historical moment, when postwar governments made a concerted effort to provide well-planned, collective solutions to issues such as housing, transport and employment. The development of Milton Keynes came at the end of this great period of postwar planning. By seeking both to draw on and learn from the experience of the earlier new towns, it brought together many competing impulses. In a British context, therefore, Milton Keynes is an atypical new town.

An early promotional brochure for Milton Keynes quoted a planner who specifically evoked the positive aspects of the non-place: 'The greatest achievement would be to make it possible to drive through Milton Keynes and never know you've been there. . . . Of course, we'll never do it.' The brochure added: 'It's nice to know they're trying' (Milton Keynes Development Corporation 1972). Such statements seem to confirm the worst prejudices about Milton Keynes as a nowhere city, but they belie the complexity of these initial discussions about what sort of place it would be. In the original plans for Milton Keynes, there were several competing influences: the championing of modernism in the showpiece flats and central office buildings; the acceptance of the popularity of redbrick and tile in much of the rest of the housing; the anti-urbanism of the Garden City movement; the romantic urbanism that sought to recreate civic life in the form of pedestrian walkways and monumental public spaces; and the notion of a 'nonplace urban realm' in which people would be freed from geographical constraints through improved transport and technology.[8] In these early incarnations, Milton Keynes was imagined simultaneously as a concrete place where a lost sense of community could be recreated and a virtual space where the limits of geography could be overcome.

Conceptions of Milton Keynes shifted in the recessionary climate of the 1970s, as the Inner Urban Areas Act of 1978 redirected money from new towns to inner-city areas. Thatcherite urban policy confirmed this trend, with the New Towns Act of 1985 ordering the development corporations to be wound up. As public funds were cut, the Milton Keynes Development Corporation turned itself into a more obviously commercial operation (Bendixson and Platt 1992: 195). A pioneer of various forms of social housing and equity sharing in its early years, Milton Keynes became dominated from the early 1980s onwards by owner-occupied dwellings, and the many jobs created in the town have been in the service sector that boomed under Thatcherism, particularly retail, banking, insurance and electronics. If the clichéd representation of Milton Keynes is of an overly regimented, symmetrical environment, its history over the last two decades has been one of adaptation to the new demands of a deregulated marketplace.

The Style Council's song, 'Come to Milton Keynes', released in 1985 at the height of the town's Thatcherite reinvention, gestures towards this historical process before falling back into caricature. Paul Weller's song laments the destruction of an initial promise of community through boredom-fuelled drugs binges, ersatz patriotism and semi-detached lives. An upbeat, pastiche-laden instrumentation, including horns, strings, snatches of cricket commentary, 'Y Viva España!' and the *Robin Hood* and *Sale of the Century* theme tunes, mimics the artificiality of the town. The song's video promo, filmed not in Milton Keynes but in a music hall theatre, assembles a montage of dystopian and anti-American images: young skinheads drawing out flick knives, a girl dressed in white lace smoking heroin and stuffing her face with a 'greed burger', a near-naked woman with her nipples covered by upturned ice cream cones, a Statue of Liberty slashing her wrists with an 'American Excess' card, and a spangly-jacketed game-show presenter revealing the star prize of a Polaris missile. Weller's critique of the new towns as a laboratory of Thatcherism segues into an undirected disdain for suburbia, which is imagined as a space of vulgarity, insularity and conformity.

'Come to Milton Keynes' is a reminder of how the poor reputation of the new towns has obscured their political significance, which both predates and anticipates Thatcherism. In the 1950s and 1960s, the unique demography of these towns made them the subject of critique from both right and left. Conservative critics saw the new towns as a threat because they broke the middle-class monopoly on living in the suburbs. They viewed places such as Crawley and Stevenage, made up of overspill from council estates, as one-class towns, socialist blemishes in the largely Conservative south-east (Waller and Criddle 2002: 269). Left-wing critics, meanwhile, saw the new towns as synonymous with a new breed of affluent, skilled workers who might be won over to Conservatism (Laing 1986: 3–30). The Blairite preoccupation with Middle England is nothing new. In the history of the Labour Party, there are significant parallels between the early 1960s and the invention of New Labour in the early 1990s. In both eras, the party was reflecting on a long period out of office and worrying about voter apathy and its outdated working-class image in an era of increasing affluence and declining class-consciousness. The 1960 Penguin Special *Must Labour Lose?* anticipated many of the concerns of Radice's 1990s pamphlets about the erosion of working-class identity through growing prosperity (Abrams *et al.* 1960). The new towns embodied these trends, then and now.

The most famous example of the new town as political barometer is not Milton Keynes but Basildon, which in the 1980s became indelibly associated with the affluent working-class Conservative voter ('Basildon Man'). This reputation was fully consolidated when Basildon reported its seat earlier than any other marginal on the night of the 1992 general election, making it hugely symbolic in John Major's surprise victory. One of the iconic images of that night was the sitting Conservative MP, David Amess, grinning mani-cally as he was unexpectedly re-elected. On the BBC election night broadcast, the Labour spokesman, Frank Dobson, tried to put on a brave face by uttering the famous words: 'I don't think even in Basildon they think the world is built on Basildon' (*Independent* 1992: 19). New Labour politicians soon made up for this slight by making Basildon, and other south-east marginals, a key element in their election strategy.

In fact, Basildon's reputation was as much to do with popular mythology as electoral science. With its high proportion of manual workers, it is not very representative of new towns in the south-east (Hayes and Hudson 2001: 14). Basildonians did not, as the myth goes, convert wholesale to Conservatism in the Thatcher–Major years; they continued to return a Labour council. But Basildon did follow the trend of other south-east new towns in switching to the Conservatives in 1979 and then reverting to Labour in 1997. The same pattern is evident in Milton Keynes, Labour winning both of its marginal seats from the Conservatives in 1997. The social mix of the new towns and the tendency of newcomers not to identify themselves as strongly with tribal loyalties have always made them politically volatile seats. New town voters tend to be more pragmatic than others, making their electoral choices according to their own short-term interests rather than traditional regional patterns or inherited allegiances (Waller and Criddle 2002: 9).

The perceived cultural marginality of the new towns belies their polit-ical and economic centrality. Milton Keynes has been very successful in attracting jobs and residents, in stark contrast to some of the other new towns, particularly those beyond the south-east such as Runcorn, Skelmersdale and Irvine. These different legacies make it difficult to accommodate the new town within Augé's notion of the non-place as anchored less in regional geography than in globalized space, an absence of territoriality that closes off questions of political control and accountability (1995: 115). One of the main reasons why Milton Keynes has flourished, in fact, is its prime location, halfway between London and Birmingham, and right next to the Glasgow–London railway line, the M1 and the A1. If Milton Keynes is one of the fastest growing areas in the country, it is not so much because it is a 'non-place', but because it connects crucially with the more local contexts of quotidian life: housing, work and commuting.

Wish we weren't here: boring postcards

These different kinds of 'non-place' are the subject of Martin Parr's *Boring Postcards* (1999), a collection of British postcards, produced mainly in the 1950s and 1960s, of motorways, service stations, shopping precincts, airport terminals and new towns (See Figure 4.3). These postcards were often cheaply produced, and their generic instinct to prettify their subject matter is undermined by overprocessed colour, clumsy tinting and cheap lithography. Parr's anthology draws on a serial aesthetic pioneered by the pop and conceptual artists of the 1960s. Its most obvious precursor is the work of Ed Ruscha, in photographic collections such as *Twentysix Gasoline Stations* (1963), *Every Building on the Sunset Strip* (1966) and *Thirtyfour Parking Lots in Los Angeles* (1967). Like *Boring Postcards*, Ruscha's books are made up of cheaply reproduced images of the mundane environment, grouped together by type, with no commentary except for brief identifying captions. The same interest in the everyday is evident in the work of American photographers emerging in the

Figure 4.3 'The M1 Motorway'.
© Martin Parr Collection/Magnum Photos.

1960s and 1970s such as Stephen Shore, William Eggleston, Lewis Baltz and Robert Adams, who produced images of gasoline stations, parking lots and roadside diners. More recently, Catherine Opie's untitled photographs of roads and flyovers ('Freeways' (1994–5)) and deserted shopping precincts ('Mini-Malls' (1997–8)) in Los Angeles form part of this same tradition of the deadpan, unblinking portrayal of vernacular spaces. A common characteristic of these photographers is their tendency to picture these 'non-places' without cars and people, so that they seem almost like ancient ruins, opened up to questions of memory and history. Parr's wordless investigation of the postcard aesthetic, a form that is associated with touristic utopias but that has also consistently shifted our understandings of the picturesque, represents an implicit engagement with this body of work.

In his own photographs of the everyday, Parr uses high-colour film and a ring-flash camera, a type normally reserved for medical photographs, to produce an unforgiving, precise image. He suggests that this aesthetic is an attempt to evade the nostalgic impulses of much photographic work:

> I'd look at the output of British documentary work [in the 1970s and 1980s], and think, this is nothing to do with the type of life that I lead, or the lives that most people lead. Most of it was very exotic: the last thatcher in Norfolk, that kind of thing. Documentary photographers love to photograph things that are about to disappear. . . . That's why I decided to do things like supermarkets. Or petrol pumps. I was looking at a photograph of a petrol pump that I took in 1989. It's unrecognizable when compared with a petrol pump of today.
>
> (Sweet 2003)

Boring Postcards arises from the same interest in invisible historical change. When compared with Parr's American and German versions of Boring Postcards, these images of British 'non-places' reveal them not simply as sites of nascent globalization but as repositories of cultural memory. Boring Postcards USA (2000) is largely made up of photographs from the 1960s and 1970s of the interstates, toll bridges, truck stops and motels created in the wake of the 1956 Highways Act. Although these postcards are undeniably boring, the American tendency to celebrate rather than denigrate roadside culture means they do not have that same aura of sadness and disappointment infecting the British versions.[9] Langweilige Postkarten (2001), a series of postcards of East and West German autobahns, petrol stations, shopping precincts, airports and tower blocks, has a specific cold war context. These photographs reveal the propagandistic use of new buildings and technologies as triumphal testaments to the different versions of social progress in East and West. The images of Britain in Boring Postcards also have a distinctively national context. They belong to a period in which national governments and local councils made major investments in public spaces that were seen as symbols of modernity and progress. The pedestrianized shopping precinct in Stevenage, for example, was one of the most photographed sites in Britain for several years after its completion in the late 1950s (Ward 1993: 78).

There are two main senses to the word 'routine': it is an unchanging and often unconscious series of actions in everyday life, or a well-rehearsed sequence, as in a dance or stand-up routine. This latter sense reminds us that, in fact, all routines are learnt: in the mundane practices of daily life, the memory of the learning process has simply been erased. The construction of a public service infrastructure in Britain in the 1950s and 1960s – including the building of 'non-places' such as motorways, service stations and new towns – was accompanied by numerous newsreel and public information films, shown in cinemas and on television; articles in the specialist and mainstream press; and booklets and press releases prepared by governments, local authorities and contractors (see Merriman 2003: 125). The purpose of these texts was partly promotional, particularly in the case of the new towns, which needed to attract residents and investment. But they were also designed to inform people about the unfamiliar routines that these new environments would demand. When the first service station opened on the M1, for example, an architect, F. H. Carter, appeared on television to explain how the opposite sides of the road were linked by bridges, and how drivers should exit and return to the motorway via slip roads (Lawrence 1999: 23–4). The building and opening of the M1 in the late 1950s similarly led to many celebratory newsreels about this 'safe, fast and beautiful' road (Pathé 1958):

> The great highway will never look empty again. It'll be a crowded road of speed. In keeping is ultra-modern signposting. Plenty of notice of the next filling station. Flyovers ensure that no traffic fights for crossing-rights. This is the motoring we used to dream about.
>
> (Pathé 1959)

The modern viewer can find the plum-voiced paternalism of these films hilariously condescending, but they do bring home the learned nature of routines that we tend to practise unthinkingly and situate outside history and memory.

Parr's postcards have a similar kind of kitsch appeal to these public information films. From a contemporary perspective, it is difficult to imagine what anyone could have found visually interesting about the pedestrianized town centre in Basildon, the departure lounge at Manchester Airport or a portmanteau image of the M1, and it seems strange that these postcards once formed part of semi-touristic cultural practices. Motorists bought postcards of service stations from vending machines in the cafeterias, and sent them to friends and family with scrawled accounts of strange new customs on the back: 'We are having a cup of coffee on our way back along the motorway'

(Phillips 2000: 286). Laughing at the strange rituals of the recent past, though, is perhaps the least interesting way of reading boring postcards. In their retro-futurism, their evidence of abandoned processes of modernization, they reveal that quotidian routines are always the product of changing socio-political contexts. As a cultural historian of the M1 points out, we should be careful not to make too simple a contrast between the 'rather shabby, dull, overly-familiar and repetitive *supermodern* place experienced by today's drivers' and the 'exciting, new, *modern* place' opened in November 1959 (Merriman 2001: 335). The building of the M1 provoked fierce arguments between planners and preservationists, and many lobby groups balked at the unabashed modernity of the concrete bridges, flat-roofed service stations and road signs. But the early motorways, like other 'non-places' built around the same time, were still seen as alluring, progressive developments, and were generally viewed as necessary and inevitable even by their detractors (Merriman 2001: 175–6). Parr's 'boring' postcards commemorate the inauguration of these environments. For all their quaintly dated feel, they reveal a more complicated relationship between commerce, planning and public space than is usually conceded in stereotypical characterizations of this period of postwar reconstruction as one of centralized 'bureaucratic nannying'.[10]

The historian Pierre Nora has claimed that in contemporary societies we tend to see memory as a symbolic way of recovering the irreversible, linear time of modernity. In an increasingly mobile and accelerated world, we try to corral memory into what he calls *lieux de mémoire* (places of memory). These monuments, museums and heritage sites are 'how modern societies organize a past they are condemned to forget because they are driven by change' (Nora 1996: 2). Memory has to function as a series of external prompts in this way because there are no longer any '*milieux de mémoire*' where it can be experienced from within a culture, as something embedded in tradition, habit and custom. Augé draws heavily on Nora's work, extending his insights into an analysis of the 'non-place'. Augé's non-place is an anaesthetized, ephemeral environment in which everything happens 'as if there were no history other than the last forty-eight hours of news' (1995: 104). Historical understanding can only now be found in 'places of memory', as towns are turned into museums and tourist attractions, and bypasses and high-speed trains relieve us of the need to actually visit them (1995: 73).

Both Nora and Augé offer a carefully delimited notion of memory that seems to overlook traces of the past that are neither subsumed into commodified heritage nor embedded in timeless tradition. As Lefebvre suggests, this notion of memory serves to close off questions about the historical development of quotidian life. Memory and the everyday tend to be viewed as opposites, the former being seen as 'a typical process of accumulation and therefore an essential component of mechanisms that materialize and technicalize such a process', and the latter as not cumulative. . . . Everyday life, when it changes, evolves according to a rhythm that does not coincide with the time of accumulation. . . . Thus an illusion is created of the unbroken continuity of houses, buildings and cities from the oriental town of proto-history down to the present day.

(Lefebvre 1971: 61)

Parr's postcards destroy this illusion of the timelessness of everyday life, revealing old routines and unrealized potential in a way that refuses the catharsis of nostalgia. Their boringness works against itself, producing images that are both funny and sad because they subvert our traditional ways of reading the 'non-place'. These postcards represent the non-place not as the site of supermodernity but of banalized modernity, cultural change assimilated into daily routine. One of the strengths of Augé's notion of the non-place is that it manages to avoid the more hyperbolic emphases of postmodern theory, its tendency to focus on the cutting-edge contemporaneity of flagship architecture, high-end consumerism and state-of-the-art technology. Augé shows that non-places, while locked into the accelerated processes and increased mobility of global capital, are also the mundane, repetitive spaces in which we live our daily lives. He does not always acknowledge, though, how the blankness of non-places – which is as much mythic reputation as actual experience – obscures both their histories and the necessarily political questions about how they are organized and inhabited.

Chapter 5

LIVING SPACE
Housing, the market and the everyday

As A DENSELY POPULATED COUNTRY with some of the oldest and most dilapidated homes in Europe and a largely unrestrained property market, Britain is a good place to begin thinking about a universal site of daily life: the house. The most important development in housing in Britain since the war has been a dramatic shift towards owner-occupation, from 29 per cent of dwellings in 1951 to 71 per cent in 2003 (*Social Trends* 2004: 152, 154). The traditional Conservative policy of encouraging homeownership, encapsulated in Anthony Eden's espousal of a 'property-owning democracy' in the 1950s, gradually became a cross-party consensus in the 1960s and 1970s. A 1971 government White Paper announced that homeownership 'satisfies a deep and natural desire on the part of the householder to have independent control of the house that shelters him and his [*sic*] family' (Short 1982: 119). Although the cultural meanings that have developed around the house in recent years have endorsed the naturalness of this desire, there is in fact nothing natural about it. Levels of homeownership have been historically variable and, although they are rising throughout Europe, differ greatly across individual countries.

The increase in homeownership in Britain over the course of the last century was the result of particular historical circumstances and political interventions, such as the growing strength of building societies, the increasing rent controls that encouraged private landlords to sell up, and the introduction of tax incentives for mortgage-holders. Thatcher's government greatly reinforced and accelerated this overall trend. It raised the ceiling for mortgage interest tax relief, essentially a gigantic subsidy to homeowners, while drastically reducing expenditure on public housing; its deregulation of the financial system created favourable conditions for borrowing and encouraged huge speculation in the housing market; and its 1980 Housing Act gave millions of council tenants the right to buy their homes at huge discounts, partly in the expectation that these new homeowners would be more likely to vote Conservative. Thatcher's housing policy, one of the most popular aspects of her programme, was arguably more socially divisive than other areas of policy such as health and education, where public expenditure actually increased in these years. But Thatcherism only anticipated and mirrored developments in much of the rest of Europe and America in the 1980s and 1990s, where government funding of public housing declined and financial deregulation created massive credit and mortgage booms. In many of the advanced economies, social housing is increasingly seen as a safety net and property ownership is almost a prerequisite of citizenship.

This chapter is divided into six sections, which all examine how ideas and representations of the house have both mirrored and obscured these realities of the housing market. First, it explores Lefebvre's notion of the 'pseudo-everyday', a kind of self-conscious domesticity that conceals the house's quotidian life. Second, it considers the politics and symbolism of location, with particular reference to terraced housing. Third, it discusses the tower block, both in relation to its traditionally negative representation and its more recent (but only partial) reinvention as a model for chic urban living. Fourth, it explores the cultural meanings and political contexts of new housing on private estates. Fifth, it shows how a close examination of the visual logic of such houses, in the work of Patrick Keiller, David Rayson and my own viewings of an Essex housing estate, can help to draw out these buried meanings and contexts. Finally, it examines the representation of the housing market in property shows, newspaper stories, DIY stores and other aspects of the cultural economy.

Houses and the pseudo-everyday

Houses are different from the cultural phenomena that I have discussed so far in this book because, instead of being dismissed as boring and residual, they have been desired and meaningful objects. Lefebvre used the term 'pseudo-everyday' to describe the ways in which the routines of daily life were 'reconstructed in caricature' in postwar consumer society, and he saw the house as a prime site of this reconstruction (2002: 84, 44). Writing in the 1950s, in the middle of France's 'âge du nylon', he focused on the phenomenon of the Ideal Home, the self-advertising modernity of electrical gadgetry, synthetic fibres and streamlined surfaces. For Lefebvre, this 'pseudo-everyday' helped to naturalize the economic and political transformations of capitalism by linking them to timeless, routine tasks. The touch-button, gizmo-filled kitchen hid the disjointed and unequal development of capitalist societies behind the promise of technological 'progress', while also domesticating modernity, making it seem both inexorable and unthreatening (Lefebvre 1971: 50–1).[1]

More recently, we can see the same process at work in the seamless alternation between modernity and nostalgia in interior design. Contemporary kitchens, for example, combine the modern (Maytag fridges, chrome worktops, built-in espresso machines) with the retro (cast-iron range cookers, *batteries de cuisine*, fireclay sinks, butcher's blocks), bringing together labour-saving devices with gadgets such as juicers, coffee grinders, pasta makers and balance scales, which actually increase workload but suggest culinary 'authenticity'.[2] The enlargement of kitchens since the 1960s – either by building extensions or 'knocking through' into dining rooms – is also partly an effect of this reinvention of domesticity as 'lifestyle'. Although women have increasingly undertaken paid work outside the home in these years, they still do a disproportionate share of the cooking and housework in dual-income families. This rearrangement of the kitchen has therefore been about valuing 'women's work' as creative and valuable, without making it as demanding or time-consuming as the daily grind of the traditional housewife. As the kitchen has been transformed into the main eating area and social hub of the home, cooking has become a familial activity integrated into the rest of the household, rather than simply a domestic chore.

This performative domesticity, though, has gone hand in hand with a certain embarrassment about the house's quotidian life. The remaking of the home as a form of domestic theatre may value the habitual and routine, but only in their more congenial, low-maintenance forms. Extractor fans take away kitchen smells, disposal units incinerate waste in a few seconds, integrated appliances are hidden behind doors, surfaces are easily wipeable, catalytic liners keep ovens clean, 'Servosoft' drawers glide silently open and shut, and dishwashers are quieter than a ticking clock. This has allowed the middle classes to embrace a comfortable version of the below-stairs life of the servants they might have employed in a previous era, while robotizing more tedious tasks or offloading them to cleaners and au pairs. The anti-clutter aesthetic of modern interior design can also be seen as a reworking of the Corbusian ideal of the 'law of Ripolin' (whitewash), with its dislike of the dirt and mess of the quotidian (Le Corbusier 1987: 189). Furniture stores such as IKEA promise to relieve us of the drudgery of daily life through clean lines, easy-care materials and imaginative solutions to storage problems.

This 'pseudo-everyday' culture is almost entirely interiorized, focusing on the inside of the house at the expense of its more predictable, routine facade. The DIY and interior design industries that have emerged as by-products of the homeowning boom have left the house's exterior relatively untouched – with the exception of the back garden, which has generally been treated as another room in the house ripe for reinvention. The 1990s and early 2000s saw a huge wave of home makeover programmes in the UK, a format exported successfully to other countries. These programmes were occasionally about grand designs, building new homes from scratch or converting old industrial buildings and barns into modern living spaces. More usually, they involved superficial but dramatic attempts to redesign the interiors of houses.

In the classic of the genre, *Changing Rooms* (BBC1, 1996–2005), two pairs of neighbours redecorate one room in each other's homes, assisted by professional designers, with a time limit of two days and a budget of £500. The time constraints and limited costs mean that corners are inevitably cut: old chairs and sofas are recovered or resprayed rather than replaced; new fireplaces are made from MDF and covered with teabag stains and smudged pencil lines to create a cheap marble effect; table lamps are decorated with tessellated post-it notes, stuck on with glue. When the rooms are finished, the presenter interviews the two designers, who give the design a name inspired by their particular theme ('Bollywood bedroom', 'Parisian boudoir', 'Rustic retro'). The dramatic transformation of the room is indicated by the merging of 'before' into 'after' shots. Participants are then led into their changed rooms with their eyes closed, and are either appalled or delighted when they open them.

The makeovers in *Changing Rooms* and similar programmes are not generally motivated by a concern with how the room will be lived in after the dramatic 'reveal'. To employ Judy Attfield's useful distinction, such shows elevate a notion of *design*, which she defines as 'things with attitude', over the banal reality of *material culture*, which she calls 'design in the lower case'. This concept of design specifically excludes 'the disordered everyday clutter of the mundane', the vast majority of objects and materials that do not form part of the conspicuous display of taste or style (Attfield 2000: 5–6).[3] Houses are where we spend most of our quotidian lives, and undertake the basic tasks of maintenance and sustenance such as cleaning, cooking, eating, washing, sleeping and childcare. These tasks are invariably distributed unevenly, according to the political economies of particular families and the wider inequalities of societies. The 'pseudo-everyday' – the carefully arranged tableaux of the show home, interior design catalogue or home makeover programme – conceals both the mundane life of the house and the labour that goes into maintaining it.

This interest in the house as a space for privatized consumption exists alongside a denial of the sameness of mass housing. According to the *Guardian Media Directory*, there are currently 44 British magazines dealing with the interior refurbishment and redecoration of homes, but only two magazines, *What House?* and *Your New Home*, concerned with the purchase of new houses (Alden 2005: 81–2). New-build British homes are often dismissed as 'Noddy boxes', 'toy-town houses' or 'rabbit hutches'. In fact, this anxiety about the blank uniformity of mass housing has a long history. Georgian terraces, with their classical regularity, were boringly repetitive to Victorians. Late-Victorian terraces were condemned by Edwardians as 'endless rows of brick boxes, looking out upon dreary streets and squalid backyards' (Unwin 1909: 4). The Stockbroker Tudor houses of interwar suburbia were criticized by contemporaries for their unimaginative homogeneity. The modern disdain for volume building is both a denial of the longstanding nature of these anxieties, and a response to newer concerns about the nature of the housing market.

This dislike of the uniformity of mass housing is also evident in Lefebvre's work on the house, which aims to critique Gaston Bachelard's and Martin Heidegger's notions of the house as dwelling – a kind of sacred, eternal space that links us to our existential needs and humanity's shared past (Lefebvre 1991b: 121). Lefebvre suggests that the *pavillons*, the single-family, detached suburban houses or bungalows built in France in the interwar period, were popular with ordinary people because 'in a detached house (no doubt in a small-minded way) modern man "dwells poetically"' (2003a: 130). The owner-occupied house allows the dweller to rearrange space according to personal taste, while also representing the natural, ageless order of everyday routines. For Lefebvre, though, these feelings are illusory:

> Every occupant of a *pavillon* . . . believes they find in objects their own thoroughly 'personalized' microcosm, and their own happiness. But these microcosms, these 'systems' share a strange resemblance. The same suppliers sell these goods, these objects, these houses in the 'Normandy', 'Basque' or 'modern' style. Every subject could move somewhere else and feel just as comfortable.
>
> (Lefebvre 2003a: 132)

In his 1957 foreword to the first volume of his *Critique of Everyday Life*, Lefebvre again discusses the *pavillons* when he describes looking up from his writing in an unnamed location and seeing the western suburbs of Paris out of his window. It is an idyllic scene, with barges moving slowly along the broad curve of the Seine and rows of cars gleaming in the sunshine as they drive across the Pont de Saint-Cloud. Lefebvre then describes how new houses have blighted this landscape:

> But nearer, tumbling down the groove of the valley of the Sèvre like insects, in a prosaic disorder, little houses separated by kitchen gardens where guard-dogs bark and cats wail at night. They are called 'pavilions', but no irony is intended. . . . Their owners' superficiality oozes forth in an abundance of ridiculous details, china animals on the roofs, glass globes and well-pruned shrubs along the miniature paths, plaques adorned with mottos, self-important pediments. . . . On Sunday mornings, especially when the weather is fine, these little houses open their entrails to the sun with strings of eiderdowns, sheets, blankets. They

spread over the hillside like hundreds of dead chickens in an immense shop window.

(Lefebvre 1991a: 43)

Lefebvre sees these family houses as the home of an expanding French middle class. The new suburbs have successfully brought factory workers and taxi drivers together with the petite bourgeoisie, but only in the defence of an impoverished everyday life. These 'appendixes' of the city have none of its poverty – no space here for the Algerian workers from the nearby Renault factory at Billancourt, for whom these modest houses would be palaces – but also none of its 'tumult, power, creation, luxury' (1991a: 43). Lefebvre claims to be reluctant to dismiss the uneventful lives of these neo-suburbanites, 'decent folk' who cannot be blamed for 'not wanting the "world" in which they feel reasonably at home to be transformed'. By separating themselves from the squalor and poverty of the city, though, the *pavillon* dwellers have found only a form of happiness 'tinged with mediocrity' (1991a: 43). Lefebvre's analysis of the chaotic spread of the *pavillons*, which has ruined one of the most beautiful landscapes in Paris, is as much to do with aesthetics as political economy, and seems at least partly motivated by metropolitan condescension. His discussion of the 'ideology' of the *pavillon* fails to address the more intractable realities of housing markets, and in particular the crucial politics of location.

Location, location, location

The politics of location are particularly evident in the fate of the terraced house, the dominant form of mass housing in Britain over the last few hundred years. Although few were built after the First World War, the surviving terraces still dominate the landscape of much of Britain's towns and cities, particularly in the north of England. These houses were constructed by speculative builders, who emerged in Britain much earlier than in the rest of Europe. For these private builders, terraces were fast and cheap to put up, and allowed them to use standard layouts and newly mass-produced materials such as sawn timber, tiles and window frames (Woudhuysen and Abley 2004: 132–3). The uniformity of terraces was also an effect of planning regulations, which increased in strictness throughout the nineteenth century. The key piece of legislation was the 1875 Public Health Act, which gave local councils the powers to introduce bylaws controlling the layout of new streets. After this act, houses were no longer built back-to-back or randomly in courts and alleys. Every dwelling had to have rear access, and the width of the street had to be at least the same as the height of the building's front wall. These bylaws produced endless parallel streets running off main roads, with rows of identical houses along them.

Cultural representations of the terraced house in Britain are often inflected with class and regional associations. The monolithic terraced row has long been part of the iconography of northern working-class life, in L. S. Lowry's paintings, Shirley Baker's street photographs, television programmes (*Open All Hours*, *Bread*) and films (*East is East* (1999) and *Billy Elliot* (2000)). In the opening titles of the soap opera *Coronation Street*, the camera pans over terraced houses, back alleys and outbuildings in Salford, near Manchester, before homing in on the eponymous street with a pub and corner shop at either end. Chris Waters describes such images as 'urban pastoral', a way of looking at working-class daily life that makes it a source of anthropological curiosity and aesthetic contemplation (1999: 131). Rachel Whiteread's cast of the insides of a late-nineteenth-century dwelling in London's East End offered a more unsettling take on the terraced house. With its concrete facade revealing evidence of the accumulated residues of daily routines – soot-blackened fireplaces, joist ends rotten from damp, indentations left by light switches, old plug sockets and door latches – *House* (1993) was a silent rebuke to a housing market that promotes more carefully managed nostalgia.[4] As the last surviving 'house' in a former row of near-identical dwellings, it served as a counterpoint to two common phenomena of contemporary urban landscapes: the empty spaces left by demolished houses, and the modern-day slums, the whole streets of bricked-up terraces located in the deprived areas of British towns and cities.

The development of an unfettered private housing market in the Thatcher era created huge variations in house prices, which rose spectacularly in certain areas while going into freefall in others. It accelerated a process in which many terraced houses have been dismissed as slums, while others have been modernized as 'town houses' for middle-class families. These town houses might be a cut above the average terrace, with a pocket front garden or some form of setback such as iron railings, and double bay windows rather than a flat front. But they are structurally very similar to the 'slum' houses that have been demolished or allowed to fester as modern-day ruins. In London, in particular, these renovated late-Victorian terraces are occupied by an increasingly homogeneous group of urban professionals. The gentrified area of Fulham in south-west London, for example, consists largely of geometric grids of two- and three-storey bay-windowed terraced houses, their redbrick monotony occasionally relieved by pastel-coloured paint. But nobody criticizes these houses for their uniformity or arrangement in regimented rows; they are prized possessions in the housing market. The varying fate of Britain's terraced houses shows how their external sameness has been secondary to their capacity for interiorized reinvention and capital accumulation.

In June 2003, the government announced a scheme to refurbish 3,000 terraced houses in the Langworthy area of Salford, with the help of private developers. One of the developers was Urban Splash, the company renowned for converting warehouses and other old industrial buildings in Liverpool and Manchester into city-centre loft apartments. Urban Splash agreed to redevelop over 400 houses near Chimney Pot Park, the iconic area featured in the opening credits of *Coronation Street*. This area was now full of empty, boarded-up properties, with negative equity and social problems such as vandalism and drug addiction. Urban Splash aimed to radically transform the interior of the houses, with an open-plan living room and galley kitchen upstairs, the two bedrooms switched to the ground floor, and fully glazed elevations at the back looking out on to communal gardens *(The Guardian* 2003). In the 1950s and 1960s, these houses would simply have been demolished and replaced by new public housing funded by taxation. In more recent years, the various bodies spearheading urban regeneration seek to work *with* the market, using public money to stimulate private investment and change public attitudes. Since the housing market is partly fuelled by collective psychology, the calculation is that the refurbishment of a relatively small number of houses will turn round the market in the whole area, making perfectly serviceable terraces seem habitable again. House prices in surrounding streets did indeed rise dramatically once Urban Splash had announced its involvement in the scheme *(Manchester Evening News* 2004).

Writings on the house within cultural studies have tended to focus on the meanings and desires associated with it, in a way that underestimates these powerful market forces. In *Sex and Real Estate*, for example, Marjorie Garber examines what she sees as the erotic charge of the housing market, its transformation into forms of 'yuppie pornography' (2001: 3). With a methodology rooted in textual criticism, Garber offers a series of extended metaphors ('The House as Body', 'The House as Beloved'), the persuasiveness of which is largely dependent on the sheer accumulation of cultural analogies, historical precedents and literary parallels. This connective style presents the meanings of the house as cross-cultural and historically continuous. In fact, although her textual sources are diverse, her real-life examples belong almost exclusively to a specific cultural economy, that of affluent middle-class professionals with spacious houses in New York and New England, and second homes in Cape Cod or Martha's Vineyard. For these cash-rich and time-poor people, the house is a site where 'space comes to substitute for time' and we can 'stage the life we wish we had time to live'. Her approach to the house overlooks its more mundane aspects and makes it instead a repository for a desire that is always unsatisfiable in that it 'cannot be contained within explanation or need' (2001: 207). For Garber, the monetary value of the house is secondary to its cultural meanings, so that the nature of house buying as the transfer of capital makes it an arena of erotic flirtation and enticement.

The housing market, of course, has a vested interest in stimulating the dreams and desires that we literally 'buy into' when we purchase houses.

This may be easier to do in a country such as the US, where houses are relatively spacious and plentiful. British homebuyers may be less convinced by Garber's account of househunting as sublimated erotic desire. It is something of a media truism in Britain that the process of buying and moving house is the most traumatic life experience after divorce, childbirth or the death of a loved one. While such an assertion is difficult to prove, its constant reiteration shows that the anxieties provoked by housemoving are just as culturally potent as the fantasies and desires associated with the house itself. Housemoving is stressful because it brings ordinary people into direct contact with the competitiveness and injustices of the market, forcing them to become small-time speculators in a way that can be frightening as well as exhilarating.

The increasingly cut-throat housing market of the 1980s found an obvious cultural expression in the transformation of the estate agent into folk devil. This stereotype, which presented the estate agent as a sharp-suited, smooth-talking young man, driving a flashy car paid for by excessive commission fees from his clients, has its origins in an unregulated marketplace. In their study of estate agents, Michael Clarke, David Smith and Michael McConville show that attempts *within* the industry to professionalize itself were effectively scuppered in the 1980s by Thatcherism's promotion of the unrestrained market and its suspicion of professions as 'a conspiracy against the laity' (1994: 7, 47). Unlike other people involved with selling houses, such as solicitors and surveyors, estate agents do not need to have any qualifications or experience, or be regulated by a professional body. They are simultaneously selling a commodity and providing a service, a conflict of interest that was heightened in the 1980s and 1990s when independent estate agents were bought out by large corporations, who also wanted to sell us insurance, mortgages and pensions (Clarke *et al.* 1994: 44).

One of the main reasons that estate agents are mistrusted, though, is that they are not just selling the physical entity of a house but, in their well-known mantra, 'location, location, location'. The location of a house is crucial because it embodies three interrelated factors: the concrete advantages of particular areas (such as closeness to the city centre, good transport links or nearby parks), the more nebulous advantages of social differentiation and status, and, most importantly, the potential of both these factors to commute into rising house prices. In most cities, though, residential areas are not neatly segregated according to class or income. London, in particular, has extremely complex gentrification patterns. There are two main reasons for this: the density of the city, as generations of speculative builders have built houses on any available piece of infill; and house price rises over the last few decades, which have pushed middle-class homeowners out of certain areas and into less salubrious ones. To use Alan Warde's distinction, gentrification in London has typically occurred through the 'collective social action' of middle-class pioneers rather than through organized capital, with the exception of the Docklands (1991: 224). This means that smart househunters need to become amateur ethnographers in order to note the telltale signs of so-called 'hot spots' and 'up-and-coming' areas: shops selling different varieties of coffee, the presence of skips in the road suggesting refurbishment, four-wheel-drive cars, a deli selection in the local mini-market. Estate agents are invaluable but unreliable interpreters of this constantly shifting landscape. Their demonization encapsulates our anxieties that we might be on the wrong side of this knowledge economy.

The promotional work that estate agents undertake to sell houses in particular locations is often slippery and inconsistent. In London, for example, they will try to cash in on the good reputation of desirable areas such as Chelsea, Wimbledon and Dulwich by transferring their glamour to adjoining areas – rechristening Raynes Park as 'West Wimbledon', Herne Hill as the 'North Dulwich Triangle', or Pimlico as 'Chelsea's new quarter'. The less fashionable area of Kilburn, meanwhile, has virtually disappeared from estate agents' details, as it is nomenclaturally colonized by West Hampstead to the North, Maida Vale to the South and Queen's Park to the West (Segrave 2004: 404). Estate agents will also try to carve out much smaller, exclusive areas, by naming them after groups of desirable roads or topographical features: 'Crouch End Heights', 'the Tonsleys' in Wandsworth, 'the Greeks' in West Hampstead or 'Between the Commons' (the area between Clapham and Wandsworth Commons, also known as 'Nappy Valley' for its association with fecund young middle-class couples).

Carrie Segrave's *New London Property Guide*, the recognized bible for househunters in the capital, offers in-depth analysis of no less than 480 neighbourhoods. As well as discussing the concrete benefits and downsides of living in certain areas – school league tables, transport links, council tax rates, green spaces, crime figures – she also deals with the less tangible aspects of house location, such as the kudos and potential for rising equity attributed to particular postcode areas. Postcodes are much more than simply alphanumeric devices to help with the mechanical sorting of mail. They have become a crucially significant actuarial shorthand, used at no cost to themselves by banks and insurance firms to classify potential customers, and by public and private agencies to target services (see Raper *et al.* 1992). So-called 'golden postcodes' can add thousands of pounds to the value of a property, and there are often startling price anomalies between virtually identical houses on either side of postcode boundaries.

This is ironic because, when the Royal Mail gradually introduced the postcode system throughout Britain between 1959 and 1974, upmarket residential areas attached a considerable stigma to having a postcode at all, in the same way that the well-to-do have traditionally preferred to have house names rather than numbers (*Independent* 2002). This situation has now been dramatically reversed, as postcodes have to be literally decoded for their social connotations. London's postcodes, in particular, are a representational minefield, with many estate agents often quoting just postal districts in property advertisements. If you are going to succeed as an amateur property speculator, which is what you will have to become if you want to buy a house, then you had better know your EC1 (chi-chi Clerkenwell) from your E1 (the mixed East End heartland), your W11 (stylish Notting Hill) from your W10 (edgier north Kensington), your N6 (leafy Highgate) from your N7 (gritty Holloway).

Postcodes are unstable, contentious signifiers not just because they arbitrarily overlap the 'natural' divisions of local councils or neighbourhoods, but because they are interpreted inexactly. Estate agents, valuers and insurers concentrate all the symbolic weight on the outward code (the first part, which shows the broad destination of the letter) and ignore the inward code (the second part, separated by a space, which guides the letter from its final sorting office to the individual address). The inward code, which can pinpoint streets and groups of houses, would actually be a much more accurate indicator of class and status in the cheek-by-jowl divides of London neighbourhoods. Implicitly acknowledging that this emphasis on the outward code imposes a false coherence on residential patterns, the director of a leading property consultancy has argued that there are 'clean', 'confused' and 'polluted' postcodes, depending on the extent to which they are infiltrated by downmarket neighbourhoods (Braid 2002). In this strange estate-agent speak, the codes themselves take on anthropomorphic qualities. The postcode's instability means that its meanings have to be reasserted ever more forcibly by interested parties.

These postcode battles are much more than a matter of simple snobbery. The nature of houses as financial investments and the importance of rising property values in our society turn all homeowners into compulsory participants in this game of status-seeking. Postcodes have an anonymously agreed value that everyone simply accepts as a prerequisite for participation in the housing market. Postcode symbolism is a prime example of market group-think, a kind of representational vortex in which there is a circular relationship between cultural meaning (what makes a 'desirable' area) and monetary value. In this self-fulfilling system, a valuable house or address is one that is already 'sought-after' or 'desirable'. Housebuying is consequently one of the few areas of British life where overt class snobbery remains socially acceptable, reflecting an unquestioned value system in which a 'nice' or 'up-and-coming' area is always a middle-class one. In London, this represents a source of great cultural anxiety for the middle classes who rarely make up a majority of the population, even in the leafiest or most assiduously rebranded areas (Butler, with Robson 2003: 1). As the New London Property Guide puts it regretfully, 'poor people cannot be uninvented' (Segrave 2004: 320).

The limits of tower-block chic

This entanglement of housing-market psychology with class-consciousness is also apparent in the reputation of the tower block. High-rise housing has long been characterized as a visible cautionary tale about the folly of centralized state planning. Indeed, Lefebvre's writings on the slab blocks of the HLMs (*habitations à loyer modéré* or low-rent housing), which were built in the new towns and suburbs around Paris in the 1950s and 1960s, largely anticipate the received wisdom about tower blocks today. For Lefebvre, the HLMs are homogeneous 'cages' or 'dwelling machines' characterized by their soulless functionalism and 'threshold of tolerability' (2003b: 81; 1991b: 314).

Lefebvre's writings on the HLMs need to be seen in a specifically French context. In France in the postwar period, central government became heavily involved with housing provision because of rising homelessness and the development of shantytowns (*bidonvilles*) on the edges of cities. France embarked on a mass housing programme later than other major European countries, so the housing was more uniform, with widespread use of system-building (Power 1993: 86). In Britain, most tower blocks were built in the inner cities, because of resistance to influxes of ex-slum dwellers in suburban areas, and attempts by city councils to prevent population loss within their boundaries (Glendinning and Muthesius 1994: 157–93). In France, though, the HLMs were built in the suburbs, as part of what Lefebvre saw as the development of new, semi-colonial relationships between city centres and their peripheries. He viewed the uniformity of modernist housing as a product of the hierarchical, coercive impulses of planners, technocrats and politicians – what he called 'the dictatorship of the right angle' (Lefebvre 2003b: 98).

In contemporary Britain, though, the tower block has taken on new significance within a housing market that places an extraordinarily high value on private ownership. Whatever the failures of the high-rise as a form of mass housing – and there were undoubtedly significant problems of design, construction and maintenance – its universally awful reputation also reveals the power of the marketplace to define the cultural value of housing. The tower block is routinely seen as a disastrous form of housing that has aged badly and that people never wanted to live in anyway. The visual impact of the tower blocks has allowed them to function more readily as symbols of misguided social engineering. First, their height gives them an embarrassing visibility. Although they never constituted more than a quarter of all public housing units built in Britain at any one time (Ramsden 2002: 645), their conspicuousness makes them seem more common than this. Second, they are relatively uniform throughout the country, with the same basic elements of a reinforced concrete or steel framework, infilling or cladding, and prefabricated sections. Third, their often untreated concrete tends to stain, streak and blister in the rain, is an absorbent surface for car fumes and other forms of pollution, and offers a flat and expansive canvas for spraycan graffiti. Such visible signs of dilapidation seem to convey the inadequacy of all forms of social housing, in a way that belies the often surprisingly good interior state of the flats.

In this anti-mythology, the tower block belongs to an earlier period in which dogmatic, paternalist state planners formed an unholy alliance with elitist, avant-garde architects. It is true that tower blocks in Britain were pioneered by the architectural department of the London County Council, which included a number of avant-garde architects interested in working in the area of mass housing. But once the design formulae of the tower blocks had been established, and they began to be built in other areas of Britain, a complicated relationship developed between avant-garde design and mass production. Tower blocks were less the product of architects than large contracting firms such as Wimpey, Laing and Concrete Ltd, with their standard designs, in-house engineers, and 'package deal' contracts with local authorities (Glendinning and Muthesius 1994: 200–17). The British tower block was also primarily the creation of ambitious local politicians rather than a centralized state. Even the infamous 1957 Housing Act, which granted increased subsidies to high-rise buildings, was the product of lobbying by local politicians (Pawley 1998: 48).

Despite this complex history, the primary 'lesson' learnt from the tower blocks has been a simple one: social housing, which dominated the market between the Second World War and the 1970s, is a bad thing (Dunleavy 1981: 2). Since the tower blocks have generally been occupied by poorer social groups, they have been characterized as a betrayal by professional experts of (that always politically charged term) 'ordinary people'. Prince Charles's frequent attacks on modern architecture invariably pit the misguided expertise of architects and planners against the more trustworthy instincts of ordinary people. In a now famous speech at Hampton Court in May 1984, he said: 'Architects and planners do not have a monopoly of knowing best about taste, style and planning. Ordinary people should not be made to feel guilty or ignorant if their natural preference is for more traditional designs' (Pawley 1998: 212).

The tower block has a poor image largely because it is excluded from a private housing market that confers value and meaning not merely on houses but the people who live in them. Buildings designed to bring about roughly equal standards in housing have done exactly the opposite, placing their occupants squarely outside a validating market economy. As Britain's chronic housing shortage lessened from the early 1970s onwards, the people in high-rise estates were primarily those excluded from the now universal aspiration towards owner-occupation. Tower-block flats were almost never sold under the policies introduced by the Thatcher government that allowed council house tenants to buy their properties (Power 1998: 46). These difficult-to-let estates have become dumping grounds for those people – young single mothers, unemployed workers, immigrants, asylum seekers – who cannot be accommodated elsewhere. Many mortgage companies will not lend money for apartments in blocks higher than around six or seven storeys, or in buildings that use certain types of prefabricated construction, or where a sizable number of the other flats are council-owned. The down-valuing of these flats becomes self-fulfilling, confirming and reproducing their position at the bottom of the housing market.

But the demonizing of the tower block represents a retreat from the market as well as an embracing of it. Although the mass-production methods used in the building of tower blocks were fairly ad hoc and piecemeal, they have contributed to a suspicion of modern forms of prefabrication that has had a lasting effect on British housebuilding (Glendinning and Muthesius 2004: 160). Since tower blocks were part of the putative globalization of the industry, with a relatively small number of systems patented (mainly in France and Sweden) and used throughout western Europe, the eastern bloc and the developing world, there may also be a sense that prefabricated building represents a standardization that is fundamentally alien and 'un-British'. In the years since the tower blocks were built, prefabricated methods have been increasingly used in commercial buildings but have hardly impinged at all on private housing.

Both Patrick Wright and Joe Kerr note that the ceremonious dynamiting of tower blocks has been a common visual trope in inner-city areas since the mid-1980s, with local authorities often placing adverts in newspapers, arranging seats for onlookers and inviting celebrities along to detonate the charge (Wright 1991: 95; Kerr 2003: 192). Such events serve to reinforce the notion of the tower block as 'a generator of infernal meanings for people who only look at it from outside. . . . a monstrous emblem of the futility of all State-led social reform' (Wright 1991: 68, 90). Wright and Kerr both focus on the borough of Hackney, which in the 1980s was demonized as a case study in the problems of the inner city but which achieved new notoriety in the 1990s for demolishing more tower blocks than any other borough. The cheering crowds at these demolitions were partly made up of the residents of Hackney's gentrified town houses, who no longer had to suffer the polluting effects of the high-rise estates on their property values (Kerr 2000: 261). The pulling down of the tower blocks symbolically consigns these buildings to the dustbin of history, along with a now discredited, dystopian socialism.

In his manifesto for postmodern architecture, Charles Jencks makes a celebrated reference to the dynamiting of the 1950s slab blocks on the notorious Pruitt-Egoe housing development: 'Modern architecture died in St Louis, Missouri on July 15, 1972 at 3.32pm' (1991: 23). Despite the dramatic images of demolitions, though, only a small proportion of high-rises in Britain (and the rest of the world, for that matter) has actually been blown up. Most have survived because local authorities have calculated that demolishing them would create a still greater housing crisis (Power 1998: 3–8). The confident postwar belief in large-scale housing created unwieldy constructions that could not be easily replaced without incurring huge expense and creating massive re-housing problems. Housing survives long after it has ceased to be part of a particular architectural movement – long enough, in fact, for it to be rehabilitated in response to changing fashions.

If one needed further evidence of the way in which the market deter-mines the value of housing, it can be found in the more recent reinvention of the high-rise as a desirable residence for young urban professionals. In London, this is seen not only in new developments such as Richard Rogers's Montevetro building at Battersea and other high-rises along the Thames, but also in a select number of the older tower blocks, such as Ernö Goldfinger's Trellick Tower. In the late 1990s and early 2000s, Trellick Tower was the must-mention in a series of articles in the broadsheet press about how high-rise flats were now fashionable dwellings for well-off urbanites. These articles reported that pictures of Trellick Tower were now used on T-shirts and indy-label R&B CDs as a stamp of urban cool; it was being celebrated in pop songs such as Blur's 'Best Days' (1995); and people were placing cash offers for the flats on the communal noticeboard in the lobby (Dyckhoff 2003; Bueno 1999).

The Grade II-listed Trellick Tower is indeed a distinctive building, with a separate lift and service shaft joined by walkways to the main building, and a slim footprint only one flat wide. But the main reason for its new-found fashionability is its Notting Hill address, and in particular the bourgeois-bohemianization of Golborne Road, with its fashion stores, coffee shops and gastro-pubs. Location has been similarly important in the rehabilitation of the World's End Estate in Chelsea, and Keeling House in up-and-coming Bethnal Green. There has been no similar reinvention of the high-rise council estates in down-at-heel areas such as the Isle of Dogs, South Thamesmead and Deptford. Goldfinger's other London high-rise, Balfron Tower near the Blackwall Tunnel, is not a fashionable address. Significantly, no other British cities have experienced a similar transformation in the reputation of the tower block. 'Tower-block chic' is entirely a London phenomenon, its escalating property values putting a high premium on anywhere near the city centre and quelling the anxieties of the most conservative mortgage-lenders. The partial transformation of the high-rise is yet another indicator of the significance of 'location, location, location'.

The politics of housebuilding

As housebuilding by local councils came to a virtual halt from the late 1970s onwards, the trend swung decisively towards private building. The new houses built since then are different from earlier mass-produced private housing in Britain, such as the hundreds of thousands of suburban semi-detached dwellings built in the interwar years. In 1930, 84 per cent of housebuilders had less than ten employees and completed only a few houses each year, which ensured different designs even when the builders were using similar pattern books (Oliver *et al.* 1981: 98). From the early 1980s onwards, though, a wave of conglomeration created a small number of national housebuilding companies with central offices, in-house architects and rationalized production lines. This new type of housebuilding could be seen as part of the belated development of tract building on the American model, the prototypes for which were the Levittowns, the mass estates built between the late 1940s and early 1960s in New York, Pennsylvania and New Jersey by Levitt and Sons. Like the Levittowns, the modern British housing estate is characterized by structural sameness with small concessions to individual difference. Since the 1980s, there has been a standard type of vernacular house style, with a pantiled, pitched roof, orange brick walls, white-painted garage doors, window sills and skirting. These standard features are then embellished with more 'individual' touches, such as Tudorbethan timber, stucco, two-tone bricks and neo-Georgian doors.[5]

The iconic image of housing in the 1980s and 1990s was a cul-de-sac on an edge-of-town estate with a cluster of these identikit homes. The preponderance of the cul-de-sac was largely the product of *Design Bulletin 32*, a series of guidelines for laying out residential roads devised by the Department of the Environment in the late 1970s as a way of stopping motorists using quiet residential areas as rat runs (Noble *et al.* 1977). The sameness of these environments was not just an effect of standardized housing but planning regulations that stipulated minimum road and pavement widths, turning circles and distances between houses. Mindful of homeowners' concern for property values, developers also tended to impose identical restricted covenants on residents that prevented them from making any changes to the fronts of their properties.

The high premium paid for detached houses in Britain has as much to do with the symbolic resonances of detachment (wealth, property, exclusivity) as its actual advantages (privacy, noise reduction, bigger houses). In these modern 'executive homes', detachment is a key selling point, although they are often separated by just a few feet from adjoining houses. The horseshoe arrangement of houses also betokens an enforced communality, which connects with influential ideas of 'defensible space' developed by the American criminologist Oscar Newman (1972: 126–8, 182–5) and the British urban geographer Alice Coleman (1985: 13–17). The notion of 'defensible space' suggests that small groups of residents need a clearly defined, semi-private territory outside their front doors where they can be collectively vigilant against crime and anti-social behaviour – an idea supported by the police and reinforced in schemes such as Neighbourhood Watch, which began in Britain in 1982 after originating in America in the 1970s. For its detractors, the cul-de-sac became a byword for curtain-twitching suburban respectability, self-interest and withdrawal from the social sphere. Many cul-de-sacs are not even properly marked on maps, reinforcing the impression that they represent a retreat from civic space into privatized experience. Jonathan Glancey sees the cul-de-sac as the ultimate manifestation of bland suburbia:

> That suburban non sequitur, that dead end of neo-Georgian fanlight doors and leaded lights has long been one of the most subversive features of the British townscape. It is the denial of the city spirit and urbanity and, if you like, of civilisation itself. For those of us who have long thought it a conspiracy against architecture, a kind of thumb-cocking at urban good manners, the cul-de-sac is a thorn in the side.
>
> (Glancey 1998: 16)

Barratt was the housebuilding firm that became indelibly associated with these new houses, especially small 'starter homes' for young couples. Its emblematic status was confirmed when the chief architect of the homeowning boom, Margaret Thatcher, bought a Barratt home in 1985, albeit a more upmarket model in a gated development in Dulwich. Paul Barker suggests that Barratt's transformation of Britain's vernacular landscape is of much greater cultural significance than the more critically acclaimed, flagship architecture of regenerated city centres:

> When the social history of our times comes to be written, he [Lawrie Barratt, the company's founder] will get more space than Norman Foster. You can search out Foster masterpieces here and there. But Barratt houses are everywhere. Foster buildings are the Concordes of architecture. Barratt houses fly charter.
>
> (Barker 1998: 54)

Barratt reproduced many of the working methods and marketing tools of American tract housing developments. Like Levitt and Sons, Barratt altered the basic features in its houses each year in response to market demands and technical innovations; it made extensive use of show homes, marketing suites and glossy brochures; and it bundled all the elements of buying a house (such as the mortgage, solicitor's and surveyor's fees) into a single, one-stop financial package. Barratt homes came with virtually everything included, even carpets, white goods and furniture. All first-time buyers needed to bring, the brochures claimed, were the crockery and the bed linen. Barratt was a pioneer in using market research in housebuilding, surveying its existing customers and scanning census data and government statistics for emerging trends.

In Lawrie Barratt's words, the company sold and built rather than built and sold (Spring 1983: 28), seeking to match Fordist production methods to consumer needs:

> We looked at what people earned, worked out a multiple of three times their income – or three-and-a-half times or whatever – and from that we could work out what people could afford to buy. . . . Then we worked backwards to how many square feet of house we could afford to build. We wrapped the whole thing up into a package and that gave people a certainty about what their house was going to cost them.
>
> (Laurance 1997: 9)

Barratt's name recognition, though, was always greater than its impact on the housing market. Barker's quote, above, refers partly to the firm's less well-known role as a pioneer of apartment building on brownfield inner-city sites and Marina projects. Barratt is only one of several big housebuilding companies in the UK. It became synonymous with new houses largely because of an aggressive national press advertising campaign and famous television commercial of the late 1970s and early 1980s, featuring Patrick Allen, an actor from the 1960s series *Crane*, who promoted the merits of new homes from a helicopter flying over Barratt estates. This advert was unusual because British housebuilders only rarely promote their products on television. They tend to advertise locally, stressing their native knowledge and expertise. One of Britain's biggest companies, Bellway, promotes itself as 'the local national housebuilder'. In *Building* magazine in 1983, Martin Spring claimed that Barratt had 'transformed private house-building from an ultra-conservative, soil-bound drudge to dynamic manufacturing of consumer products' (1983: 28). In truth, 'the Barratt revolution' was only partially successful; it did not modernize housebuilding and homebuying in Britain in the way that the Levittowns and their imitators did in the United States.

Buying a house in Britain remains a tortuously complicated economic and legal process. Only the builders of new houses, accounting for a small proportion of house purchases each year, simplify this process with 'no-hassle, move-in free deals' offering minimum deposits, waived stamp duty and legal fees, and part-exchange with older homes. The technology of housebuilding in Britain also remains old-fashioned. It is true that almost all new houses have machine-made bricks, synthetic roof tiles and factory-produced windows, and that computer-aided design allows housebuilders to fill available land with new houses in a few months. But Britain has been slow to adapt to the prefabricated methods pioneered by Levitt in the 1940s. Modular, off-site building only represents about 1 per cent of the market, in contrast with countries such as the US and Japan where it is widely practised (Hetherington 2003).

There is a deep-seated cultural bias in Britain against the idea of the house as simply another mass consumer product. New houses have to pretend to be old, mixing together variations of traditional English architectural forms (Medieval, Tudor, Georgian, Arts-and-Crafts). The most obvious example of this traditionalism is the survival of brick, either in traditional masonry construction or cladding for timber-framed houses, over more economical and practical alternatives such as clapboard. Raphael Samuel sees the 'return to brick', and other signifiers of the neo-vernacular style such as tiled roofs and pedimented windows, as part of a more general trend towards 'retrochic', also evident in the nostalgic refitting of house interiors. For Samuel, brick houses signify solidity, permanence, traditional craftwork and a distinctively British heritage (1994: 129).

It is unlikely, though, that housebuyers either know or care that their new home is mimicking a medieval yeoman's house or an eighteenth-century town house. What is interesting is how this buried semiology of heritage and nostalgia connects with the nature of the house as a major financial investment, creating an aesthetic inertia based on a series of agreed assumptions about what a 'house' looks like. Housebuyers tend to have traditional tastes because, unlike the more innovative housing associations, they have to consider resale. Local authority planning restrictions also tend to militate against innovative new designs. Most importantly, professional surveyors, naturally wary of claims against their indemnity insurance, will tend to down-value houses that deviate from the traditional norm.

The most significant consequence of this anti-modern bias, though, is that people prefer period homes to new dressed up as old. The dislike of new houses tends to increase with ascension up the social scale, with the upper and middle classes almost invariably preferring to live in older properties. To educated metropolitans who would not dream of living in one, a 'Barratt home' is shorthand for a monotonous suburban tract house, regardless of which company built it. This value system even extends to the fixtures and fittings associated with new houses, hence the widespread middle-class disdain for uPVC windows. It is almost unheard of in Britain to demolish an existing owner-occupied house and build a new one in its place. This is in spite of the fact that new houses are unquestionably better built than ever before, with deep foundations, certified and tested materials, technical specifications running to hundreds of pages and regulations governing their construction that fill whole volumes. Many housebuyers, though, persist in the belief that 'they don't build houses like they used to' (Rivers 1992). The contrast with America, where it is common to demolish perfectly presentable homes in smart areas to make way for swanky rebuilds, could not be more marked.

The most remarkable feature of the British housing market since the 1980s has been its resistance to neo-liberal globalization, and its failure to transform the physical landscape in the way that the American subdivisions have done.

In the early 1980s, housebuilders organized themselves into the House Builders Federation to campaign for the expected new development, and nine private housebuilders grouped together to form Consortium Developments to lobby for a number of private enterprise new towns in the counties around London. But this group dissolved itself in 1992 after most of the proposals were rejected on appeal following prolonged planning inquiries. Thatcherite planning deregulation may have transformed the peri-urban landscape in the form of out-of-town retail developments and office parks, but there was no similar revolution in housing (Hall 2002: 133).

One of the reasons for this disparity can be found in an acronym that achieved media prominence in Britain from the mid-1980s onwards: Nimby. This term originated in the US in 1980, the phrase it abbreviated ('not in my back yard') revealing its American derivation. Initially, it referred specifically to a person opposed to the siting of something polluting or dangerous in their own area, such as waste facilities, who was in favour of similar developments elsewhere. But it quickly came to mean someone who objected to many forms of development, and in a British context this particularly meant new house-building. The figure of the Nimby was especially associated with the creeping urbanization of south-east England, in the area immediately outside the Green Belt within commutable distance of London.

Although the term 'Nimby' had an initially pejorative connotation, by the 1990s and 2000s it was also being used positively to describe heroic conser-vationists pitted against voracious developers. One *Daily Mail* article, for example, described Nimbys as 'freedom fighters', manning the new front line in 'an age of political apathy and dwindling turn-outs'. Nimbyism, it claimed, was 'beautifully socially inclusive', bringing together old and young, 'tree-huggers' and homeowners, in their opposition to 'town hall numpties [idiots] and bossy quango bosses' (*Daily Mail* 2002). A similarly sympathetic article, this time in the left-wing *New Statesman*, argued that

> the Nimby is not the enemy of progress but its begetter. In a land, and increasingly a world, where democracy is bought and where the global trumps the local every time, the Nimbys – those prepared to defend what they know and love against the depredations of the distant and the disengaged – are the true heroes.
>
> (Kingsnorth 2004: 22–3)

As these articles suggest, the figure of the Nimby seems to refute the notion that citizens in modern liberal democracies are politically apathetic: when people feel threatened, and goals seem clear and achievable, they are more than ready to fight their corner.

Nimbys could be seen as a symptom of what Ulrich Beck calls the 'repressed sociality' of modern life, which manifests itself in apparently isolated, sporadic issues such as 'the planned highway in the vicinity of one's own back yard, the worsening school situation for children, or the atomic waste storage dump being built nearby which cause aspects of a "collective fate" to penetrate into consciousness' (1992: 134). As such, Nimbys are politically ambiguous figures who cannot be assigned easily to left or right. There has been much recent work in cultural studies on campaigns by ravers, squatters, eco-warriors and anti-globalization protestors (see McKay 1996, 1998). But this work has rarely included discussions of middle-class Nimbys, even though they are a highly successful case of direct action, and their concerns sometimes overlap with those of radical groups on issues such as land ownership, environmentalism and opposition to big business. From a right-wing perspective, Nimbys also highlight the tension between neo-liberal economics and traditional Conservativism. Tory ministers in the 1980s and 1990s often found themselves torn between support for the private enterprise of the housebuilders and sympathy for the preservationist residents of 'the shires'.

The most important factor in the growing cultural significance of the Nimby is the changing public image of housebuilding. In the 1950s and 1960s, housebuilding was often represented as a heroic activity, and political parties competed with each other to set higher national targets. In election campaigns, politicians exploited the sod-turning and ribbon-cutting photo opportunities provided by the building of new homes. Housing starts and completions were big news stories in the same way that changes in mortgage rates are today. As Martin Pawley puts it:

> In those days, when house-building was not so much a market as a mixture of social service and heavy industry, the idea of council housing off the production line was as much a vote-getter as mortgage-subsidized investments-for-living-in were to become twenty years later.
> (Pawley 1998: 46)

Labour's gradual rejection of socialist policies such as nationalization and redistributive taxation during its long period in opposition in the 1980s and 1990s is well documented. Its abandonment of a housebuilding policy is less acknowledged but is arguably as significant. In its election manifestos of the 1980s, Labour promised to end council house sales, and aid local authorities in ambitious programmes of housebuilding and renovation (Balchin and Rhoden 2002: 13). But it abandoned these plans in the 1990s, tailoring its policies more to existing homeowners. New housebuilding has scarcely been mentioned in recent general election campaigns, despite there being general agreement that there is a shortage of houses because of the rising number of single, divorced and elderly people. Yet new housebuilding has sunk to its lowest levels since the Second World War, with annual output since the mid-1990s fluctuating around the 150,000 mark (Barker 2003: 3).

New Labour's housing policy has recognized the need for new houses but shown an unwillingness to offend key voters in the south-east with too much actual housebuilding. Planning permission for new housing is usually negotiated locally through a legally ambiguous notion of 'planning gain', where local councils can ask developers to provide social amenities, or money to fund them, in return for consent. The Labour government, and the London Mayor, have sought to use planning gain to force developers to provide more 'affordable housing', usually for rent by housing associations, alongside more expensive private houses. From the early 2000s, the government also introduced a number of initiatives that allow carefully designated categories of 'key workers' (public-sector employees such as nurses, teachers and police officers) in the south-east to purchase homes through bigger loans or shared equity. 'Affordable housing' and 'key workers' are subjective terms that largely owe their existence to an inflationary housing market. They have been formulated in response to the perceived political difficulty of solving the related problems of housing shortages and exorbitant house prices by building more homes for everyone, rather than just these narrowly defined groups.

Labour also inherited the policy of the Major government of shifting housebuilding from greenfield to brownfield sites. Although this strategy of re-using formerly derelict urban buildings or sites may have been influenced by the call of Richard Rogers's Urban Task Force for an 'Urban Renaissance' (1999), it is also a response to voter opposition to new housebuilding in key marginal seats in the south-east. Labour increased minimum-density thresholds in order to squeeze more homes from each site, reducing the amount of land dedicated to car parking and encouraging the building of smaller houses and flats, or upwards building in the Georgian townhouse style. In February 2000, employing the most famous televisual example of the suburban cul-de-sac, the deputy prime minister, John Prescott, announced that he was 'declaring war on the wasteful use of land' in the '*Brookside*-style housing estate', with its detached houses, generous front lawns, garages and driveways (Prescott 2000).[6]

Although a 2004 government report (the Barker Review of Housing Supply) recommended easing restrictions on greenfield construction, the idea of an extensive programme of public and private housebuilding, as happened in Britain in the 1950s and 1960s, is not on the political agenda. Some of the new housebuilding will take place in designated, relatively uncontentious areas – Milton Keynes, Ashford, the Thames Gateway – but these will be nothing like the planned new towns of the postwar era. The housing shortage is largely being addressed by the leverage of private finance to fund public building, and piecemeal infilling in towns and villages in dispersed locations. Housebuilding is no longer a heroic endeavour but a delicate game of politics between the housing haves and have-nots, played out by proxy in media representations of the battle between 'development' and 'conservation'. It is unlikely that we will see footage of smiling ministers cutting ribbons on new housing estates in the near future.

House viewings

Much of this media and political discourse on the house seems to rely on a morally charged aestheticism, with its narratives of the mass-market uniformity of suburban box housing and its invasion metaphors about the 'concreting' or 'bulldozing' of south-east England. Recent visual representations of the house, such as in the work of the artist David Rayson and the filmmaker Patrick Keiller, offer a different perspective on these discourses through their patient attention to the ordinariness of mass housing. Rayson's house paintings are based primarily on his memories of the Ashmore Park housing estate in Wolverhampton on which he grew up in the 1970s and 1980s. Paintings such as *Griffiths Drive* (Figure 5.1) are based on extraordinarily detailed draughtsmanship, and borrow from the aesthetics of vernacular photography in their unstinting depiction of ordinary life and their revelation of normally unnoticed details in commonplace environments.

Figure 5.1   David Rayson, *Griffiths Drive*, 110 × 122 cm, 2000.

Reproduced by permission of the artist, Wolverhampton Art Gallery and Maureen Paley/Interim Art, London.

151

Rayson's work has some similarities with Dan Graham's photographic project on American tract housing. Graham began photographing suburban houses in his native New Jersey in 1965 with a cheap Kodak Instamatic, a model that had just come on the market. This camera, which was fixed-focus, cartridge-loading and generally idiot-proof, marked a key moment in the vernacularization of photography. By using the Instamatic, Graham made it clear that he was interested less in visual aesthetics than a deliberately banal 'anthro-photography' that would exploit the capacity of rolled film for serial repetition (Graham 2001: 11). Like other American photographers such as Lewis Baltz (*The New Industrial Parks near Irvine, California* (1974)), Robert Adams (*The New West* (1974)) and Garry Winogrand ('New Mexico, 1957'), Graham found that the neutrality and automatism of the photograph, and its natural proscenium frame, were particularly able to convey the supply-and-demand logic of tract housing.

In *Homes for America*, an evolving work first published in *Arts Magazine* in 1966, Graham accompanies his photographs with a text that describes, in flat, unsurprised prose, the different types of mass-produced housing in a New Jersey development. Graham shows how the houses are placed in plots of exactly the same size and in uniform sequences, either regular rows or staggered setbacks. This sameness is then concealed by covering the wooden shell of the house in some form of cosmetic cladding such as vinyl or a half-stone brick facade; giving the houses nostalgic or evocative names such as 'Cape Cod', 'Ranchhouse' or 'Colonial'; and naming the developments in a way that gives the impression of well-established communities ('Fair Lawn', 'Greenfields Village', 'Pleasantville') rather than tracts built quickly to fill up vacant land.[7] Instead of being simply disdainful of mass suburban housing, Graham aims to show how its repetitions produce complex variations and haunting absences.

Like Graham, Rayson focuses on the bland exteriors and serial logic of houses as a way of revealing their collective life. His paintings convey the silence and emptiness of commuter estates in the daytime, with the lives of their residents implied only by surface appearances. The title of the exhibition that brought Rayson to wider public attention is 'Somewhere else is here'.[8] It is reminiscent of a line from Philip Larkin's poem 'I remember, remember' about his nondescript childhood in the featureless suburban streets of pre-war Coventry: 'Nothing, like something, happens anywhere' (1988: 82). As this title suggests, Rayson's work often explores the tension between the generic features of housing estates, and the unspoken ways in which they reveal the small traces of individual lives.

In his study of still-life painting, Norman Bryson argues that historical art criticism has tended to divide painting into two spheres: a highly valued megalography (concerned with grand narratives, historical events and great figures) and a less esteemed rhopography (concerned with the unremarkable routines and objects of everyday life) (1990: 15). Bryson suggests that rhopography (from the Latin *rhopos*, meaning trivial objects) has a tendency to turn into megalography. Rhopographic paintings often aim at a 're-education of vision', a looking again at overlooked objects so as to make them seem unfamiliar and unique, which is actually a 're-assertion of painting's own powers and ambitions' (1990: 88, 90). But certain artists avoid this tendency by undermining the rules of visual composition, refusing to direct the viewer's gaze towards particular elements in the picture at the expense of less 'significant' elements. The works of the eighteenth-century still-life painter, Jean-Siméon Chardin, for example, 'cultivate a studied informality of attention, which looks at nothing in particular'. Chardin produces an overall, uncentred image that suggests that nothing needs to be 'vigilantly watched' (1990: 91–2). Rayson's paintings work in a similarly inclusive way. The viewer is not sure which area of the painting to focus her gaze on, or how to divide the frame into accented foreground and unaccented background. In the exhibition catalogue, the preparatory drawings for these paintings have grid squares underlying them, suggesting a non-judgemental methodicalness that gives each element in the picture equal weight.

Rayson's paintings are composites, drawn from his own childhood memories of Ashmore Park and speculations about what it might look like today. Ashmore Park is a former council estate which, in Rayson's work, now reveals the unmistakable signs of owner-occupation: uPVC windows, a conservatory built on to a kitchen, a new car on a gravel drive, a satellite dish. Even smaller details suggest the lack of ownership of the public spaces that connect these private environments: stubbed-out cigarettes, crushed lager cans, crisp packets, cracked paving stones and graffiti tags. Maurice Blanchot writes that the everyday is ordinarily invisible because 'one has always looked past it . . . the everyday is what we never see for a first time, but only see again' (1987: 14). The value of boredom is that it represents 'the everyday become manifest: as a consequence of having lost its essential – constitutive – trait of being *unperceived*' (1987: 16). The studied 'boredom' of Rayson's paintings allows them to hint at the human stories behind the blank surfaces of these newish houses.

Patrick Keiller's *The Dilapidated Dwelling* (2000)[9] also explores the hidden politics of housing through its investigation of an aesthetic problem: how to capture the static object of the house in the fundamentally kinetic medium of film. Like Keiller's earlier *London* (1994) and *Robinson in Space* (1997), *The Dilapidated Dwelling* is a fictionalized documentary-essay consisting of a series of long-held shots of buildings and public spaces, over which an actor (in this case, Tilda Swinton) provides deadpan narration. Swinton is a researcher who returns to Britain after spending two decades with a little-known Arctic people who build enormous snow houses that can be quickly demolished and rebuilt. She works for an organization whose aim is to 'anticipate the future', and has been recalled home to investigate 'the predicament of the house in Britain'. The nature of this predicament soon becomes clear: unlike the nomadic Arctic people, the British have not learnt to rebuild their dwellings. While consumer technologies have become much cheaper in real terms over the last few decades, the price of housing has risen dramatically and old housing has not been replaced. At the existing rate of replenishment, Keiller's narrator calculates that Britain's current housing stock will have to last 5,600 years.

Although the main tenet of the film seems to be that we should use new technologies to build more houses more quickly,[10] *The Dilapidated Dwelling* stops short of producing a developed argument. Instead, it follows the pattern of Keiller's earlier films in using the juxtaposition of words and images to explore historical connections and spatial relationships in everyday life. The film is interspersed with archive footage of Buckminster Fuller introducing his Dymaxion and Wichita houses, Constant Nieuwenhuys discussing his 'New Babylon', and the films made by the architectural collective Archigram in the 1960s. These architects and cultural critics all suggest that technologies developed in the military and aerospace industries should be re-employed to transform domestic space. Keiller's narration introduces these clips without making their connection to the rest of the narrative explicit. But it is clear that, even though the idiosyncratic ideas of these theorists were rarely translated into practical forms, Keiller does not expect us to read them in the kitsch register that is often reserved for old newsreels. When set against the contemporary images of dilapidated housing, in fact, they suggest the missed historical opportunities and failed potential of mass housebuilding.

The Dilapidated Dwelling plays down the kinaesthetics of film in its depiction of the house. Its shots of houses are typically medium or long-range, frontal and static. These unemphatic, exterior images capture the house's ordinariness as an object, stripping it of its usual associations with nostalgia, desire and speculative capital, which are more usually related to house interiors. Keiller films a number of examples in order to show how houses have often been quickly assembled, ordinary artefacts: seventeenth-century timber-framed houses; early-twentieth-century self-build homes in the Essex marshes; and post-Second World War Arcon prefabs. Another recurring motif in *The Dilapidated Dwelling* is speeded-up film of suburban houses taken from moving cars, such as the interwar semis built along the A40 out of London. Fast motion tends to be a filmic cliché conveying the frenetic activity of city life, but here it communicates the boredom and deadness of these landscapes, their apparent disconnection from more dynamic parts of the British economy and society.

As in *Robinson in Space*, the narrator in *The Dilapidated Dwelling* undertakes a formless journey around the country, exploring the survival of rundown housing even in areas that are most integrated into a globalized, high-tech economy. Keiller writes the narration for his films after the footage has been compiled (Keiller 2002: 40). The slowness of the holding shots and their sometimes puzzling relationship to the voiceover point to tensions in everyday life that might normally be overlooked: the alternation between mobility and stasis, the co-existence of dilapidation and cutting-edge modernity, the siting of crucial economic activities in peripheral spaces.

The Dilapidated Dwelling offers a reverse image of the house in its frequent shots of so-called LSSBs (Large Single-Storey Buildings) or 'Big Sheds', the warehouse, office and retail spaces built near motorway intersections. These buildings are a growing feature of contemporary landscapes but are largely ignored, carrying none of the symbolism of the private house. Unlike the house, they are swiftly assembled, easily dismantled and largely recyclable (Pawley 1998: 184). Keiller's film points to the structural connections between the older space of residential areas and these newer spaces that have sprung up on the edge of towns. During one shot looking out on to Oxford from a Cowley car park, Swinton's voiceover describes the scene: 'There are houses, few built later than the 1950s, and enormous sheds which retail the products with which they are continually modified.' Keiller suggests that capitalism sustains itself not merely through the voracious search for new markets but through the selling of atavistic counter-dreams of domesticity and retreat.

In the summer of 2003, I did my own house viewings. I visited Chafford Hundred in Essex, one of the new housing estates filmed in *The Dilapidated Dwelling*. There are some rather forlorn shots of the town in Keiller's film that lead the narrator to wonder why Britain has remained resistant to mass-produced housebuilding methods: they are of almost deserted building sites, with a few workers in hardhats carrying solitary planks across duckboards, shovelling sand into batch mixers or knocking bricks into place with trowels. According to the London *Evening Standard*, though, Chafford Hundred was 'Britain's most coveted address' in 2001 (Curtis 2001). If Chafford Hundred is a property hotspot, it is not because it is architecturally innovative or trendily exclusive, but because it provides relatively affordable homes in an otherwise stratospheric London housing market. Inaugurated in 1986 when Thurrock borough council gave planning consent for the reclamation of 600 acres of ex-industrial land in the Essex marshes, Chafford Hundred now has several thousand houses built by every major housebuilder in Britain.

Developers and buyers are attracted to Chafford Hundred for the same reasons that Levitt was attracted to Long Island in the 1940s – huge areas of unused land, government subsidies, proximity to the metropolis and the promise of good transport connections. The town now forms part of the Thames Gateway, an area pinpointed by the government for new building to solve the south-east's housing deficit, in the most ambitious building programme since the postwar slum clearances. In a logical extension of the London Docklands development, the Thames Gateway project aims to create a 'linear city' on the largest area of brownfield land in the country, a 43-mile stretch of post-industrial no-man's land from east London to estuarine Kent and Essex. But since its inauguration as the East Thames Corridor in 1991, the development of the Thames Gateway has been slow, bedevilled by arguments about planning gain, affordable housing and the cost of decontaminating recycled land. The Gateway incorporates seven London boroughs and ten local councils in Kent and Essex, creating inevitable bureaucratic problems (Puckett 2003: 26).

The first thing I notice, when being shown around the 'starter homes' in Chafford Hundred, is their smallness. They are essentially two-storey flats, with a living room and kitchen downstairs and two bedrooms upstairs. The one-size windows are tiny, with ledges so narrow that one resident has had to bracket a window box to the wall. Housebuilding companies will often build to the minimum specifications required to comply with building regulations and sell the house, using the smallest dimensions, the thinnest walls and the least amount of building material. When builders work with huge economies of scale, this apparently insignificant miserliness over a few square feet makes a big difference to profit margins. Everything in Chafford Hundred suggests newness: endless 'For Sale' signs, recently planted saplings mulched with pulverized bark, bare trellising, show homes and marketing suites. But the town also conveys the housing market's embarrassment about the nature of the house as a commodity. The street names – Saffron Road, Swallow Close, Maunder Close – imply instant *rus in urbe*. Most houses have plaques, standardized for each street, with names such as The Briars, The Brindles, Haystacks or Sundial Cottage. The houses have timber frames concealed by brick casing, redundant chimneys and nostalgic signifiers such as old-fashioned coaching lamps and artificially archaized bricks.

Apart from a few enclosed areas with security cameras and 'Keep Out' signs, there has been an admirable attempt in Chafford Hundred not to hive off residents into separate income pods: flats, starter homes and double-garaged executive houses are often situated on the same street. There are two sets of shops, a 'Chafford Hundred Campus' providing education from nursery to adult level, a library, a medical centre, a restaurant and other amenities. But these good intentions have come up against the harsh realities of the housing market. Chafford Hundred is clearly a commuter estate; when I came on a Friday afternoon, the place was deserted. Its main attractions to residents are its closeness by car to the Lakeside shopping centre, a nearby mega-mall; the A13, one of the busiest trunk roads in Europe, which follows the Thames from Essex into the centre of London; the M25 motorway; and a railway line leading directly into London's Fenchurch Street station.

Every house in Chafford Hundred has either a carport or a garage, or both. The town's entire layout is designed to accommodate the car, segregating traffic from houses by access-only streets with speed humps, and then allowing for ease of movement around the town through perimeter roads and endless roundabouts (Figure 5.2). There are giant signs in the middle of the roundabouts, announcing 'Triumph Gate' or 'Castle Gate', presumably in an attempt to turn them into local landmarks. Road design is a prime consideration in new housing estates, not simply because the residents depend so much on their cars, but because planners and developers rely on risk-averse standard practice, fearing prosecutions if accidents occur. Hence the large turning circles, wide roads and over-sized roundabouts in towns such as Chafford Hundred (Commission for Architecture and the Built Environment (CABE) 2004: 16, 44–5). As one report on new housing estates recently put it, 'the public realm effectively becomes a "technical" area for storing and manoeuvring cars, rather than spaces or places in their own right' (CABE 2004: 44).

Walking around Chafford Hundred, it is not long before I am completely lost – partly because the sameness of the houses provides no landmark, and partly because the curvilinear streets are disorientating. Invented in American tract developments to close off the vista and protect the viewer from the unwelcome sight of an endless row of subdivisions (Kunstler 1994: 128), the curvilinear street has the unfortunate side effect of destroying any sense of direction. These difficulties of orientation and legibility are significant. For all their entanglement with the mythologies of the property market, houses

Figure 5.2   Chafford Hundred.
Photograph by the author.

remain the silent necessity of everyday life. Everyone needs one, but the politics of housing have meant that many new homes have been built in residual, maze-like estates. Although I eventually find my way to the station with the aid of several of the town's residents, getting lost in Chafford Hundred seems like a metaphor for housebuilding as a political black hole.

If you follow the A13 east out of Chafford Hundred, the next big town you reach is Basildon, the largest of the first group of new towns built around London after the Second World War. In October 1948, Lewis Silkin, Minister of Town and Country Planning, set out his vision for Basildon to an audience in Laindon, a village that would form part of the new town:

> Basildon will become a city which people from all over the world will want to visit, where all classes of the community can meet freely together on equal terms and enjoy common cultural and recreational facilities. Basildon will not be a place that is ugly, grimy and full of paving stones like many large modern towns. It will be something which the people deserve; the best possible town that modern knowledge, commerce, science and civilisation can produce.
>
> (Hayes and Hudson 2001: 20)

Silkin may have overestimated Basildon's international impact (as well as its resistance to paving stones). But at least almost everyone in Britain has heard of Basildon. The new towns were publicly designated, and the subject of intense discussion and debate. Who has heard of Chafford Hundred? It is barely known in Essex, let alone the rest of Britain. When I mentioned my visit to friends and colleagues, even those who lived in London had never heard of it. They were surprised when I told them it was one of the largest private housing estates in Europe. Much of the new housebuilding in Britain remains unexamined because it is taking place not in concentrated areas but in fragmented, dispersed places. Iain Sinclair has called Chafford Hundred 'amnesia-ville . . . an empty-by-day enclave with no centre and no purpose' (2002: 400).[11] In fact, the town does have a purpose, but it is not one that is being publicly discussed, because it is unlikely that anyone would have occasion to visit it unless they lived there. It is a *terra nullius*, an improvised and unnoticed 'solution' to a runaway housing market that has left many prospective home-owners priced out of even modest accommodation.

Reading the market

Inflation is the bête noire of neo-liberal economics. Why, then, are vertiginous house prices (which, significantly, are excluded from the Retail Prices Index, which calculates UK inflation rates) commonly seen as an indicator of a healthy economy, with little consideration given to those who might be unable to afford them? The answer lies largely in a contemporary obsession with property speculation, which reflects the ascendancy of finance capital over manufacturing and production in modern capitalist economies. Huge financial industries have developed to fund house purchases in these economies, locking people into systems of debt and equity. This means that many different groups have a vested interest in maintaining the buoyancy of the market: estate agents, mortgage brokers, solicitors, housebuilders, banks and building societies. The housing boom has also spawned huge subsidiary industries based on interior design, furnishings, refurbishment and conversions, which homeowners have partly funded through the release of equity due to rising house prices. By far the biggest and most profitable area of the building trade is the repair and maintenance of old houses (Barker 2003: 8), and DIY is also a growing, multi-billion pound industry. According to one survey, the London homeowner spent an average of £2,454 on DIY during 2003, while the first-time buyer spent an average of £5,250 (*What House?* 2004: 12). A whole cultural economy has evolved, consisting of out-of-town stores, television programmes and books, to persuade us that DIY is a source of pleasure and profit, instead of a form of unpaid labour in which an economic system that has singularly failed to replenish an aged housing stock sells us back the tools to patch up our dilapidated houses.[12]

In Britain, house price rises have been so dramatic that many homes actually earn more money in capital accumulation than their occupants do in their jobs (Pawley 2002: 34). Rising house prices are part of the small change of everyday conversation, and few homeowners can resist looking in estate agents' windows and property ads to keep track of them. The right-wing press has aggressively promoted the 'good' news about house price rises, while presenting the slightest evidence of a slowdown as a calamity. This has often amounted to little more than puffery or scaremongering, with the help of surveys of dubious legitimacy produced by interested parties such as banks and building societies. It has also produced some startling inconsistencies. On 30 June 2003, for example, the *Daily Express* ran a front page story, 'Survey reveals how your home is hit', that contained a stark warning: 'The property boom has come to a halt – and house prices could be set to nosedive' (O'Grady 2003). Less than a week later, the *Express* had a very different front-page headline, '10% rise forecast this year: new hope on house prices', and a more optimistic message: 'Home owners got a massive boost yesterday with a major bank predicting house price growth of more than ten per cent this year' (Chapman 2003). The satirical magazine *Private Eye* has poked fun at this media fixation by running a series of parodies of tabloid stories linking momentous world events to the price of property in Middle England: 'Saddam captured – good news for house prices.'

In recent years, this interest in the value of houses has found a new outlet in the popularity of television property shows. These shows, which regularly attract four or five million viewers on minority channels such as BBC2 or Channel 4 (C4), fall into two main types. The first type follows ordinary people as they look for houses, with experts offering them advice. The template for this genre, *Location, Location, Location* (C4), films househunters with varying budgets and gives some fairly straightforward advice about making offers, surveys and planning permission. Later variations are more directly aspirational, showing prosperous homeowners trying to exploit the investment potential of rising equity. *A Place in the Sun* (C4) and *A Place in France* (C4) follow Britons looking for a second home abroad. *Escape to the Country* (BBC2) and *Relocation Relocation* (C4) trail city-based professionals as they sell up and buy a home in the country (while, in the latter case, retaining a smaller urban residence as well). Since these shows largely deal with people in the overpriced south-east property market cashing in their equity to move abroad or to cheaper parts of the country, the dream of expat or rural bliss is only open to those on the right side of a geographical and class divide. But the light-hearted, gently diverting nature of these programmes means that they rarely dwell on such problematic issues. Despite their titles, they are not actually about the subtleties of location: issues such as the class composition of particular areas, or the symbolic value of particular postcodes, are rarely discussed.

The second type of programme is about ordinary people trying to make their houses more alluring to potential buyers, or doing up properties for a profit, with experts again on hand to offer advice. While the location/relocation genre has friendly estate agents helping couples to fulfil their dreams, the presenters of the second type of show invariably practise 'tough love'. This genre often overlaps with the makeover genre, but unlike *Changing Rooms*, it is not about people using interior design to express their hidden creative urges. In these programmes, quirky is out and bland is in. In *House Doctor* (Channel 5), the presenter, a Californian 'Real Estate Stylist' called Anne Maurice, frequently advises her clients to paint the walls beige so as not to deter potential buyers. Sarah Beeny, the advice-dispenser on *Property Ladder* (C4), similarly tells her charges to use neutral colours and avoid any idiosyncratic personal flourishes. *Property Ladder* episodes are often cautionary tales of people who ignore Beeny's advice, design the property according to their own personal preferences and lose money accordingly.

The most mercenary of these shows is *Selling Houses* (C4), which is 'about selling your house as quickly as you can, and for as much money as you can'. The estate agent-turned-presenter Andrew Winter has a simple value system in which aesthetic decisions are related to potential profit: 'Remember, light means space means cash.' If the explicit agenda of *Selling Houses* is money, its hidden one is class. Winter persuades working-class homeowners to make their houses more 'upmarket' and 'aspirational' (in other words, middle-class) in order to sell them. He tells them to replace their garish wallpaper with tasteful magnolia and pistachio paint; get rid of 'clutter'; replace their tatty carpets with hardwood floors; and display strings of garlic and extra virgin olive oil in the kitchen. These shows essentially present the housing market as a pain-free gateway to instant riches, once certain tricks of the trade have been learnt. In another example of the circular nature of the search for market 'confidence', the investment bank Durlacher created a 'TV index' in 2004 that tracked the number of these shows dedicated to making money out of property deals. In a note to its clients, Durlacher observed: 'Probably the best indication of difficulties in the market will be when *Property Ladder* is no longer commissioned' (Doward 2004).

In this climate, the housing market is often represented ambiguously. On the one hand, it is reassuringly reified, as a labyrinthine but identifiable entity to which various recognized authorities (bankers, mortgage-lenders, estate agents, television presenters) can bring their professional expertise. In an era of pensions scandals, poor savings rates and erratic share prices, the permanent structure of the house has been seen as offering a form of financial security, the relative solidity of 'bricks and mortar' (a phrase that itself suggests the backward-looking nature of British housebuilding). On the other hand, the housing market is worryingly virtual, an unstable amalgam of public-relations hype, consumer confidence and guesswork about the future state of the economy. Hence the anxieties about overborrowing, negative equity and house price crashes that draw on memories of the early 1990s, when there were hundreds of thousands of house repossessions. In both these representations of the market, though, there is one constant: it is seen as uncontrollable and unstoppable, something that cannot be altered by political intervention, except perhaps a little tinkering with interest rates. The market can be anticipated and interpreted but never questioned.

In his classic work about speculative bubbles and crashes, the economist Charles P. Kindleberger questions this received wisdom. He argues that markets are not rational and predictable as neo-classical economics and neo-liberal ideology have it, but susceptible to rumour and panic. Speculative frenzies follow certain stages: an initial exogenous event such as the end of a war, a revolutionary invention or financial deregulation; a period in which investors pile in, aided by the expansion of credit; a 'euphoric' stage in which later investors buy assets not for their intrinsic value but out of fear they will lose out; and a 'panic' stage in which a few insiders, followed by a stampede of smaller investors, take their profits and sell out. Kindleberger's book makes a case for strong interventions by governments or lenders of last resort to cool the market – the very interventions that are least welcomed in the euphoric stages of financial mania (1989). The tabloid championing of rising house prices and the more understated endorsement of the market in lifestyle television programmes make it politically difficult for governments to consider measures such as increased property taxes, which might help to restrain the euphoria.

The skewed media representation of the housing market could be seen as an inevitable effect of an economy in which the haves (mortgage-holders, property developers and housing financiers) outnumber the have-nots (first-time buyers, long-term renters, the homeless). But the housing market impoverishes rich and poor alike. Rising equity may give homeowners a sense of increasing wealth, but all most of them have at the end of the process is an object that they need – a house – which they can only exchange for another equally expensive house. The enormous sums of money that have flowed into housing in Britain in recent years have focused almost entirely on demand rather than supply. More than 90 per cent of the money advanced each year for mortgages is used to fund 'transfer expenditure' rather than 'resource expenditure': in other words, to buy old houses rather than new ones (Balchin and Rhoden 2002: 108, 23). The so-called 'property boom' over the last few decades has essentially consisted of the buying and selling of an almost unchanging stock of period houses. In London, the only real winners in this process have been professional investors, many from the Far East and Russia, who make cash purchases of large numbers of houses. Even rich people are spending an extraordinary amount of their incomes on old, cheaply built, overpriced properties. The cultural meanings that accrue around the house – as a space of nostalgia, belonging and security, both existential and financial – conceal this inconvenient fact.

Chapter 6

CONCLUSION
The everyday and cultural change

ONE OF THE CENTRAL DIFFICULTIES of 'reading the everyday', as I have argued in this book, is that daily life seems to exist outside historical change. Where the everyday is seen as 'a natural atmosphere of a familiar reality', as Karel Kosík puts it,

> history appears as a transcendental reality occurring behind its back and bursting into the everyday in the form of a catastrophe into which an individual is thrown as 'fatally' as cattle are driven to the slaughterhouse. . . . While the everyday appears as confidence, familiarity, proximity, as 'home', history appears as the derailment, the disruption of the everyday, as the exceptional and the strange. . . . History changes, the everyday remains.
>
> (Kosík 1976: 44)

It is interesting, then, how many of the theorists of everyday life I have discussed in this book were formulating these theories in periods of change and revolution. Kracauer's work on office life was conducted during the death throes of Weimar Germany, as the aftermath of the 1929 Crash destroyed the fragile social reforms and economic recovery of the Stresemann era; and his theories of film and photography were forged out of his subsequent experiences of fascism and exile. Lefebvre wrote his first book on everyday life in France in the immediate postwar period, when fuel, food and housing shortages made the simplest matters of quotidian life of pressing concern.[1] He continued this work in the France of the 1950s and 1960s, against the backdrop of dramatic changes in daily life wrought by Americanized consumerism and bureaucratic state planning (Kelly 1997: 88–90). Certeau's writings on

163

everyday life are partly an attempt to find new ways of thinking about political action and historical change after the 1968 *évènements*, a period in which 'from everywhere emerged the treasures, either aslumber or tacit, of forever unspoken experiences' (quoted in Ward 2000: 4). Augé formulated his theories about non-places in response to what he saw as the acceleration of history and shrinkage of space in 'supermodernity', and the subsequent difficulty of distinguishing between substantive change and mere 'events'. These theorists all argued, in their different ways, that the apparent continuum of the everyday was a space for unnoticed but profound transformations. In this concluding chapter, I want to offer some final thoughts on the relationship between everyday life and historical change.

In recent years, the massive upheavals in the post-communist countries of eastern Europe have once again shown not only that apparently eternal routines can come to an end abruptly but that these routines can themselves function as the impetus for social change. It was not just the confinement within national borders, the privileges of the *nomenklatura* or the surveillance of the secret police that ordinary east Europeans could no longer live with, but the impoverishment of everyday life: the shoddily built tower blocks without running hot water or central heating; endless queuing for basic necessities; interminable waiting lists for consumer 'luxuries'; and unfulfilling work routines. In the last years of the German Democratic Republic (GDR), the attempts by the regime to suggest that waiting, that seminal experience of East German life, was a practical lesson in collectivity – describing a queue, for example, as a *Wartekollektiv* (waiting collective) or a *sozialistische Warte-gemeinschaft* (socialist waiting-association) – came to seem like the laughable death-knell of an increasingly ineffective thought police.

A central argument of this book has been that we can see the reality of, and potential for, historical change in the most ordinary phenomena. One of the icons of the fall of the Berlin Wall in November 1989 was the Trabant P601 car, or Trabi. During the cold war, this vehicle seemed to embody the differences between East and West. While West Germany's car manufacturers (Mercedes, Audi, Volkswagen) were credited with spearheading the country's economic success, the Trabi was dismissed as 'the command economy on wheels'. It was nicknamed 'the cardboard car' because it was made from Duroplast, an unrecyclable phenolic resin strengthened by Soviet cotton wool waste and compressed brown paper. Its two-stroke Otto engine burned a petrol and oil mix producing ten times as much pollution as Western cars, which gave it its distinctive cough and splutter. Its accelerator pedal even had a point of resistance part of the way down to discourage excessive fuel consumption. The Trabi was an embarrassment to the global car community because it represented all the mundanity of cars with none of their escapist counter-narratives of speed, status and freedom.

Remaining in production, essentially unchanged, for a quarter of a century, the Trabi was characterized by its perpetual sameness. There were, though, slightly comical attempts to differentiate between particular models. The Trabant P601 was produced as either a 'limousine' or 'estate' car, in 'standard', 'special request' and 'de luxe' versions, the latter having such exciting additional features as a different-coloured roof, chromium-plated bumpers and headrests. There was even a convertible Trabi with the trendy name, 'Tramp', which was essentially a civilian version of the GDR army jeep. Minor improvements to the Trabi, such as changes to the ventilation system or slight increases in engine performance, were promoted as major technological breakthroughs. But in terms of their overall design, these different models were indistinguishable from each other. When the new Trabant 1.1 with four-stroke Volkswagen engine was finally launched in autumn 1989 with great fanfare, it was hidden under an old Trabi's body. There was no clearer visual representation of the tendency of the everyday to lag behind the possibilities of modernity than the endless stream of identical, mustard-yellow Trabis trundling through the Berlin Wall checkpoints in November 1989.

After the fall of the wall, the East German market was flooded with used Volkswagens and Mercedes and, no longer protected by the government, the Trabant factory in Zwickau quickly went bust. By the time of monetary union in July 1990, East Germans were abandoning their Trabis in the street or exchanging them for more valuable currency such as Western cigarettes. But the process of kitsch recuperation had already begun, with street artists making impromptu sculptures from abandoned Trabis. Berlin shops today sell Trabi souvenirs such as die-cast models, T-shirts and key rings; Trabi parts are recycled as furniture in smart cafe bars; and trendy young Berliners drive Trabis with jazzy paint jobs and new engines. The Trabant is now being celebrated for precisely the same reason that it had once been such an embarrassment: its ability to *traben* (trot along) behind the more spectacular achievements of Western consumerism. Of course, such *ostalgie* (a neologism used to describe nostalgia for the old East Germany) never acknowledges this uneven development as a problem: the everyday is simply registered as that which always lags behind.

For all the excitement of November 1989, this brief utopian moment was not translated into a more permanent revolution in everyday life. Jürgen Habermas pointed out that East Germans generally interpreted the fall of the wall not as an opportunity to create a radically new kind of society, but as a *nachholende* revolution, a 'catching up' with Western countries (1990). This game of 'catch up' has continued in the years since unification, as East Germans have been urged simply to accept an inevitable process of neoliberal Westernization. The Trabi's fate is instructive because the global car industry epitomizes this uneven development in everyday life. Car manufacturers foist their obsolescent, high-polluting models on African and Latin

American markets, and are often assisted in this by block purchases from governments in these regions (Howe 2002: 115–16). In 2003, a German business group announced the Afri-Car project – the development of a cheap, low-maintenance 'people's car' for the developing world, based on the Trabant (Hall 2003). In contrast with its status in the united Germany, this relaunch of the Trabi seems to be untainted by postmodern irony.

Neo-liberalism makes sense of this uneven development by viewing modernization as a linear process in which the benefits of Euro-American societies will slowly filter through to developing countries. As Kristin Ross argues, this view 'presents the West as a model of completion, thus relegating the contingent and the accidental – the historical, in a word – to the exterior' (1995: 196).[2] These global inequalities are both lived out and obscured in the practices and mythologies of daily life. The everyday, whether dismissed as boringly residual or validated as the heroically ordinary, is routinely seen as apolitical. This has made it all the more open to the cultural meanings and political investments that I have sought to examine in this book. More recently, in a global economy in which the smooth running of daily routines relies on integrated technologies, complex infrastructures and the cooperation of large numbers of people, the everyday has become the prime focus for anxieties about the management of risk.

In the last few years, these anxieties have particularly centred on the threat from international terrorism. al-Qaida and its affiliated groups are distinguished from earlier terrorist organizations by a new ruthlessness about civilian casualties. Their aim is not merely to cause as many deaths as possible but to achieve the disruption and breakdown of everyday life by reducing people to a state of permanent anxiety. Recent terrorist attacks, or attempted attacks, have taken place in the spaces of daily life – subways, trains, aeroplanes, office blocks – at the height of the working day. A particularly shocking aspect of news reports of these attacks is the accounts of violent death when set against the prosaic details of quotidian routines: paperbacks, umbrellas and laptops found in the wreckage, unclaimed cars left in car parks, mobile phones ringing unanswered, office stationery raining down on surrounding streets. Follow-up news stories of these atrocities often focus on individual people, fleshing out their journey to work or the uneventful morning at the office that was cruelly interrupted. These accounts are haunting because they involve people going about daily lives that seem so similar to our own.

In New York after September 11, 2001, the normal routines of daily life were disrupted. Many subway trains and buses stopped running; bridges, tunnels, roads and schools were closed; the courts, mailbox pickup and street cleaning were suspended; motorists were given a 30-day reprieve from the city's normally stringent parking rules; and the New York Stock Exchange ceased trading for the longest period since the Depression. At the same time, the Mayor of New York, Rudolph Giuliani, urged New Yorkers to get back to their normal routines, claiming that the best way to defy the terrorists was to show that 'the life of the city goes on' (Perez-Pena 2001). President George Bush repeated this message, urging that 'tomorrow the good people of America go back to their shops, their fields, American factories, and go back to work' (Johnson *et al.* 2004: 181). The resumption of everyday life became a political issue, infused with patriotic symbolism and grounded in economic necessity. A market founded largely on consumer confidence needed to be reassured that ordinary people would behave as they had always done, particularly by spending money on travel and shopping. The ringing of the opening bell on the New York Stock Exchange at 9.30am on 17 September was thus a defiant statement of 'business as usual'. This everyday event was now drenched with symbolism: the crowd observed a two-minute silence, a US Marine sang 'God Bless America', and a police officer, firefighter and emergency services worker rang the bell together.

The more problematic aspect of these mourning and coping narratives is that, even as they politicize the everyday, they confront us with an 'ordinary life' whose normativity is never questioned. It is more difficult to make a similar imaginative connection with Iraqis or Afghans killed by bombs dropped from fighter planes, because their daily lives are not so easily recognizable or represented. There is none of the concreteness and specificity of quotidian detail, the small acts of daily life that seem both surreally trivial and newly symbolic in the context of tragedy. In one newspaper article about the sense of fear in everyday life produced by the threat from terrorism, foreign wars could be reduced to a subordinate clause: 'Bombing raids on Afghanistan apart, what we're left with is a domestic Phoney War with the prospect of it suddenly becoming very unphoney indeed' (Betts 2001). The abstractions used by Western politicians to justify these recent wars – 'democracy', 'the free world', 'civilized society', 'way of life' – depend partly on unexamined identifications with 'our' everyday lives.

Richard Johnson points out that the term 'way of life', which has a particular resonance in cultural studies and was constantly reiterated by politicians such as Tony Blair and George Bush in the months after September 11, 'resists instant and "fundamentalist" moral (or aesthetic) claims to superiority without letting go of evaluation entirely'. It conflates 'the necessary sustaining practices of daily living and the more particularly "cultural" features – systems of meaning, forms of identity and psycho-social processes – through which a world is subjectively produced as meaningful' (Johnson 2002: 211). The valorization of our 'way of life' is based on an implicit identification between daily routines and cultural values that conceals the intimate relationship between the most mundane aspects of our lives (car journeys, office life, buying a house) and much broader forces of global capital (oil hikes, company share prices, international property speculation). As I have argued throughout this book, this politics of everyday life has been consistently obscured by the tendency in media and political discourse to see the public sphere as intrusive, threatening or simply uninteresting.

One of the most influential critics of this retreat from the public sphere in recent years has been the American political scientist Robert Putnam. His work discusses the decline in 'social capital' – the value, financial and otherwise, of communal solidarity and associational life – in the United States over the last few decades. Putnam sees this trend primarily in falling electoral turnouts and declining membership of civic groups such as sports clubs, churches and charity leagues, hence the memorable title of his book, *Bowling Alone*, which refers to the dramatic fall in the number of organized leagues in one of the most popular participation sports in America, ten-pin bowling. Putnam's argument rests largely on the accumulation of an extraordinary range of survey material on diverse types of communal behaviour such as church attendance, membership of parent teacher associations (PTAs), charity work, volunteering and driving etiquette.

Putnam's emphasis on the importance of social capital could be seen as a reaction against the free-market individualism and moral authoritarianism of the Thatcher–Reagan years. He certainly rejects the traditional right-wing explanations for social fragmentation, such as the decline of the nuclear family and the growth of welfare dependency. For a political scientist, though, he seems relatively uninterested in politics and policy-making. Instead, he sees the decline of social capital as an effect of long-term societal trends: the impact of television; the stresses of two-career families; the amount of time spent commuting in a suburbanized society; and the dying off of the socially concerned generation that lived through the challenges of the Depression and the Second World War. Although the first three of these developments are not confined to America, Putnam tends to view social capital in terms of national trends rather than 'global economic transformations'. There is no obvious reason, he argues, why 'corporate delocalisation' should influence 'our readiness to attend a church social, or to have friends over for poker, or even to vote for president' (Putnam 2000: 283). Putnam's is essentially a bottom-up approach that suggests that ordinary people need to be given the space and time to forge stronger connections within their own communities.

Most strikingly, perhaps, Putnam does not examine the role of media and political discourses in generating or depleting social capital, which (as he acknowledges) is a nebulous entity found not only in empirically observable behaviours but also in attitudes, ideas and representations. One of the main arguments of my book, in fact, has been that these representations are crucially important in establishing parameters of public debate, and suggesting how much power, or little power, we have to change our everyday lives. The authority of these representations lies in the fact that they have rarely been seen as politically motivated or ideologically contentious. In recent years, neo-liberal ideology has largely succeeded in taking the everyday out of the sphere of politics and attaching it to the naturalized, inexorable logic of the market-place. In such a context, the relative popularity of policies or ideologies is less relevant than their general acceptance as part of the landscape of daily life – so that, in Colin Leys's words, 'within two decades the omnipresence of business and business culture ha[s] become as commonplace and apparently inevitable as the rain' (2001: 54).

The real value of a critique of everyday life is that it can challenge this apparent inevitability, by showing how the quotidian brings together inertia and change, enslaving routines and sublimated desires, unseen transformations and unfulfilled possibilities. Lefebvre criticized the 'great modern myth of the Revolution as total act, radical break, absolute renewal' (1991a: 65), empha-sizing that real change had to occur through a more far-reaching transfor-mation of the spaces and practices of daily life. For Lefebvre, the boredom of the everyday could serve as a force for both radicalism and conformism. He liked to point out that the 1968 *évènements* originated not on the radical Left Bank but in the new suburban university at Nanterre (the French title of his account of May 1968 was *L'Irruption de Nanterre au sommet*) – a bit like an English revolution starting in Croydon or Milton Keynes. The *évènements* were ultimately unsustainable, though, because Parisians eventually got sick of the disruptions and privations, and longed to get back to a normality that they defined in politically neutral terms, preferring 'boredom at "zero point"' to 'the hazards of desire' (Lefebvre 1969: 89; Lefebvre 1971: 186).

One of the central insights of Lefebvre's work is that 'the only genuine, profound human changes are those which cut into this substance [of everyday life] and make their mark upon it'. We cannot simply break through the facade of daily existence and discover some more exalted plane or higher truth about ourselves: 'Man must be everyday, or he will not be at all' (Lefebvre 1991a: 228, 127). Real social change, this critique of everyday life suggests, comes about in how we catch buses and trains, spend time at our work desks, drive along motorways, get stuck in traffic jams, park our cars and live in our houses. My aim in this book has been to show how the cultural materials that have been representing our everyday lives over the last few decades have often served to deny or obscure this potential for change. If we want to begin to transform our everyday lives for the better, perhaps we need to consider more closely how we think, talk about and represent them: to see the everyday not as the eternally tedious or bathetically comic residue of contemporary life, or simply as a sphere of overlooked ordinariness, but as the real space in which we lead our actual lives.

Notes

Preface and acknowledgements

1   Gardiner (2000) and Highmore (2002a), for example, provide invaluable surveys of cultural theorists of everyday life. Highmore (2002c) collates many of the key readings, and special issues of *New Literary History* (2002) and *Cultural Studies* (2004) present stocktakings of this area. Chaney (2002), Bennett and Watson (2002) and Silva and Bennett (2004) discuss everyday life in relation to more traditional sociological concerns such as class, work, consumption and leisure.

1 Introduction: waiting, cultural studies and the quotidian

1   For a similar take on buses in the US, where they have been dubbed 'loser cruisers', see Hutchinson (2000) and Lipsitz (2004). Hutchinson and Lipsitz both argue that the poor status of the bus in Los Angeles, where it is the principal means by which low-paid black women commute to their jobs, is a product of its racial and class politics.

2   See Roberts (1999: 27–8) for a critique of this notion within cultural studies of everyday life as the site for 'a politics of feints, dodges and ludic subversion'.

3   Of all the key figures in early cultural studies, Hoggart has been the most consistently interested in the quotidian. See, for example, *Townscape with Figures* (1994), a survey of the town of Farnham in Surrey that Stefan Collini aptly calls 'a kind of *Uses of Literacy* for the garden-centre age' (1999: 228). Hoggart covers such banal subjects as shop windows, supermarket check-outs, commuters on railway platforms, post office queues and 'executive'

housing developments. His abiding interest, in this book and elsewhere, is how quotidian activities are based less on beliefs or ideologies than on unquestioned habits and dispositions (1994: 30, 170), which makes them particularly open to manipulation by dominant media and political cultures. With particular relevance to my own research, Hoggart's work from *The Uses of Literacy* onwards has criticized the media's 'well-known cant of "the common man"', 'a grotesque and dangerous flattery' (1958: 179) that valorizes a repressive notion of 'ordinary life' in the name of an uncritical populism.

4   Rita Felski similarly argues that everyday life 'is chock-full of *idées recues*, unexamined hunches, arguments taken on faith, habitual judgements, unjustified generalizations, metaphors which we have forgotten are metaphors' (2002: 616). Felski is responding to what she sees as a tendency within cultural studies to see the everyday as more concrete, immediate and 'real' than traditional objects of academic inquiry, a kind of 'escape route from the rarefied realm of abstract ideas and esoteric knowledge' (2002: 607). She draws here on the work of Agnes Heller (1984), who argues that daily life is both concrete and abstract, reliant on embodied practices and unthinking assumptions.

5   On the fertile tradition of writing about the quotidian in France, which incorporates not only sociology and cultural theory but also more general non-fiction and fiction, see Gumpert (1997), Sheringham (2000) and Highmore (2003–4).

6   For further discussion of this term, see chapter four.

7   Laurie Langbauer (1999: 234–5) argues that Certeau and Lefebvre's notion of the everyday is a rhetorical construction, conjured up 'like a charm' in order to provide us with the illusion of unmediated access to the real. Tony Bennett and Elizabeth B. Silva (2004: 6) also criticize Lefebvre's notion of 'moments' for its belief in a 'pure sociality' that temporarily escapes the influence of bureaucracy, capitalism and the state.

8   See, for example, Kracauer's essays on boredom, waiting and waiting rooms (1995a, 1995d and 1997).

9   A number of other recent writers have explored cinema's relationship to the everyday. Yvette Bíró argues that cinema quickly 'worked out the ritual of big-city life, making our most common activities consensually accepted and recognized'. In the cinema the most desultory elements of daily life become, simply by virtue of being watched, 'extraordinary and comprehensive experiences' that are 'charged with the emotional content of ceremonies' (1982: 79–80). Lesley Stern similarly points to the tension in film between two propensities, the histrionic and the quotidian, which she links to the inflation or deflation of cinematic codes such as cross-cutting, camera movement and mise-en-scène (2001: 324). Stern argues that, alongside its more spectacular effects, film can capture periods of boredom and 'hanging around wasting time' (2001: 336). But no matter how unhistrionic cinema tries to be, 'everyday, habitual gestures, caught by the moving camera, are

Critical Enquiry 28 (1)

potentially framed, put into quotation marks, hypostasized' (2001: 354). Andrew Klevan (2000) also explores the revelation of the everyday in undramatic moments in the films of Satyajit Ray, Robert Bresson and others. Like Kracauer, all these writers suggest that the unique mechanical qualities of film allow it to represent normally unseen aspects of quotidian life.

10 Highmore (2002a: 22) also discusses these methodological problems, suggesting that we need something like an 'avant-garde sociology' to capture the simultaneously concrete and elusive aspects of quotidian life.

11 For a more extended discussion of historiography and the everyday, see Harootunian (2004) and Moran (2004).

2 Workspace: office life and commuting

1 *Alladeen* was conceived by Keith Khan, Marianne Weems and Ali Zaidi, and jointly produced by the Builders Association and Motoroti. It was performed at numerous venues in the UK, Europe, America and Asia between 4 April 2003 and 15 May 2005. The production was linked to a multimedia website at www.alladeen.com (accessed by the author on 29 December 2003).

2 Released on DVD by 20th Century Fox.

3 The first series of *The Office* was shown on BBC2 between 30 August and 4 October 2001; the second series on BBC2 between 30 September and 4 November 2002; and the two episodes of *The Office Christmas Specials* on BBC1 on 26 and 27 December 2003. These have been released by the BBC on DVD/video as *The Office: The Complete Series 1* (2002), *The Office: The Complete Series 2* (2003) and *The Office: The Christmas Specials* (2004).

4 In an essay on the historical development of Japanese rail commuting, James A. Fujii (1999: 117) similarly argues that 'the commute served to homogenize passengers, regardless of their pursuits, to common rhythms of city life. . . . The commute, in this sense, is an *activity*, a qualitatively new part of everyday life that had hitherto not existed. The ambivalence we feel toward it as convenience and *in*convenience reflects our awareness that such transport primarily serves the ends of increased production of goods, surplus labor, and profits.'

5 See Latour (1993: 100–1) for a critique that suggests that Augé needed to do more traditional anthropological fieldwork on the Métro; and Sheringham (1995) for a more positive account of Augé's distinctive form of 'ethno-analysis'.

6 1930s critics of the map argued that the real purpose of representing the Underground system as a grid of roughly equidistant points, with the more commonly used central stations on a larger scale so that the map is less cluttered, was to deceive prospective commuters into thinking that the suburban stations were closer to the centre than they actually were (Garland 1994: 7). It is unlikely that there was any such conspiracy by the Transport

Board, which was initially unsympathetic to Beck's map precisely because its distorted scale gave no sense of distance or location. For Janin Hadlaw, though, the activity of commuting is made up of 'dead time' that is not valued by society and brings no financial reward, so 'not recognizing its duration in representation is completely logical' (2003: 34). Simon Patterson's artwork, *The Great Bear* (1992, displayed in London's Tate Gallery), makes a play on the diagrammatic nature of the Tube map. Using Beck's design as a base, Patterson replaces the names of the lines with different categories (philosophers, footballers, explorers) and the names of the stations with those of famous figures who match these categories. *The Great Bear* suggests that the Tube map has become its own reality, entirely abstracted from what it ostensibly represents.

3 Urban space: the myths and meanings of traffic

1   Willesden is an unglamorous area of north-west London.
2   Ian Parker discusses some of these driver myths in an essay on London traffic (1999).
3   For more about this complex 'everyday ecology of driving', see Katz (1999: 48). Featherstone (2004: 12) and Thrift (2004: 47) also discuss the ambiguity of hand signals, horns and headlights as a way of conveying information or intent to other drivers.
4   To complicate matters further, school-run mums are also associated with four-wheel-drive cars. It is often implied (or even explicitly stated) that women are not strong or skilful enough to deal with these unwieldy vehicles. During his 2004 campaign for re-election as London Mayor, Ken Livingstone entered this debate when, in an interview on GMTV on 23 May, he said that four-wheel-drive vehicles were 'largely a status symbol . . . bad for London and unnecessary', and described parents trying to manoeuvre them through school gates as 'complete idiots'. See Sheller (2004: 231) for a discussion of how similar gender and class assumptions circulate in the US around SUVs (sports utility vehicles).
5   Ross (1995: 138–9) gives an account of Poujadism in relation to the politics of daily life in France in the 1950s.
6   On these shifting meanings of 'congestion', see McCreery (2002).
7   Actor Network Theory has developed this idea of a 'black box' in which mundane technologies conceal the complicated processes of daily life. See Latour (1987: 130–1) and Michael (2000: 24, 131).
8   There is a more detailed discussion of the car's relationship to its 'externalities' in Miller (2001a: 12–17).
9   Macgregor Wise (2004) explores the capacity of webcams to defamiliarize the quotidian through their poor quality, disjointed images.
10   Phillips has given a lecture and slideshow based on this project at irregular intervals at the Tate and South London Galleries since September 1977.

Selected images are reproduced in Phillips (1992: 138–63), and on his website at www.tomphillips.co.uk (accessed by the author on 31 March 2004).

11 Wigoder (2001) has some interesting reflections on photography and the everyday, particularly in relation to images of people waiting in public places. For a fuller account of these different traditions of street photography, see Westerbeck and Meyerowitz (2001). Roberts (1998) uses the concept of 'the everyday' as a way of exploring much larger debates about the relationship between photography and realism.

12 Felski (1999–2000: 28) argues that this idea of the city as 'a chaotic labyrinth of infinite possibilities' overlooks more routine pedestrian movements.

4 Non-places: supermodernity and the everyday

1 Tomlinson (1999: 108–13) and Frow (1997: 75–7) have also sought to ground Augé's theories in more concrete sociological and historical contexts. The historical geographer Peter Merriman uses the example of the building and opening of the M1 in the late 1950s to argue that Augé overlooks 'the complex habitations, practices of dwelling, embodied relations, material presences, placings and hybrid subjectivities associated with movement through such spaces' (2004: 154). Edensor (2003) offers a further critique of the notion of motorway placelessness in his detailed study of the mundane landscape of a small section of the M6, including its embankments, hard shoulders, cones and road signs. John Urry's concept of 'automobility' represents a more general challenge to Augé's notion of 'non-places' by suggesting that such environments are not self-contained but form part of a system of 'dynamically interdependent' practices organized around the car, such as petrol refining and distribution, roadbuilding and roadside service industries (2004: 26).

2 *London Orbital*, an Illuminations film for Channel 4 television, was first broadcast on Channel 4 on 27 October 2002, and has also been shown at various cinema venues. It is available on DVD/video from Illuminations.

3 For a more detailed discussion of the political symbolism of 'Mondeo Man', see McKibbin (1999).

4 Edensor (2004) argues that the mundane aspects of motorway culture, such as roadside furniture, road markings and service stations, can contribute to a sense of national identity. He draws on Billig's notion of a 'banal nationalism' (1995) constituted from the habitual practices of daily life.

5 Franks (2000) explores the ambivalent position of the 'non-plan' manifesto within New Left and New Right discourses.

6 See Attfield (2000: 221–2) for an account of local campaigns against proposed service stations with 'intrusive' modern designs.

7 In a discussion of his home town of Crawley, Sam Appleby suggests that the new town became an 'imagined site of anomie' (1990: 27) with the

development of a new kind of political culture in the Thatcher era that attacked an earlier era of state planning and promoted a highly specific notion of national heritage (1990: 40–1).

8   This term, which is probably the first scholarly reference to 'non-places', was coined by Melvin Webber, a professor of urban and regional development at Berkeley who served as a consultant to the team that drew up the plans for Milton Keynes. Webber argued that, whereas cities were places of concentrated, static settlement with the unique advantages of accessibility and proximity, 'nonplace urban realms' used improved transport and electronic technologies to create more flexible, voluntary associations. He recognized that it was the professional classes, by virtue of their greater reserves of cultural and economic capital, who were able to maintain these far-flung 'nonplace' communities (Webber 1964: 112–13). Webber saw Milton Keynes as an opportunity to make the benefits of the 'nonplace' open to all by creating an intelligent city with advanced technological and transport networks.

9   Jakle and Sculle (1994, 1999) and Jakle et al. (1996) provide exhaustive surveys of the architecture and iconography of these American gas stations, motels and roadside restaurants. In doing so, they acknowledge the influence of John Brinckerhoff Jackson and the field of cultural landscape studies that he inaugurated in the early 1950s. Jackson writes positively about those vernacular, unplanned environments that might be described as 'nonplaces', such as trailer parks, parking lots, strip malls and filling stations. He argues that these environments form part of an 'accessible landscape' that challenges older forms of territoriality, and creates nebulous but still significant forms of community, 'a kind of sodality based on shared uses of the street or road, and on shared routines' (1994: 9–10).

10 See Mandler (1999: 209) for a critique of this stereotypical characterization of the postwar period.

5 Living space: housing, the market and the everyday

1   See Ross (1995: 71–105) for a more extensive discussion of this relationship between modernization and domesticity in 1950s France.

2   Luce Giard contrasts the prosaic activity of cooking, 'a zone of silence and shadow, hidden within the indefinitely repeated detail of common existence' (1998: 179), with these attempts to remake the kitchen as a place of domestic theatre and clinical efficiency. See Highmore's discussion of Giard's work (2004: 317–22).

3   The essays collected in Miller (2001b) also employ the concept of 'material culture' to challenge this dominant idea of the house as a site of conspicuous consumption and social aspirationalism.

4   For a more detailed discussion of Whiteread's sculpture in relation to the politics of memory and the everyday, see Lingwood (1995).

5   Comparatively little has been written in the fields of architectural history and theory about this kind of commercial vernacular building. Upton (2002) explains this omission in terms of the professional identities of architects and architectural critics, which partly rely on the valuing of specialized expertise and unique commissions over everyday practices and volume building.

6   The Channel 4 soap opera *Brookside* (1982–2003) was set in an actual cul-de-sac of 'Barratt-style' houses on a Liverpool estate and made innovative use of the homes as permanent, live-in sets.

7   Graham (1993: 14–23) reproduces images and text from this project.

8   This exhibition was held at Kettle's Yard, University of Cambridge, from 3 May to 15 June 2003. See Rayson (2003) for the exhibition catalogue.

9   *The Dilapidated Dwelling* was made by Illuminations Films for Channel 4 but has not yet been broadcast on television. It has been shown in various venues and is available on video from Illuminations.

10   Keiller develops this position more explicitly in an article in *Architectural Design* (1998).

11   See Barker (1999) for a more positive account that seeks to rescue Chafford Hundred from what it sees as metropolitan and professional disdain.

12   Davidson *et al.* (1997) discuss the relationship between the DIY boom and the poor state of British housing.

6 Conclusion: the everyday and cultural change

1   Ross (1997: 19–20) discusses the unique historical conditions in postwar France that helped to produce these new ideas about everyday life.

2   Harry Harootunian, a historian of modern Japan, similarly suggests that the study of everyday life presents a challenge to Western historians who have seen modernity as an inevitably linear process in which 'peripheral' societies always lag behind Europe and America. For Harootunian, the everyday is 'the site of unevenness' (2000: 56), undermining this continuist notion of history that relies 'on the fixity of the past and its capacity to yield a historical knowledge that can reveal how the present developed from it' (2000: 15).

Bibliography

Abrams, Mark, Rose, Richard and Hinden, Rita (1960) *Must Labour Lose?*, Harmondsworth: Penguin.

Adams, Tim (ed.) (2001) *City Secrets: London*, New York: The Little Bookroom.

Ahearne, Jeremy (1995) *Michel de Certeau: Interpretation and its Other*, Cambridge: Polity.

Alden, Chris (2005) *Guardian Media Directory 2005*, London: Guardian Books.

Amiel, Barbara (2002) 'Blunkett and Livingstone are planning to run our lives', the *Daily Telegraph*, 8 July.

Appleby, Sam (1990) 'Crawley: a space mythology', *New Formations* 11 (Summer): 19–44.

Appleyard, Donald, Lynch, Kevin and Myer, John R. (1964) *The View from the Road*, Cambridge, MA: MIT Press.

Ardagh, John (1988) *France Today*, Harmondsworth: Penguin.

Arthur, Charles (2003) 'Congestion charging: firms blame each other for chaos', *The Independent*, 14 February.

Attfield, Judy (2000) *Wild Things: The Material Culture of Everyday Life*, Oxford: Berg.

Augé, Marc (1995) *Non-Places: Introduction to an Anthropology of Supermodernity*, trans. John Howe, London: Verso.

—— (1998) *A Sense of the Other: The Timeliness and Relevance of Anthropology*, trans. Amy Jacobs, Stanford, CA: Stanford University Press.

—— (2000) 'Roundabouts: the revenge of the local', in Steve Pile and Nigel Thrift (eds) *City A-Z*, London: Routledge, pp. 206–7.

—— (2002) *In the Metro*, trans. Tom Conley, Minneapolis, MN: University of Minnesota Press.

Baillie, Kate and Salmon, Tim (2001) *The Rough Guide to Paris*, London: Rough Guides.

Balchin, Paul and Rhoden, Maureen (2002) *Housing Policy: An Introduction*, 4th edn, London: Routledge.

Baldry, Christopher (1997) 'The social construction of office space', *International Labour Review* 136, 3: 365–78.

Ballard, J. G. (1974) *Concrete Island*, London: Jonathan Cape.

—— (1995) *Crash*, London: Vintage.

Banham, Reyner (1968) 'Disservice areas', *New Society*, 23 May: 762–3.

Banham, Reyner, Barker, Paul, Hall, Peter and Price, Cedric (1969) 'Non-plan: an experiment in freedom', *New Society*, 20 March: 435–43. Reprinted in Jonathan Hughes and Simon Sadler (eds) (2000) *Non-Plan: Essays on Freedom, Participation and Change in Modern Architecture and Urbanism*, Oxford: Architectural Press, pp. 13–21.

Barker, Lynsey (ed.) (2003) *Housebuilding: Market Report*, London: Key Note.

Barker, Paul (1998) 'Observations', *New Statesman*, 6 March: 54.

—— (1999) 'In praise of suburbia', *Blueprint* 159 (March): 28–32.

Barthes, Roland (1993) *Mythologies*, trans. Annette Lavers, London: Vintage.

Baum, Dan (2001) 'The ultimate jam session', *Wired* 9, 11 (November): 170–81.

Bayley, Stephen (2003) 'Cacotopia rules', *Blueprint* 206 (April): 66–70.

BBC Radio 4 (2004) *Routemasters*, presented by Joe Kerr, 11 May, 8 June.

BBC1 (2003) *Imagine: The World According to Parr*, 3 December.

Beck, Ulrich (1992) *Risk Society: Towards a Future Modernity*, London: Sage.

Bendixson, Terence and Platt, John (1992) *Milton Keynes: Image and Reality*, London: Granta.

Benjamin, Walter (1979) 'A small history of photography', in *One-Way Street and Other Writings*, trans. Edmund Jephcott and Kingsley Shorter, London: NLB, pp. 240–57.

Bennett, Tony and Silva, Elizabeth B. (2004) 'Everyday life in contemporary culture', in Elizabeth Silva and Tony Bennett (eds) *Contemporary Culture and Everyday Life*, Durham: Sociology Press, pp. 1–20.

Bennett, Tony and Watson, Diane (eds) (2002) *Understanding Everyday Life*, Oxford: Blackwell.

Berman, Marshall (1983) *All That is Solid Melts into Air: The Experience of Modernity*, London: Verso.

Betts, Hannah (2001) 'Nothing to fear but fear', *The Times*, 12 October.

Betts, Ian (2003) 'Before too long', *Surveyor*, 23 October: 14–16.

Billig, Michael (1995) *Banal Nationalism*, London: Sage.

Bíró, Yvette (1982) *Profane Mythology: The Savage Mind of the Cinema*, trans. Imre Goldstein, Bloomington, IN: Indiana University Press.

Blanchot, Maurice (1987) 'Everyday speech', *Yale French Studies* 73: 12–20.

Boggan, Steve (2001) 'Farewell to "dark, satanic" image of UK's call centres', the *Independent*, 11 December.

Boltanski, Luc and Chiapello, Ève (1999) *Le Nouvel Esprit du Capitalisme*, Paris: Gallimard.

Bonnett, Alastair (2000) 'Buses', in Steve Pile and Nigel Thrift (eds) *City A-Z*, London: Routledge, pp. 26–8.

Braid, Mary (2002) 'Sending a coded message', *The Times*, 28 July.

Brown, Mike (1995) *The Design of Roundabouts*, London: HMSO.

Brown, Paul (2003) 'Park land', *The Guardian*, 23 April.

Bryson, Norman (1990) *Looking at the Overlooked: Four Essays on Still Life Painting*, London: Reaktion.

Buck, Nick, Gordon, Ian, Hall, Peter, Harloe, Michael and Kleinman, Mark (2002) *Working Capital: Life and Labour in Contemporary London*, London: Routledge.

Bueno, Julia (1999) 'Moving on up', the *Independent*, 25 July.

Bull, Michael (2000) *Sounding Out the City: Personal Stereos and the Management of Everyday Life*, Oxford: Berg.

Butler, David and Kavanagh, Dennis (1997) *The British General Election of 1997*, Basingstoke: Macmillan.

Butler, Tim with Robson, Garry (2003) *London Calling: The Middle Classes and the Re-making of Inner London*, Oxford: Berg.

Cameron, Deborah (2000) *Good to Talk? Living and Working in a Communication Culture*, London: Sage.

Carney, Ray (2000) *The Films of Mike Leigh: Embracing the World*, Cambridge: Cambridge University Press.

Carr-Brown, Jonathan (2000) 'Tories want to let drivers turn left at red lights', *The Sunday Times*, 19 November.

Castoriadis, Cornelius (1988) 'Modern capitalism and revolution', in *Political and Social Writings, Volume 2, 1955–1960: From the Workers' Struggle Against Bureaucracy to Revolution in the Age of Modern Capitalism*, ed. and trans. David Ames Curtis, Minneapolis, MN: University of Minnesota Press, pp. 226–315.

Certeau, Michel de (1984) *The Practice of Everyday Life*, trans. Steven F. Rendall, Berkeley, CA: University of California Press.

Chambers, Iain (1994) *Migrancy, Culture and Identity*, London: Routledge.

Chaney, David (2002) *Cultural Change and Everyday Life*, Basingstoke: Palgrave.

Chapman, John (2003) '10% rise forecast this year: new hope on house prices', *Daily Express*, 5 July.

Chevalier, Louis (1994) *The Assassination of Paris*, trans. David P. Jordan, Chicago, IL: University of Chicago Press.

Ciulla, Joanne B. (2000) *The Working Life: The Promise and Betrayal of Modern Work*, New York: Times Books.

Clapson, Mark, Dobbin, Mervyn and Waterman, Peter (eds) (1998) *The Best Laid Plans: Milton Keynes since 1967*, Luton: University of Luton Press.

Clark, Andrew (2003) 'Minister wades into row over London traffic lights', *The Guardian*, 28 April.

—— (2004) 'London goes into reverse on speed humps', *The Guardian*, 15 April.

Clarke, Michael, Smith, David and McConville, Michael (1994) *Slippery Customers: Estate Agents, the Public and Regulation*, London: Blackstone Press.

Clarkson, Jeremy (2003) 'Now I c sense', the *Sun*, 8 March.

Clear Channel Adshel (2004) Adshel website. Online. Available at www.adshel. com (accessed 4 January 2004).

Cohen, Stanley (2002) *Folk Devils and Moral Panics*, 3rd edn, London: Routledge.

Coleman, Alice (1985) *Utopia on Trial: Vision and Reality in Planned Housing*, London: Hilary Shipman.

Collini, Stefan (1999) 'Critical minds: Raymond Williams and Richard Hoggart', in *English Pasts: Essays in History and Culture*, Oxford: Oxford University Press, pp. 210–30.

Collins, Christopher (ed.) (1999) *Margaret Thatcher: Complete Public Statements on CD-ROM*, Oxford: Oxford University Press.

Commission for Architecture and the Built Environment (CABE) (2004) *Housing Audit: Assessing the Design Quality of New Homes: London, the South East and the East of England*, London: CABE.

Compston, Emily and Nixson, Matt (2003) 'Red Ken is driving our children out of school', *Mail on Sunday*, 19 January.

Couldry, Nick (2001) 'The umbrella man: crossing a landscape of speech and silence', *European Journal of Cultural Studies* 4, 2 (May): 131–52.

Cowie, Ian (1988) 'Nearly time to fly the nest', the *Daily Telegraph*, 24 October.

Cultural Studies (2004) Special issue on everyday life, 18, 2/3 (March/May).

Curtis, Nick (2001) 'Britain's most coveted address', *Evening Standard* (London), 12 September.

Cusick, James (1996) 'Ten slow years on the road to hell', the *Independent*, 30 October.

Daily Mail (2002) 'Hurrah for all the nimbys in our back yards', *Daily Mail*, 29 August.

Daily Mirror (1999) 'Internet news', *Daily Mirror*, 10 September.

Davidson, Maggie, Redshaw, Justine and Mooney, Alex (1997) *The Role of DIY in Maintaining Owner-Occupied Stock*, Bristol: Policy Press.

Deans, John (1995) 'You dreadful human beings', *Daily Mail*, 9 February.

Debord, Guy (1981) 'Perspectives for conscious alterations in everyday life', in Ken Knabb (ed.) *Situationist International Anthology*, Berkeley, CA: Bureau of Public Secrets, pp. 68–75.

Department for Transport (1998) *From Workhorse to Thoroughbred: A Better Role for Bus Travel*, London: HMSO.

—— (2003) 'Road Accidents Great Britain 2001'. Online. Available www.dft. gov.uk/ (accessed 3 May 2004).

—— (2004) *National Travel Survey 2002*, London: Department for Transport (April). Online. Available www.dft.gov.uk/ (accessed 4 May 2004).

Design (1959) 'Which signs for motorways?', *Design* 129 (September): 28–32.

Doward, Jamie (1999) 'Motorway meccas get mall makeover', the *Observer*, 22 August.

—— (2004) 'Property collapse feared as landlords sell up', the *Observer*, 25 April.

Dowling, Tim (2002) 'Sick of the Tube? There is a better way', *The Guardian*, 2 September.

Downs, Anthony (1992) *Stuck in Traffic: Coping with Peak-Hour Traffic Congestion*, Washington, DC: Brookings Institution.

Dunleavy, Patrick (1981) *The Politics of Mass Housing in Britain 1945–1975*, Oxford: Clarendon Press.

Dyckhoff, Tom (2003) 'A lot of fuss about slabs of concrete', *The Times*, 25 March.

Eden, Richard (2001) 'Waiting game pays off for £20-an-hour queuing agency', the *Daily Telegraph*, 12 October.

Edensor, Tim (2003) 'M6 – junction 19–16: defamiliarizing the mundane land-scape', *Space and Culture* 6, 2 (May): 151–68.

—— (2004) 'Automobility and national identity: representation, geography and driving practice', *Theory, Culture and Society* 21, 4/5 (August–October): 101–20.

Edwards, Adam (1999) 'Service gets the hard shoulder', *The Times*, 10 July.

Edwards, Brian (1997) *The Modern Station: New Approaches to Railway Architecture*, London: E and FN Spon.

Epstein, Richard A. (2002) 'The allocation of the commons: parking on public roads', *Journal of Legal Studies* 31 (June): 515–44.

Esher, Lionel (1981) *A Broken Wave: The Rebuilding of England 1940–1980*, London: Allen Lane.

Featherstone, Mike (2004) 'Automobilities: an introduction', *Theory, Culture and Society* 21, 4/5 (August–October): 1–24.

Felski, Rita (1999–2000) 'The invention of everyday life', *New Formations* 39 (Winter): 13–31.

—— (2002) 'Introduction', *New Literary History* 33, 4 (Autumn 2002): 607–22.

Fiske, John (1989a) *Reading the Popular*, London: Unwin Hyman.

—— (1989b) *Understanding Popular Culture*, London: Unwin Hyman.

Fogg, Elaine (1992) 'Train idea cheap but not cheerful', *The Times*, 11 January.

Ford Motor Company (2003) *New Look Ford Mondeo Catalogue*, Brentwood, Essex: Ford Motor Company.

France, Julie (2002) 'Glass war', *The Guardian*, 18 November.

Frank, Thomas (2001) *One Market Under God: Extreme Capitalism, Market Populism, and the End of Economic Democracy*, London: Secker and Warburg.

Franklin, Adrian and Crang, Mike (2001) 'The trouble with tourism and travel theory?', *Tourist Studies* 1, 1 (June): 5–22.

Franks, Ben (2000) 'New Right/New Left: an alternative experiment in freedom', in Jonathan Hughes and Simon Sadler (eds) *Non-Plan: Essays on Freedom, Participation and Change in Modern Architecture and Urbanism*, Oxford: Architectural Press, pp. 32–43.

Fraser, Jill Andresky (2001) *White-Collar Sweatshop: The Deterioration of Work and its Rewards in Corporate America*, New York: Norton.

Freeman, Vaughan (1993) 'Mondeo makes its mark', *The Times*, 22 January.

Friedman, Milton (1996) 'How to plan and pay for the safe and adequate high-ways we need', in Gabriel Roth, *Roads in a Market Economy*, Brookfield, VT: Ashgate, pp. 223–46.

Frow, John (1997) *Time and Commodity Culture: Essays in Cultural Theory and Postmodernity*, Oxford: Clarendon Press.

Fujii, James A. (1999) 'Intimate alienation: Japanese urban rail and the commodification of urban subjects', *Differences* 11, 2 (Summer): 106–33.

Gaber, Ivor (2004) *Driven to Distraction: An Analysis of the Media's Coverage of the Introduction of the London Congestion Charge*, Goldsmiths College, University of London: Unit for Journalism Research.

Garber, Marjorie (2001) *Sex and Real Estate: Why We Love Houses*, New York: Anchor.

Gardiner, Michael E. (2000) *Critiques of Everyday Life*, London: Routledge.

Garland, Ken (1994) *Mr Beck's Underground Map*, Harrow Weald, Middlesex: Capital Transport.

Garreau, Joel (1991) *Edge City: Life on the New Frontier*, New York: Anchor.

Gauntlett, David and Hill, Annette (1999) *TV Living: Television, Culture and Everyday Life*, London: Routledge.

Geertz, Clifford (1973) *The Interpretation of Cultures: Selected Essays*, New York: Basic Books.

Giard, Luce (1998) 'Doing-cooking', in Michel de Certeau, Luce Giard and Pierre Mayol, *The Practice of Everyday Life, Volume 2: Living and Cooking*, trans. Timothy J. Tomasik, Minneapolis, MN: University of Minnesota Press, pp. 149–247.

Gibbons, Fiachra (1996) 'Strange goings-on in West Sussex', *The Guardian*, 12 April.

Gill, A. A. (2000) *Starcrossed*, London: Black Swan.

Glancey, Jonathan (1998) 'End of the road', *The Guardian*, 27 November.

—— (2001) *London: Bread and Circuses*, London: Verso.

Glendinning, Miles and Muthesius, Stefan (1994) *Tower Block: Modern Public Housing in England, Scotland, Wales and Northern Ireland*, New Haven, CT: Yale University Press.

—— (2004) 'Architecture versus building in the 1960s housing boom', in James Woudhuysen and Ian Abley, *Why is Construction so Backward?*, Chichester: Wiley-Academy, pp. 132–62.

Glinert, Ed (2003) *The London Compendium: Exploring the Hidden Metropolis*, London: Allen Lane.

Goffman, Erving (1971) *Relations in Public: Microstudies of the Public Order*, London: Allen Lane.

Graham, Dan (1993) *Rock My Religion: Writings and Art Projects 1965–1990*, ed. Brian Wallis, Cambridge, MA: MIT Press.

—— (2001) Interview with Mark Francis, in Birgit Pelzer, Mark Francis and Beatriz Colomina (eds) *Dan Graham*, London: Phaidon, pp. 6–35.

Graham, Stephen and Marvin, Simon (2001) *Splintering Urbanism: Networked Infrastructures, Technological Mobilities and the Urban Condition*, London: Routledge.

Gramsci, Antonio (1971) 'The study of philosophy', in *Selections from the Prison Notebooks*, ed. and trans. Quintin Hoare and Geoffrey Nowell Smith, London: Lawrence and Wishart, pp. 323–77.

Grayling, A. C. (2002) 'How to make the traffic flow', *New Statesman*, 4 March: 14.

Grayling, Tony (1999) 'Don't let it pass you by', *The Guardian*, 10 November.

Grimston, Jack (2003) 'Livingstone plans London of boulevards', *The Sunday Times*, 6 July.

Gross, Donald and Harris, Carl M. (1974) *Fundamentals of Queueing Theory*, New York: John Wiley.

Guardian (2003) 'Reinventing the terraced house', *The Guardian*, 24 September.

Gumpert, Lynn (1997) 'Beyond the banal: an introduction to the art of the everyday', in Lynn Gumpert (ed.) *The Art of the Everyday: The Quotidian in Postwar French Culture*, New York: New York University Press, pp. 11–17.

Habermas, Jürgen (1990) 'What does socialism mean today? The rectifying revolution and the need for new thinking on the Left', *New Left Review* 183 (September/October): 3–21.

Hadlaw, Janin (2003) 'The London Underground map: imagining modern time and space', *Design Issues* 19, 1 (Winter): 25–35.

Hagerty, Bill (2002) 'Mail man', *The Guardian*, 9 September.

Hall, Allan (2003) 'The Trabant legend chugs back to life', the *Scotsman*, 7 May.

Hall, Peter (1963) *London 2000*, London: Faber and Faber.

—— (1989) *London 2001*, London: Unwin Hyman.

—— (2002) *Urban and Regional Planning*, 4th edn, London: Routledge.

Hall, Stuart (1983) 'The great moving right show', in Stuart Hall and Martin Jacques (eds) *The Politics of Thatcherism*, London: Lawrence and Wishart, pp.19–39.

—— (1988) *Hard Road to Renewal: Thatcherism and the Crisis of the Left*, London: Verso.

Halliday, Stephen (2001) *Underground to Everywhere: London's Underground Railway in the Life of the Capital*, Stroud: Sutton.

Hann, Michael (2001) 'Leave my town alone', *The Guardian*, 7 August.

Hardman, Robert (2003) 'How I see it', *Daily Mail*, 18 February.

Harootunian, Harry (2000) *History's Disquiet: Modernity, Cultural Practice, and the Question of Everyday Life*, New York: Columbia University Press.

—— (2004) 'Shadowing history: national narratives and the persistence of the everyday', *Cultural Studies* 18, 2/3 (March/May): 181–200.

Hartley, John (2003) *A Short History of Cultural Studies*, London: Sage.

Hatakeyama, Naoya (2002) *Slow Glass*, Winchester: Light Xchange and The Winchester Gallery.

Hayes, Dennis and Hudson, Alan (2001) *Basildon: The Mood of the Nation*, London: Demos.

Hearn, D. (1971) 'Motorway service areas', in Joyce C. Davis (ed.) *Motorways in Britain Today and Tomorrow: Proceedings of the Conference Organized by the Institution of Civil Engineers in London 26–28 April 1971*, London: Institution of Civil Engineers, pp. 83–5.

Heath, Anthony F., Jowell, Roger M. and Curtice, John K. (2001) *The Rise of New Labour: Party Policies and Voter Choices*, Oxford: Oxford University Press.

Heath, Christian, Hindmarsh, Jon and Luff, Paul (1999) 'Interaction in isolation: the dislocated world of the London Underground train driver', *Sociology* 33, 3 (August): 555–75.

Heffer, Simon (2003) 'Treachery that's killing democracy', *Daily Mail*, 22 February.

Heller, Agnes (1984) *Everyday Life*, trans. G. L. Campbell, London: Routledge and Kegan Paul.

Henderson, Mark (2003) 'Daft science cashing in on the bleeding obvious', *The Times*, 31 December.

Hennessy, Patrick (2002) '999 chiefs: congestion charge may cost lives', *Evening Standard* (London), 14 August.

Hermer, Joe and Hunt, Alan (1996) 'Official graffiti of the everyday', *Law and Society Review* 30, 3: 455–80.

Hetherington, Peter (2003) 'Here's one I made earlier', *The Guardian*, 19 February.

Highmore, Ben (2002a) *Everyday Life and Cultural Theory: An Introduction*, London: Routledge.

—— (2002b) 'Introduction: questioning everyday life', in Ben Highmore (ed.) *The Everyday Life Reader*, London: Routledge, pp. 1–34.

—— (ed.) (2002c) *The Everyday Life Reader*, London: Routledge.

—— (2003–4) 'Mind the gap', *New Formations* 51 (Winter): 149–54.

—— (2004) 'Homework: routine, social aesthetics and the ambiguity of everyday life', *Cultural Studies* 18, 2/3 (March/May): 306–27.

Highways Agency (2001) 'M25 leaflet: advance notice of roadworks and traffic information', April–June.

Hoggart, Richard (1958) *The Uses of Literacy*, Harmondsworth: Penguin.

—— (1994) *Townscape with Figures: Farnham: Portrait of an English Town*, London: Chatto and Windus.

Home Office (2003) *Respect and Responsibility – Taking a Stand Against Anti-Social Behaviour*, London: HMSO (March).

Howe, John (2002) 'Vehicle of desire', *New Left Review* 15 (May/June): 105–17.

Hughes, David and Massey, Ray (1999) 'War on the motorist', *Daily Mail*, 18 November.

Hutchinson, Sikivu (2000) 'Waiting for the bus', *Social Text* 63 (Summer): 107–20.

Hutton, Will (1996) *The State We're In*, 2nd edn, London: Vintage.

Independent (1992) 'Election 1992: in the heat of the night', the *Independent*, 12 April.

—— (2001) 'Unhappy eaters', the *Independent*, 14 December.

—— (2002) 'A short history of the postcode', the *Independent*, 26 January.

—— (2003) 'A capital success?', the *Independent*, 18 February.

Information Commissioner (2000) *CCTV Code of Practice*, Wilmslow, Cheshire: Information Commissioner's Office.

Institution of Highways and Transportation (2003) *The Motorway Archive*. Online. Available www.ukmotorwayarchive.org/ (accessed 5 July 2003).

Jackson, John Brinckerhoff (1994) *A Sense of Place, A Sense of Time*, New Haven, CT: Yale University Press.

Jakle, John A. and Sculle, Keith A. (1994) *The Gas Station in America*, Baltimore, MD: Johns Hopkins University Press.

—— (1999) *Fast Food: Roadside Restaurants in the Automobile Age*, Baltimore, MD: Johns Hopkins University Press.

—— (2004) *Lots of Parking: Land Use in a Car Culture*, Charlottesville, VA: University of Virginia Press.

Jakle, John A., Sculle, Keith A. and Rogers, Jefferson S. (1996) *The Motel in America*, Baltimore, MD: Johns Hopkins University Press.

James, Simon (2001) *Mind the Gap*, London: HarperCollins.

Jarvis, Helen, Pratt, Andy C. and Cheng-Chong Wu, Peter (2001) *The Secret Life of Cities: The Social Reproduction of Cities*, Harlow: Prentice-Hall.

Jencks, Charles (1991) *The Language of Post-Modern Architecture*, 6th edn, London: Academy Editions.

Jessop, Bob, Bonnett, Kevin, Bromley, Simon and Ling, Tom (1988) *Thatcherism: A Tale of Two Nations*, Cambridge: Polity.

Johnson, Richard (2001) 'Historical returns: transdisciplinarity, cultural studies and history', *European Journal of Cultural Studies* 4, 3 (August): 261–88.

—— (2002) 'Defending ways of life: the (anti-)terrorist rhetorics of Bush and Blair', *Theory, Culture and Society* 19, 4 (August): 211–31.

Johnson, Richard, Chambers, Deborah, Raghuram, Parvati and Tincknell, Estella (2004) *The Practice of Cultural Studies*, London: Sage.

Jones, Tim (1994) 'End of the line for bus queue bylaw', *The Times*, 21 September.

Katz, Jack (1999) *How Emotions Work*, Chicago, IL: University of Chicago Press.

Keeley, Graham (2003) 'Women voice fears on night transport', *Evening Standard* (London), 7 March.

Keiller, Patrick (1998) 'The dilapidated dwelling', *Architectural Design* 68, 7/8 (July/August): 22–7.

—— (2002) 'Architectural cinematography', in Kester Rattenbury (ed.) *This is not Architecture: Media Constructions*, London: Routledge, pp. 37–44.

Kelly, Michael (1997) 'The historical emergence of everyday life', *Sites: The Journal of 20th-Century/Contemporary French Studies* 1, 1 (Spring): 77–91.

Kerr, Joe (2000) 'Tower blocks', in Steve Pile and Nigel Thrift (eds) *City A-Z*, London: Routledge, pp. 260–2.

—— (2003) 'Blowdown: the rise and fall of London's tower blocks', in Joe Kerr and Andrew Gibson (eds) *London from Punk to Blair*, London: Reaktion, pp. 189–98.

Kindleberger, Charles (1989) *Manias, Panics and Crashes: A History of Financial Crises*, 2nd edn, Basingstoke: Macmillan.

Kingsnorth, Paul (2004) 'Nimbys are the true democratic heroes', *New Statesman*, 3 May: 22–4.

Kinneir, Jock (1980) *Words and Buildings: The Art and Practice of Public Lettering*, London: The Architectural Press.

Klevan, Andrew (2000) *Disclosure of the Everyday: Undramatic Achievement in Narrative Film*, Trowbridge, Wiltshire: Flicks Books.

Kosík, Karel (1976) *Dialectics of the Concrete: A Study on Problems of Man and World*, trans. Karel Kovana with James Schmidt, Dordrecht, the Netherlands: D. Reidel.

Kracauer, Siegfried (1960) *Theory of Film: The Redemption of Physical Reality*, London: Oxford University Press.

—— (1995a) 'Boredom', in *The Mass Ornament: Weimar Essays*, trans. and ed. Thomas Y. Levin, Cambridge, MA: Harvard University Press, pp. 331–4.

—— (1995b) *History: The Last Things Before the Last*, Princeton, NJ: Markus Wiener.

—— (1995c) 'The mass ornament', in *The Mass Ornament: Weimar Essays*, trans and ed. Thomas Y. Levin, Cambridge, MA: Harvard University Press, pp. 75–86.

—— (1995d) 'Those who wait', in *The Mass Ornament: Weimar Essays*, trans. and ed. Thomas Y. Levin, Cambridge, MA: Harvard University Press, pp. 129–40.

—— (1997) 'On employment agencies: the construction of a space', in Neal Leach (ed.) *Rethinking Architecture: A Reader in Cultural Theory*, London: Routledge, pp. 59–64.

—— (1998) *The Salaried Masses: Duty and Distraction in Weimar Germany*, trans. Quintin Hoare, London: Verso.

Kunstler, James Howard (1994) *The Geography of Nowhere: The Rise and Decline of America's Man-Made Landscape*, New York: Simon and Schuster.

Laing, Stuart (1986) *Representations of Working-Class Life 1957–1964*, Basingstoke: Macmillan.

Langbauer, Laurie (1999) *Novels of Everyday Life: The Series in English Fiction, 1850–1930*, Ithaca, NY: Cornell University Press.

Larkin, Philip (1988) *Collected Poems*, ed. Anthony Thwaite, London: Faber and Faber.

Latour, Bruno (1987) *Science in Action: How to Follow Engineers in Society*, Milton Keynes: Open University Press.

—— (1993) *We Have Never Been Modern*, trans. Catherine Porter, Harlow: Longman.

Laurance, Ben (1997) 'Mammon: half a century of houses that Lawrie built', the *Observer*, 28 September.

Laurier, Eric (2004) 'Doing office work on the motorway', *Theory, Culture and Society* 21, 4/5 (August–October): 261–77.

Lawrence, David (1999) *Always a Welcome: The Glove Compartment History of the Motorway Service Area*, Twickenham: Between Books.

Le Corbusier (1987) *The Decorative Art of Today*, trans. James I. Dunnett, London: Architectural Press.

Lefebvre, Henri (1969) *The Explosion: Marxism and the French Revolution*, trans. Alfred Ehrenfeld, New York: Monthly Review Press.

—— (1971) *Everyday Life in the Modern World*, trans. Sacha Rabinovitch, London: Allen Lane.

—— (1991a) *Critique of Everyday Life, Volume 1: Introduction*, trans. John Moore, London: Verso.

—— (1991b) *The Production of Space*, trans. Donald Nicholson-Smith, Oxford: Blackwell.

—— (1995a) 'Introduction', in *Introduction to Modernity: Twelve Preludes, September 1959-May 1961*, trans. John Moore, London: Verso, pp. 1–6.

—— (1995b) 'Notes on the new town', in *Introduction to Modernity: Twelve Preludes, September 1959–May 1961*, trans. John Moore, London: Verso, pp. 116–26.

—— (1996) 'Seen from the window', in *Writings on Cities*, trans. and ed. Eleonore Kofman and Elizabeth Lebas, Oxford: Blackwell, pp. 219–27.

—— (2002) *Critique of Everyday Life, Volume II: Foundations for a Sociology of the Everyday*, trans. John Moore, London: Verso.

—— (2003a) 'Preface to the study of the habitat of the "pavillon"', in Stuart Elden, Elizabeth Lebas and Eleonore Kofman (eds) *Henri Lefebvre: Key Writings*, London: Continuum, pp. 121–35.

—— (2003b) *The Urban Revolution*, trans. Robert Bononno, Minneapolis, MN: University of Minnesota Press.

—— (2004) *Rhythmanalysis: Space, Time and Everyday Life*, trans. Stuart Elden and Gerald Moore, London: Continuum.

Leidner, Robin (1993) *Fast Food, Fast Talk: Service Work and the Routinization of Everyday Life*, Berkeley, CA: University of California Press.

Lévi-Strauss, Claude (1987) *Introduction to the Work of Marcel Mauss*, trans. Felicity Baker, London: Routledge and Kegan Paul.

Lewis-Smith, Victor (2003) 'Going down the tubes', *Evening Standard* (London), 17 October.

Leys, Colin (2001) *Market-Driven Politics: Neoliberal Democracy and the Public Interest*, London: Verso.

Likert, Rensis (1961) *New Patterns of Management*, New York: McGraw-Hill.

Lingwood, James (ed.) (1995) *Rachel Whiteread: House*, London: Phaidon.

Lipsitz, George (2004) 'Learning from Los Angeles: another one rides the bus', *American Quarterly* 56, 3 (September): 511–29.

Lock, David (1994) 'The long view', *Architectural Design* 64, 9/10 (September/October): 83–91.

Lockwood, David (1958) *The Blackcoated Worker: A Study in Class-Consciousness*, London: Allen and Unwin.

Longstreth, Richard (1997) *City Center to Regional Mall: Architecture, the Automobile, and Retailing in Los Angeles, 1920–1950*, Cambridge, MA: MIT Press.

—— (1999) *The Drive-in, the Supermarket, and the Transformation of Commercial Space in Los Angeles, 1914–1941*, Cambridge, MA: MIT Press.

Loudon, Andrew (2000) 'The day the clampers met their matchstick', *Daily Mail*, 18 November.

Ludlow, Mark (2003) 'Rebel drivers pledge London charge "havoc"', *The Sunday Times*, 12 January.

Lydall, Ross (2003a) 'Cameras will push crime into suburbs', *Evening Standard* (London), 3 February.

—— (2003b) 'Danger alert as scooters try to beat car charge', *Evening Standard* (London), 2 January.

Macalister Hall, Malcolm (2004) 'Miles and miles of money', the *Independent*, 15 April.

MacAskill, Ewen (1999) 'Second chance: tea at no. 10 for woman who ignored PM', *The Guardian*, 22 December.

McCreery, Sandy (1996) 'Westway – caught in the speed trap', in Iain Borden, Joe Kerr, Alicia Pivaro and Jane Rendell (eds) *Strangely Familiar: Narratives of Architecture in the City*, London: Routledge, pp. 37–41.

—— (2002) 'Come together', in Peter Wollen and Joe Kerr (eds) *Autopia: Cars and Culture*, London: Reaktion, pp. 307–11.

Macdonald, Nancy (2001) *The Graffiti Subculture: Youth, Masculinity and Identity in London and New York*, Basingstoke: Palgrave.

MacGregor Wise, J. (2004) 'An immense and unexpected field of action: webcams, surveillance and everyday life', *Cultural Studies* 18, 2/3 (March/May): 424–42.

McKay, George (1996) *Senseless Acts of Beauty: Cultures of Resistance since the 1960s*, London: Verso.

—— (ed.) (1998) *DiY Culture: Party and Protest in Nineties Britain*, London: Verso.

McKibbin, Ross (1999) 'Mondeo man in the driving seat', *London Review of Books*, 30 September.

Manchester Evening News (2004) 'Money pumps back into heart', *Manchester Evening News*, 4 February.

Mandler, Peter (1999) 'New towns for old: the fate of the town centre', in Becky Conekin, Frank Mort and Chris Waters (eds) *Moments of Modernity: Reconstructing Britain 1945–1964*, London: Rivers Oram Press, pp. 208–27.

Maspero, François (1994) *Roissy Express: A Journey Through the Paris Suburbs*, trans. Paul Jones, London: Verso.

Massey, Doreen (1992) 'A place called home?', *New Formations* 17 (Summer): 3–15.

Massey, Ray (2003) 'C-day: it will be chaos', *Daily Mail*, 17 February.

Mauss, Marcel (1970) *The Gift: Forms and Functions of Exchange in Archaic Societies*, trans. Ian Cunnison, London: Routledge and Kegan Paul.

Merriman, Peter (2001) 'M1: A cultural geography of an English motorway, 1946–1965', unpublished doctoral thesis, University of Nottingham.

—— (2003) '"A power for good or evil": geographies of the M1 in late fifties Britain', in David Gilbert, David Matless and Brian Short (eds) *Geographies of British Modernity: Space and Society in the Twentieth Century*, Oxford: Blackwell, pp. 115–131.

—— (2004) 'Driving places: Marc Augé, non-places, and the geographies of England's M1 motorway', *Theory, Culture and Society* 21, 4/5 (August–October 2004): 145–67.

Michael, Mike (2000) *Reconnecting Culture, Technology and Nature: From Society to Heterogeneity*, London: Routledge.

Mikes, George (1958) *How to be an Alien: A Handbook for Beginners and More Advanced Pupils*, London: André Deutsch.

Miller, Daniel (2001a) 'Driven societies', in Daniel Miller (ed.) *Car Cultures*, Oxford: Berg, pp. 1–33.

—— (ed.) (2001b) *Home Possessions*, Oxford: Berg.

Mills, C. Wright (1951) *White Collar: The American Middle Classes*, New York: Oxford University Press.

Milner, Andrew (1999) *Class*, London: Sage.

Milton Keynes Development Corporation (1972) 'What will Milton Keynes look like', May.

Ministry of Housing and Local Government (1965) *Parking in Town Centres*, London: HMSO.

Ministry of Transport (1962) *Traffic Signs for Motorways: Final Report of Advisory Committee*, London: HMSO.

—— (1963) *Traffic in Towns: A Study of the Long-Term Problems Of Traffic In Urban Areas*, London: HMSO.

Mintowt-Czyz, Lech (2000) 'The £7,500 bus stop on the road to nowhere', *Daily Mail*, 10 August.

Monro, Alexander (2004) 'A bus that comes when you want it', *New Statesman*, 1 March: 19.

Moores, Shaun (2000) *Media and Everyday Life in Modern Society*, Edinburgh: Edinburgh University Press.

Moran, Joe (2004) 'History, memory and the everyday', *Rethinking History* 8, 1 (March): 51–68.

Morris, Meaghan (1988a) 'At Henry Parkes motel', *Cultural Studies* 2, 1 (January): 1–47.

—— (1988b) 'Things to do with shopping centres', in Susan Sheridan (ed.) *Grafts: Feminist Cultural Criticism*, London: Verso, pp. 193–225.

—— (1990) 'Banality in cultural studies', in Patricia Mellencamp (ed.) *Logics of Television: Essays in Cultural Criticism*, Bloomington, IN: Indiana University Press, pp. 14–43.

Morris, Steven (2003) 'Blunkett becomes butt of judge's anger', *The Guardian*, 4 October.

Morse, Margaret (1998) *Virtualities: Television, Media Art, and Cyberculture*, Bloomington, IN: Indiana University Press.

Mount, Ferdinand (2003) 'Traffic charging is a great way to kill cities', *The Sunday Times*, 16 February.

Mülder-Bach, Inka (1997) 'Cinematic ethnology: Siegfried Kracauer's *The White Collar Masses*', *New Left Review* 226 (November/December): 41–56.

Murray, Peter (2001) 'Introduction', in Richard MacCormac, Peter Murray and MaryAnne Stevens (eds) *New Connections, New Architecture, New Urban Environments and the London Jubilee Line Extension*, London: Royal Academy of Arts, pp. 4–7.

Mylius, Andrew (2003) 'John Baxter: the man who masterminded London's most hated road', *The Guardian*, 10 November.

Nairn, Ian (1955) *Outrage*, London, Architectural Press.

Neale, Steve and Krutnik, Frank (1990) *Popular Film and Television Comedy*, London: Routledge.

New Literary History (2002) Special issue on everyday life, 33, 4 (Autumn).

Newman, Oscar (1972) *Defensible Space: People and Design in the Violent City*, London: Architectural Press.

Nicholson-Lord, David (1992) 'No-go areas of motorway life', the *Independent*, 18 October.

Noble, John, Elvin, Keith and Whitaker, Ron (1977) *Residential Roads and Footpaths: Layout Considerations*, London: HMSO.

Nora, Pierre (1996) 'General introduction: between memory and history', in Pierre Nora (ed.) *Realms of Memory: Rethinking the French Past, Volume One: Conflicts and Divisions*, trans. Arthur Goldhammer, New York: Columbia University Press, pp. 1–20.

Norris, Clive and Armstrong, Gary (1999) *The Maximum Surveillance Society: The Rise of CCTV*, Oxford: Berg.

Nutt, Bev (1967) 'Research report on motorway service areas', *Traffic Engineering and Control* 9, 2 (June): 84–92.

—— (1968) 'Motorway service areas', *Architectural Review* 143, 853 (March): 189–94.

Oakeshott, Isabel (2003a) 'Homes on zone boundary face huge slump in value', *Evening Standard* (London), 12 February.

—— (2003b) 'Household bills to soar as tradesmen pass on charge', *Evening Standard* (London), 22 January.

Office for National Statistics (2003) *Local Bus Services: Passenger Journeys by Area 1991–2001: Annual Abstract of Statistics*, London: Office for National Statistics.

Ogborn, Miles (2000) 'Traffic lights', in Steve Pile and Nigel Thrift (eds) *City A-Z*, London: Routledge, pp. 262–4.

O'Grady, Sarah (2003) 'Survey reveals how your home is hit – house prices grind to a halt', *Daily Express*, 30 June.

O'Hagan, Andrew (2003) 'Watching me watching them watching you', *London Review of Books*, 9 October: 3–9.

Oliver, Paul, Davis, Ian and Bentley, Ian (1981) *Dunroamin: The Suburban Semi and Its Enemies*, London: Barrie and Jenkins.

Orbit (2002) *Orbit: Transport Solutions Around London: Recommended Strategy* (22 November). Online. Available www.orbitproject.com/ (accessed 13 July 2003).

Orwell, George (1970) 'The lion and the unicorn: socialism and the English genius', in Sonia Orwell and Ian Angus (eds) *The Collected Essays, Journalism and Letters of George Orwell, Volume 2: My Country Right or Left, 1940–1943*, Harmondsworth: Penguin, pp. 74–134.

Parker, Ian (1999) 'Traffic', *Granta* 65 (Spring): 10–31.

Parr, Martin (1999) *Boring Postcards*, London: Phaidon.

—— (2000) *Boring Postcards USA*, London: Phaidon

—— (2001) *Langweilige Postkarten*, London: Phaidon.

Pathé (1958) 'Motorway progress', Pathé News, 8 September, film no. 1551.11. Online. Available www.bufvc.ac.uk/databases/newsreels/ (accessed 4 June 2004).

—— (1959) 'Motorway at last', Pathé News, 29 October, film no. 1599.04. Online. Available www.bufvc.ac.uk/databases/newsreels/ (accessed 4 June 2004).

Pawley, Martin (1998) *Terminal Architecture*, London: Reaktion.

—— (2002) 'Why there's no place like home when it comes to making money', *Architects' Journal*, 9 May: 34.

Pearson, Helen (2002) 'Bus shelters to talk back', *Nature*, 16 September: 11.

People (1998) 'Boot out this joke traffic warden', the *People*, 3 May.

Perec, Georges (1999) *Species of Spaces and Other Pieces*, trans. John Sturrock, London: Penguin.

Perez-Pena, Richard (2001) 'City to create commission to oversee reconstruction', *New York Times*, 17 September.

Phillips, Alan (1993) *The Best in Science, Office and Business Park Design*, London: Batsford.

Phillips, Tom (1992) *Works and Texts*, London: Thames and Hudson.

—— (2000) *The Postcard Century: 2000 Cards and Their Messages*, London: Thames and Hudson.

Platt, Edward (2000) *Leadville: A Biography of the A40*, London: Picador.

Plowden, William (1973) *The Motor Car and Politics in Britain*, Harmondsworth: Penguin.

Poulter, Sean (2000), 'The stresses and pains of workers at "sweatshop" call centres', *Daily Mail*, 28 December.

Power, Anne (1993) *Hovels to High Rise: State Housing in Europe since 1850*, London: Routledge.

—— (1998) *Estates on the Edge: The Social Consequences of Mass Housing in Northern Europe*, Basingstoke: Macmillan.

Prescott, Michael (2000) 'Prescott to curb urban sprawl with terraces', *The Sunday Times*, 6 February.

Prynn, Jonathan (2002) 'Smithfield under threat', *Evening Standard* (London), 7 October.

Puckett, Katie (2003) 'What exactly is going on in the east of London?', *Housing Today*, 27 June: 25–7.

Putnam, Robert D. (2000) *Bowling Alone: The Collapse and Revival of American Community*, New York: Simon and Schuster.

Pyke, Nicholas (2003) 'Low-paid workers will stampede out of London, Livingstone warned', the *Independent on Sunday*, 19 January.

Radice, Giles (1992) *Southern Discomfort*, Fabian Pamphlet 555, London: Fabian Society.

Ramsden, John (ed.) (2002) *The Oxford Companion to Twentieth-Century British Politics*, Oxford: Oxford University Press.

Raper, Jonathan F., Rhind, David William and Shepherd, John W. (1992) *Postcodes: The New Geography*, Harlow: Longman.

Rawnsley, Andrew (2001) *Servants of the People: The Inside Story of New Labour*, 2nd edn, London: Penguin.

Rayson, David (2003) *somewhere else is here*, exhibition catalogue, Cambridge: Kettle's Yard.

Relph, Edward (1987) *The Modern Urban Landscape*, London: Croom Helm.

Riches, Chris (2003) 'Bus gets parking ticket at bus stop', the *Sun*, 1 March.

Richman, Joel (1983) *Traffic Wardens: An Ethnography of Street Administration*, Manchester: Manchester University Press.

Ries, Nancy (2002) 'Anthropology and the everyday, from comfort to terror', *New Literary History* 33, 4 (Autumn): 725–42.

Rivers, Tony (1992) 'Dunbuildin' the new Britain', *The Times*, 16 May.

Robbins, Tom (2003) 'Britain gets the hump', *The Sunday Times*, 19 October.

Robbins, Tom and Brooke, Simon (1999) 'On the front line of the car wars', *The Sunday Times*, 14 February.

Roberts, John (1998) *The Art of Interruption: Realism, Photography and the Everyday*, Manchester: Manchester University Press.

—— (1999) 'Philosophizing the everyday: the philosophy of praxis and the fate of cultural studies', *Radical Philosophy* 98 (November/December): 16–29.

Rogers, Richard (1999) *Towards an Urban Renaissance: The Report of the Urban Task Force chaired by Lord Rogers of Riverside*, London: Department of the Environment, Transport and the Regions.

Ross, Andrew (2003) *No-Collar: The Humane Workplace and its Hidden Costs*, New York: Basic Books.

Ross, Kristin (1995) *Fast Cars, Clean Bodies: Decolonization and the Reordering of French Culture*, Cambridge, MA: MIT Press.

—— (1997) 'French quotidian', in Lynn Gumpert (ed.) *The Art of the Everyday: The Quotidian in Postwar French Culture*, New York: New York University Press, pp. 19–29.

Samuel, Raphael (1994) *Theatres of Memory, Volume 1: Past and Present in Contemporary Culture*, London: Verso.

Sands, Sarah (2003) 'Livingstone takes his class war to school-run mothers', the *Daily Telegraph*, 23 January.

Sartre, Jean-Paul (1976) *Critique of Dialectical Reason, Volume 1: Theory of Practical Ensembles*, trans. Alan Sheridan-Smith, ed. Jonathan Rée, London: NLB.

Schwartz, Barry (1975) *Queuing and Waiting: Studies in the Social Organization of Access and Delay*, Chicago, IL: University of Chicago Press.

Segrave, Carrie (2004) *The New London Property Guide 04/05*, London: Mitchell Beazley.

Self, Will (1996) 'Do you believe in the Westway?', in Will Self, *Junk Mail*, London: Penguin, pp. 249–56.

Sellen, Abigail J. and Harper, Richard H. R. (2002) *The Myth of the Paperless Office*, Cambridge, MA: MIT Press.

Sheller, Mimi (2004) 'Automotive emotions: feeling the car', *Theory, Culture and Society* 21, 4/5 (August–October): 221–42.

Sheringham, Michael (1995) 'Marc Augé and the ethno-analysis of contemporary life', *Paragraph* 18, 2 (July): 210–22.

—— (2000) 'Attending to the everyday: Blanchot, Lefebvre, Certeau, Perec', *French Studies* 54, 2 (April): 187–99.

Short, John R. (1982) *Housing in Britain: The Post-War Experience*, London: Methuen.

Silva, Elizabeth and Bennett, Tony (eds) (2004) *Contemporary Culture and Everyday Life*, Durham: Sociology Press.

Silverstone, Roger (1994) *Television and Everyday Life*, London: Routledge.

—— (ed.) (1996) *Visions of Suburbia*, London: Routledge.

Simmons, M. (1990) 'The M25 London Orbital motorway – a case study', in David Bayliss (ed.) *Orbital Motorways*, London: Thomas Telford, pp. 51–74.

Sinclair, Iain (2002) *London Orbital*, London: Granta Books.

Slinn, Mike, Guest, Peter and Matthews, Paul (1998) *Traffic Engineering: Principles and Practice*, London: Arnold.

Smith, Giles (2000) 'Berth of a salesman', *The Guardian*, 4 December.

Smith, John (2002) *Film and Video Works 1972–2002*, Bristol: Picture This Moving Images/Watershed Media Centre.

Smithson, Alison (1983) *AS in DS: An Eye on the Road*, Delft: University of Delft Press.

Social Issues Research Centre (2003) 'The Renault "new" van man report: the evolution of silver van man', Oxford: Social Issues Research Centre.

Social Trends (2004) No. 34, London: HMSO.

Sod-U-Ken (2003) *Sod-U-Ken: The Forum About the London Congestion Charge*. Online. Available www.sod-u-ken.com/ (accessed 15 January–24 March 2003).

Soja, Edward W. (1995) 'Postmodern urbanization: the six restructurings of Los Angeles', in Sophie Watson and Katherine Gibson (eds) *Postmodern Cities and Spaces*, Oxford: Blackwell, pp. 125–37.

Spigel, Lynn (2001) *Welcome to the Dreamhouse: Popular Media and Postwar Suburbs*, Durham, NC: Duke University Press.

Spring, Martin (1983) 'Inside the Barratt machine', *Building*, 24 June: 28–9.

Spurrier, Raymond (1960) 'Road-style on the motorway', *Architectural Review* 128, 766 (December): 406–16.

Stallabrass, Julian (1996) *Gargantua: Manufactured Mass Culture*, London: Verso.

Starkie, David (1982) *The Motorway Age: Road and Traffic Policies in Post-War Britain*, Oxford: Pergamon Press.

Stern, Lesley (2001) '"Paths that wind through the thicket of things"', *Critical Inquiry* 28, 1 (Autumn): 317–54.

Stevenson, John (1991) 'The Jerusalem that failed? The rebuilding of post-war Britain', in Terry Gourvish and Alan O'Day (eds) *Britain Since 1945*, Basingstoke: Macmillan, pp. 89–110.

Stewart, Susan (1993) *On Longing: Narratives of the Miniature, the Gigantic, the Souvenir, the Collection*, Durham, NC: Duke University Press.

Sun (1992) 'Nightmare on Kinnock Street – he'll have a new home, you won't', the *Sun*, 8 April.

—— (2001) 'Victory for the *Sun* on speed cameras: end of the hidden menace', the *Sun*, 4 December.

—— (2003a) 'Road rap crop-up', the *Sun*, 5 September.

—— (2003b) 'Ken's tax hits farm machine', the *Sun*, 18 June.

—— (2003c) 'It's 2004 . . . and Big Brother is watching you', the *Sun*, 4 August.

Sutcliffe, Thomas (2000) 'Life in the human slipstream', the *Independent*, 9 December.

Sutherland, Alex (1989) 'Poster ads come in from the cold', *The Times*, 18 October.

Sweet, Matthew (2003) 'This is Britain', the *Independent*, 29 November.

Taylor, Michael A. P., Young, William and Bonsall, Peter W. (1996) *Understanding Traffic Systems: Data, Analysis and Presentation*, Aldershot: Avebury.

Taylor, Phil, Hyman, Jeff, Mulvey, Gareth and Bain, Peter (2002) 'Work organisation, control and the experience of work in call centres', *Work, Employment and Society* 16, 1 (March): 133–50.

Thompson, Ben (2004) *Sunshine on Putty: The Golden Age of British Comedy from Vic Reeves to The Office*, London: Fourth Estate.

Thrift, Nigel (2004) '*Driving* in the city', *Theory, Culture and Society* 21, 4/5 (August–October): 41–59.

Times (1996) 'We are back as the people's party, says Blair', *The Times*, 2 October.

Tomlinson, John (1999) *Globalization and Culture*, Cambridge: Polity.

Townsend, Mark (2003) 'Gadgets aim to fool cameras', the *Observer*, 19 January.

Transport for London (2003) *Congestion Charging: First Annual Report*, London: Transport for London (June).

—— (2004a) London Underground website. Online. Available http://tube.tfl.gov.uk/ (accessed 10–17 February 2004).

—— (2004b) Transport for London website. Online. Available www.transportforlondon.gov.uk/tfl (accessed 3–12 January 2004).

Transportation Research Board (1998) *NCHRP Synthesis 264: Modern Roundabout Practice in the United States: A Synthesis of Highway Practice*, Washington, DC: National Academy Press.

Travis, Alan (1992) 'Regretful minister says it with chocolates', *The Guardian*, 14 January.

Treanor, Jill (2003) 'Union calls on government to dam jobs flow', *The Guardian*, 3 December.

Unwin, Raymond (1909) *Town Planning in Practice: An Introduction to the Art of Designing Cities and Suburbs*, London: T. Fisher Unwin.

Upton, Dell (2002) 'Architecture in everyday life', *New Literary History* 33, 4 (Autumn): 707–23.

Urry, John (2004) 'The "system" of automobility', *Theory, Culture and Society* 21, 4/5 (August–October 2004): 25–39.

Vaneigem, Raoul (1994) *The Revolution of Everyday Life*, trans. Donald Nicholson-Smith, London: Rebel Press/Left Bank Books.

Venturi, Robert, Scott Brown, Denise and Izenour, Steven (1972) *Learning from Las Vegas*, Cambridge, MA: MIT Press.

Wainwright, Martin (1986) 'Zebras get the hump', *The Guardian*, 19 August.

—— (1995) 'Norris backtracks after swipe at "dreadful" fellow travellers on buses and trains', *The Guardian*, 10 February.

Waller, Robert and Criddle, Byron (2002) *The Almanac of British Politics*, 7th edn, London: Routledge.

Walters, Joanna and Harris, Paul (2002) 'Chaos hits London traffic charge plan', *The Observer*, 10 November.

Walton, William and Dixon, Peter (2000) 'The deregulation of the provision of motorway service areas in the United Kingdom and the consequent dilemmas for planning', *Town Planning Review* 71, 3 (July): 333–59.

Ward, Colin (1993) *New Town, Home Town: The Lessons of Experience*, London: Calouste Gulbenkian Foundation.

Ward, Graham (2000) 'Introduction', in Ward (ed.) *The Certeau Reader*, Oxford: Blackwell, pp. 1–14.

Warde, Alan (1991) 'Gentrification as consumption: issues of class and gender', *Environment and Planning D: Society and Space* 9, 2: 223–32.

Waters, Chris (1999) 'Representations of everyday life: L. S. Lowry and the landscape of memory in postwar Britain', *Representations* 65 (Winter): 121–50.

Webber, Melvin M. (1964) 'The urban place and the nonplace urban realm', in Melvin M. Webber, John W. Dyckman, Donald L. Foley, Albert Z. Gutternberg, William L. C. Wheaton and Catherine Bauer Wurster, *Explorations into Urban Structure*, Philadelphia, PA: University of Pennsylvania Press, pp. 79–153.

Webster, Ben (2003a) 'Tube and trains will take the strain on Monday', *The Times*, 14 February.

—— (2003b) 'Drivers "will speed to avoid toll"', *The Times*, 20 January.

—— (2003c) 'Safety fears over paying road charge by mobile', *The Times*, 7 February.

Westerbeck, Colin and Meyerowitz, Joel (2001) *Bystander: A History of Street Photography*, 2nd edn, Boston, MA: Bulfinch Press.

What House? (2004) 'Save £3000 by buying new', *What House?*, March: 12.

White, Stephen (2003) 'The Oscars: parking industry's awards night', *Daily Mirror*, 25 February.

Whittingham, Steve and MacAdam, Harry (2003) 'Greed cameras', the *Sun*, 20 November.

Whitworth, Damian (2003) 'C is for cars, cameras, charges, controversy . . . and chaos?', *The Times*, 7 January.

Whyte, William H. (1960) *The Organization Man*, Harmondsworth: Penguin.

—— (1988) *City: Rediscovering the Center*, New York: Doubleday.

Wigoder, Meir (2001) 'Some thoughts about street photography and the everyday', *History of Photography* 25, 4 (Winter): 368–78.

Williams, David (2002) 'Safety fears as car charge threatens the school run', *Evening Standard* (London), 6 September.

Williams, David and Wilkinson, Mark (2003) 'Small firms "to face £500m road toll bill"', *Evening Standard* (London), 28 January.

Williams, Raymond (1988) *Keywords: A Vocabulary of Culture and Society*, 2nd edn, London: Fontana.

—— (1989) 'Culture is ordinary', in Robin Gable (ed.) *Resources of Hope: Culture, Democracy, Socialism*, London: Verso, pp. 3–18.

Williams, Richard J. (2002) 'Pleasure and the motorway', in Peter Wollen and Joe Kerr (eds) *Autopia: Cars and Culture*, London, Reaktion, pp. 281–7.

Willis, Paul (1977) *Learning to Labour: How Working Class Kids Get Working Class Jobs*, London: Saxon House.

—— (1990) *Common Culture: Symbolic Work at Play in the Everyday Cultures of the Young*, Buckingham: Open University Press.

Willis, Susan (1991) *A Primer for Daily Life*, London: Routledge.

Wolmar, Christian (2002) *Down the Tube: The Battle for London's Underground*, London: Aurum.

Wood, Tom (1998) *All Zones Off Peak*, London: Dewi Lewis.

—— (2001) *Bus Odyssey*, ed. Sylvia Böhmer, Ostfildern-Ruit, Germany: Hatje Cantz.

Woudhuysen, James and Abley, Ian (2004) *Why is Construction so Backward?*, Chichester: Wiley-Academy.

Wright, Patrick (1991) *A Journey Through Ruins: The Last Days of London*, London: Hutchinson Radius.

Index

Page references in *italics* denote illustrations
Alphabetical order used is letter-by-letter

Wood, Tom 26–8
Worboys report on road signage
    (1963) 97
work 17, 29–60, 124, 163; corporate
    culture in *Office Space* 36–41; middle
    management in *The Office* 41–8;
    relationship to commuting 48–9; rise
    of the *Angestellten* 30–6
working class 12, 102, 122–3, 135
Working Girl (film) 36

World's End Estate 143
world wars 79
Worst Case Scenario (film) 91, *92*
Wright, Patrick 2, 142
writing/reading opposition 23

Your New Home 132
youth cultures 9, 50

Zaidi, Ali 172n1